*E*conomics Is
Everywhere

*E*conomics Is
Everywhere

5th edition

Daniel S. Hamermesh

University of Texas at Austin
and
Royal Holloway University of London

WORTH PUBLISHERS
A Macmillan Higher Education Company

Vice President, Editing, Design, and Media Production: Catherine Woods
Publisher, Social and Behavioral Sciences: Kevin Feyen
Associate Publisher, Economics and Geography: Steven Rigolosi
Associate Editor: Mary Walsh
Marketing Manager: Tom Digiano
Marketing Assistant: Tess Sanders
Art Director: Diana Blume
Director of Editing, Design, and Media Production for the Sciences
    and Social Sciences: Tracey Kuehn
Managing Editor: Lisa Kinne
Project Editor: Robert Errera
Production Manager: Barbara Ann Seixas
Text Designer: Lee Ann McKevitt
Composition: Northeastern Graphic, Inc.
Printing and Binding: RR Donnelley
Cover Photo: Tom Abraham/E+/Getty Images
Cover Designer: Joseph DePinho

ISBN-13: 978-1-4641-8539-7
ISBN-10: 1-4641-8539-5
Library of Congress Control Number: 2014935919

Printed in the United States of America

First printing

Worth Publishers
41 Madison Avenue
New York, NY 10010
www.worthpublishers.com

About the Author

Daniel S. Hamermesh is the Sue Killam Professor in the Foundations of Economics at the University of Texas at Austin and Professor in Labour Economics at Royal Holloway University of London. He received his B.A. from the University of Chicago (1965) and his Ph.D. from Yale University (1969). He taught from 1969–73 at Princeton, from 1973–93 at Michigan State, and has held visiting professorships at universities in the United States, Europe, Australia, and Asia. He is a Fellow of the Econometric Society and the Society of Labor Economists, a Research Associate of the National Bureau of Economic Research and the Institute for the Study of Labor (IZA), and past president of the Society of Labor Economists and of the Midwest Economics Association. In 2013 he received the biennial Jacob Mincer Award for Lifetime Contributions from the Society of Labor Economists. He was that biennium's recipient of the Commons Award presented by the international economics honor society, OΔE. He was also that year's recipient of the IZA Prize in Labor Economics. He authored *Beauty Pays, Labor Demand,* and *The Economics of Work and Pay,* and a wide array of articles in labor economics in the leading general and specialized economics journals. His research concentrates on time use, labor demand, discrimination, and unusual applications of labor economics (to suicide, sleep, and beauty). He has taught introductory economics since 1968 to more than 20,000 students and has won numerous university awards for his undergraduate teaching. He is a regular guest-blogger at http://www.freakonomics.com.

Contents

Preface to the First Edition

For more than thirty years I have been bringing unusual stories into my micro principles classes and commenting on them from an economic viewpoint. At the start of the fall semester of 2001, I began doing this in the usual way. One student pointed out that it would help her if I would post the stories and my comments on my Web site; that way she could look at them later and use them to help her study for exams. I began posting my comments on a regular basis, creating an entry in what I called the "Economic Thought of the Day." A few of my friends and colleagues saw these postings and pointed out that with some expansion they would make a nice supplement to a micro principles course. This is the result.

The vignettes are organized in the same order as the topics that make up my introductory microeconomics course. This arrangement corresponds quite closely to the plans of most micro principles texts. A few texts, however, include international trade (particularly, comparative advantage) as the second topic in the course, immediately after supply and demand. For teachers using such books, Chapter 20 can be assigned right after Chapter 1 or, better still, after Chapter 6.

I thank James Barbour, Valerie Bencivenga, Anne Golla, Stephen Lich-Tyler, Paul Shensa, and Max Stinchcombe for their extremely helpful suggestions and comments on the manuscript, and Lawrence Hamermesh and John Siegfried for their encouragement. A number of colleagues, students, and family members made suggestions that led to the vignettes included here, and others' behavior inspired some vignettes. This volume is dedicated to Frances W. Hamermesh, who commented on the entire manuscript, inspired many of the examples, and has encouraged and supported this project and everything else in my professional and personal lives for thirty-seven years.

Daniel S. Hamermesh

Austin

June 2002

Preface to the Second Edition

The creation of economic "stories" from real life is an on-going process—because new stories confront one every day. This new edition contains some of the stories that were generated after publication of the first edition. As with the earlier stories, some of these were inspired by family events, some by news stories, by television shows, movies, music and other facets of daily life. Some too were suggested or corrected by students and colleagues. In this last regard, I would like to thank Peter Debaere, Stephen Donald, Brittani Elliott, Robert Henderson, Ken Hendricks, Joyce Jacobsen, Stephen Lich-Tyler (again), John McGinnis, Robert Mohr, William Todd, Tsu-yu Tsao, Lucille Vaughn and students at the University of Texas at Austin, the University of Michigan and the University of New Hampshire. This edition is dedicated to the memory of Morton Hamermesh (1915-2003) who inspired several of the vignettes and who, much more important, inspired much of my professional behavior throughout my career.

Daniel S. Hamermesh

Austin

August 2004

Preface to the Third Edition

Most of the new vignettes (and nearly one third of the 400 stories in this edition are new) stem from my own experiences, observations, frustrations, and so forth. Beginning with the fall semester in 2005, however, the students in my giant Introductory to Microeconomics class have been required to write a vignette like those included in this volume. Aside from the benefits of giving freshman and sophomores in this class a rare writing assignment, this task has also provided me with a number of extremely clever vignettes that I use in this edition of the book. I thus thank Rachel Arena, Basil Awad, Elizabeth Fortson, Patrick Hyde, Shana Opperman, Brittni Svatek, and Emily Whitley for their submissions, which I have filched for this edition. The following nonstudents also made comments about incidents in their own lives that led to vignettes in this edition, and I am deeply indebted to them: Valerie Bencivenga, Jeff Biddle, Deborah Cobb-Clark, Lisa Dickson, Richard Flores, Mariesa Herrmann, Wolter Hassink, Stephen Trejo, and Tom Wiseman. Finally, I am especially grateful to Paul Shensa, to whom this edition is dedicated; he kept the faith.

Daniel S. Hamermesh

Bonn, Germany

September 2008

Preface to the Fourth Edition

Many of the new vignettes (and over one-third of the 400 stories in this edition are new) stem from my own experiences, observations, frustrations, and so forth. I continue to assign my students the task of writing a story like these, and the high quality of many of them makes grading all 500 a pleasure each year. Also, this assignment provides some material for this book, and I thank Justin Altman, Samantha Katsounas, Katie Kercher, Lucy Li, Austin Mai, Kelley Mathis, Catalina Padilla, Stuart Rubin, Jeff Stevens, Katherine Thayer, Kathryn Whitley and Justin Wu, for their stories, which I have shamelessly swiped and modified for this edition. The following non-students also made comments about incidents in their own lives that led to vignettes in this edition, and I am deeply indebted to them: Oya Pınar Ardıç, Martin Biewen, Kasey Buckles, Larry Carver, Wolter Hassink, Stephen Pudney, Pierre Weil, Tom Wiseman, Chris Wojtewicz. I am also thankful to Paul Shensa, who has shepherded this book from its beginnings. Finally, I dedicate this edition to my mother, Madeline G. Hamermesh (1918-2011), who passed away just as I was working on it, and who inspired some of the vignettes and so much else in my life.

Daniel S. Hamermesh

Austin

June 2011

Preface to the Fifth Edition

Over one-fourth of the stories in this edition are new. Spending a substantial part of each year teaching and working in Europe has allowed me to see economics in action in different ways than one sees it in the U.S. There is nothing like different institutions to provide different incentives and different behavior in response to those incentives.

I continue to require my 550 introductory economics students to write one-page stories like those in this volume. The 10 best receive extra credit on the assignment, and it is from them that I take and modify a few stories for inclusion in this volume. My students An-Vi Nguyen, Rachel Scott and Ariane Stephenson provided stories that I include here. Among my colleagues, friends and family who inspired or suggested new stories are Anne Blumofe, Marion Hamermesh, Simon Hamermesh, Jungmin Lee, Dale Singer, Ester Smith, Michael Spagat, Steve Trejo, Tom Wiseman, Kyle Young and my son, David Hamermesh. I dedicate this edition to my six grandchildren, Jonathan, Samuel, Miriam, Yonah, Noah and Rafi Hamermesh. The first four will be in college during this edition's lifetime and might have the chance to use it in class. I hope they enjoy reading these stories, many of which are based on the good times I have had with them, as much as I enjoyed writing them. Finally, as with so much in my professional life, my wife of 47 years, Frances Hamermesh, inspired both the book generally and a number of the new vignettes in this edition.

Daniel S. Hamermesh

Melbourne, Australia

July 2013

*T*hinking About Economics Everywhere

In every introductory microeconomics course, you are taught a large number of technical, jargon-type words. These words represent a form of shorthand, a way to summarize ideas about behavior. There is one word that I teach the very first day of my introductory class, and I believe it is the most important of all: *empathy*—the intellectual identification with the feelings, thoughts, or attitudes of someone else. Students should put themselves into the particular problem being discussed and ask, "How would I behave if I were confronted with those choices?" Microeconomics is very logical, and most of us think very logically in our daily lives. When confronted with economic questions, though, we too often forget our logic and get scared because somehow the questions seem different. They're not: The economic issues pose the same questions that are posed to us in many of our daily activities and that we almost always answer sensibly and correctly.

The purpose of this book is to illustrate the wide range of daily activities to which an economic way of thinking can be applied. The 400 vignettes are organized according to the topical arrangement of a typical introductory microeconomics course. That way they can tie into what you are learning from any standard introductory textbook. They can focus your ability to apply the formal analysis taught in class to the myriad examples that come out of your daily activities. After studying this book you should be able to see your own activities and the things that you read in newspapers, magazines, books, and the Web, or hear on television and radio, in a new, economic way. As a result you should be able to understand your world better.

Ideally, you should read and think about the material in this book in small bits at a time—not all at once and not even each chapter at once. Reading and thinking about a few vignettes a day is the best way to learn how to think in economic terms about everyday phenomena. After reading a vignette, you should go directly to the attached question and try answering it while the thought expressed in the vignette is fresh in your mind.

PART I

*T*rade-Offs, Supply, and Demand

CHAPTER 1

Trade-Offs and Opportunity Cost

Production possibility frontiers

1.1

Mick Jagger and Keith Richards wrote, "You can't always get what you want." This is the essence of economics: Wants are unlimited, but the resources to satisfy them are *scarce*. That's true for us as individuals, and it's also true for societies. The same song also states, "But if you try, sometimes you might find you get what you need." This statement makes no economic sense. *Need* is not an economic term. I "need" tickets to the ballet once a week, a private jet with a pilot, a home theater, and a chauffeur for my limousine. Nobody has the right to argue with my statement about what I "need." Unfortunately, I do not have the income to obtain all these things; and even if I did, the scarcity imposed by the 24-hour day would prevent me from enjoying them in the style I would like. I can satisfy my basic wants; I have the time and income for the things that are most important to me. But we all define our needs so broadly that the Rolling Stones are wrong—you can never get what you need!

> **Q:** *Make a list of ten things that you "need." Do you get them all? If not, is it because your income isn't high enough or because you haven't got enough time?*

1.2

Many improvements in technology shift the **production possibility frontier** outward. Many of these increase human happiness, and a few do this by increasing marital harmony (Viagra?). One that we

3

just acquired does all of these while saving that most precious of all things—time: Our car's GPS device. Gertrude, as we call it, led us from a rural road in Portugal back to our rented condominium with no hassle, no spousal arguments about which road to take and no wasted time driving around trying to find the correct route.

Q: *Think about two other examples of inventions that did not even exist a decade ago. Did each shift out the* **production possibility frontier?**

1.3

Small **technical changes** often shift our **production possibility frontier** outward and make a big difference in our well-being, even if they don't increase measured output. Until the price of at-home copy machines (today, often part of all-in-one printer/fax/scanner/copier combinations) fell enough to make one a sensible purchase, I took some small document to the local mailing store (or even the dry cleaner!) and paid 10 cents per page copied. The 10 cents wasn't the problem—it was my time dragging things over there. Today, I simply turn on the machine on my desk, make the copy, and get back to work (or, more often, to leisure!) With the chance to print multiple copies of PDF files, I don't need to copy something more than once a month. But each time I do, the home machine saves me easily 15 minutes. I believe similar small, technology-induced time savings are widespread, and that together the chunks of time that they save amount to a large improvement in well-being.

Q: *List two other inventions that save you a little bit of time each time you use them, but do it frequently.*

1.4

A great example of **trade-offs** comes from the life of a full-time student. Such students can be imagined as having only two uses of their time—studying and socializing—and two outputs from those uses—knowledge acquired and social satisfaction. If a student is efficient, he or she cannot increase the amount of knowledge acquired in college without giving up social satisfaction. The **opportunity cost** of one more unit of social satisfaction is some amount of forgone knowledge, and the opportunity cost of another unit of knowledge is some amount of forgone social satisfaction. This **production possibility frontier** can shift out along each axis. A speed-reading course moves the curve out along the axis for knowledge acquisition, allowing the student to obtain *both* more knowledge and more social satisfaction (because some time that can be saved from studying can be shifted to socializing). It's harder to think of improvements that move the curve out only along the social satisfaction axis. One example that my students came up with is the beer bong. Students attach a funnel to a keg of beer, attach a tube to the funnel, and are able to ingest more beer more rapidly than before. Unfortunately, I guess this does increase "fun," at least as defined by some students. It enables them to get drunk more rapidly, releasing time for learning (assuming they can sober up quickly)!

   Q: *Draw the* **production possibility frontier** *implied in this vignette. List one other example of a technical improvement that shifts the frontier out along the learning axis, and another that shifts it out along the social satisfaction axis.*

1.5

When you consider the student's **trade-off** between socializing and learning, it is possible to think of examples that would represent technological improvements in each of these "industries" separately (as Vignette 1.4 shows). During class, I just couldn't come up with an improvement that would raise productivity in both activities; that is, that would shift the **production possibility frontier** out along both axes. A student volunteered "strip-studying," as in the Adam Sandler movie *Billy Madison*. That seems like a pretty good one—essentially this change allows the student to combine learning and (some form of) socializing in the same time period. It makes each minute of a student's time more productive (in terms of the two goals of learning and "socializing").

   Q: *The* **production possibility frontier** *implied in this vignette is the same as the one you started off with in the question above. Now list one other example of a technical improvement that shifts the frontier out along BOTH axes.*

1.6

Sandy and Harry Chapin's song *Cat's in the Cradle* is one of my favorites, partly because of the beat, partly because it illustrates one of the essential **trade-offs** in life. It sings of the life of a busy man who isn't there when his son grows up and who, in old age, is ignored by the son, who is very busy and "grew up just like me [the father]." The singer regrets not having spent time with the son, yet at the same time he describes his own busy life. If he had spent more time with the son would the son have been better off? The father wouldn't have earned as much, and the son wouldn't have had the financial security that the father's earnings provided, but they would have had more time together. Except for those who inherit large fortunes, the choices are additional earnings and resources for one's family or more time with the family. One is always constrained—by both time and the ability to consume goods. We have to make a choice within these constraints that considers all the gains for us and our kids that result from that choice.

Q: *Graph the* **production possibility frontier** *implied by this discussion, labeling the axes carefully. How would that frontier shift if people do more telecommuting?*

1.7

I spent 40 minutes waiting to begin diagnostic tests prior to seeing my ophthalmologist. What a waste of my valuable time! And data from the American Time Use Survey suggest that this is a standard problem: The average adult American spends four hours per year waiting for medical or dental care, with each wait averaging around 45 minutes. Pricing this time out at even a third of the average wage rate, the cost amounts to about $4 billion per year. Seems like a lot of money, seems very **inefficient,** but what is the alternative? The only way that every medical provider could ensure no waiting would be for the provider to have downtime him or herself—to have unutilized resources, both of his or her time and the services of the capital stock used in the practice. I'm not sure what the right mix of provider and customer waiting is; but as annoying as my waiting is, the current system may be economically **efficient.**

Q: *Let's say you are really rich and your time is very valuable. How could you minimize the waste that would otherwise occur because of waiting time?*

1.8

Many students believe that professors are either good researchers or good teachers, but not both. This belief implies that there is a negative relationship between research and teaching across different professors. I don't believe this is true at all: The better researchers are often better teachers. This doesn't mean that professors have no **trade-offs** in their activities. Instead, those who are good at one thing are good at the other, and those who are mediocre at one are typically mediocre at both. There is a **trade-off** for each individual, but the overall level of ability differs among professors so that some professors can perform better in both areas.

>   **Q:** *Draw the production possibility frontiers for a high-ability professor and a low-ability professor that are implied by this vignette. Label the axes carefully.*

1.9

Whenever I travel in other wealthy countries, I am a bit embarrassed about the dollar bill's insignificance compared with other countries' smallest bills: A five-pound note, worth $8; a five-euro note, worth $6.50, the thousand-yen note, worth $10. At the same time, no rich country has a coin as worthless as the U.S. penny. Imagine my surprise that the U.S. issued four new versions of the penny in honor of the Lincoln Bicentennial. What a waste of resources—what a move inside the **production possibility frontier!** Each penny costs much more than 1 cent to manufacture. Many people have called for the demise of the penny; it should go, but so should the dollar bill. After all, at 2 percent annual inflation, by 2050 the dollar's value will have fallen by half. Will we still be using dollar bills (and even more worthless pennies) then?

>   **Q:** *What do you think is the right set of coins and bills to make transactions easier? Or doesn't it matter anymore, since we do more things with debit and credit cards?*

1.10

A student e-mailed an interesting question: "You spent all the time in class talking about technical progress and how it shifts the **production possibility frontier** outward. Has there ever been a case of technical regression that shifted it inward?" My university has issued a dictum severely limiting faculty seeking authorization to travel to "dangerous countries" (including Israel and Mexico). This represents a clear inward shift in the **production possibility frontier.** I doubt it will have a big effect, though. First, many others and I will certainly ignore the regulation if a good trip to Mexico, Israel, or elsewhere arises and our way is paid from non-University sources. Also, current faculty members who might possibly obtain grants requiring travel to these areas will be more likely to run their grant money through other organizations—thus reducing the amount of overhead funding the University can obtain to help cover the costs of the very administrators who have propagated this policy. Worse still from the University's point of view, by making research more difficult this regulation will, if fully effective, reduce the attractiveness of the University to potential faculty. In my forty-two years as a University professor, I have seen many administrative stupidities; but this one is a strong contender for the dumbest.

> **Q:** *Technical regression for a society is extremely rare. Cases where a household sees an inward shift in what it can produce are more common. List some things that might cause such an inward shift to occur for a single household.*

Opportunity Cost

1.11

My sixteen-year-old grandson is complaining that he spent 5 hours stranded in an airport because United Airlines couldn't find a replacement airplane for one that had mechanical problems. I asked why his Dad didn't book him on Delta instead, which has many more flights from his home to his destination. He answered, "The Delta flight cost $500 more." So I asked whether his time wasn't worth $100/hour—whether his **opportunity cost** in his Dad's mind wasn't $100. "Regrettably, no," he answered.

> **Q:** *Would your father or mother pay for the more expensive ticket for you? What does this say about how they value your time?*

1.12

In the movie *The Hand That Rocks the Cradle*, a female character makes the comment, "Today's woman has to do three things: bring home at least $50,000 per year, [...], and cook homemade lasagna." It is unlikely that many women will be able to do all three because the first and third are probably **substitutes.** A woman who is earning that much money is unlikely to have the time to cook homemade lasagna because there is a **scarcity** of time, her most important resource. The opposite side of the coin is that a woman who has chosen to spend time rolling homemade pasta is unlikely to have enough time to earn this much. (I've omitted the second thing because it probably can be done by both high-earning women and those who have chosen to stay at home.) But fixed resources—24 hours in the day—make it unlikely that most women will be able to do all three things.

Q: *Are the* **opportunity costs** *of earning and cooking constant over the day and the week, or can women (and men, too) find times when one is relatively cheap and the other is relatively costly? What are these times?*

1.13

One of my female colleagues commented on the previous entry, stating, "I earn more than $50,000, and I also make homemade lasagna." My response was that **production possibility frontiers** differ, depending on a person's or country's resources and technology. She is very efficient at many things and can both earn a lot and make great home-cooked lasagna. Nonetheless, even she faces a **trade-off,** assuming that she is working and enjoying leisure efficiently. If she works more, she can earn more, but she will have less time for home cooking. If she cooks more, she won't be able to earn so much.

Q: *Draw her* **production possibility frontier** *in these two activities. Now draw a point that accounts for the fact that she spends one hour a day doing absolutely nothing.*

1.14

Where has all the Viagra spam gone? Same for Nigerians seeking to transfer millions of dollars to you (if you give would just give them your bank account number)? I haven't gotten one of these in several years, and there often used to be several a day. I assume that the spammers realized that the return per period of time—the price of the activity—was less than the **opportunity cost** of their time. They have shut down the business and moved to other activities that might yield higher returns. Economists proposed taxes on mass e-mailing, but the market seems to have solved the problem. Spam still exists, though; the latest is the e-mail saying I'm the nearest surviving relative of X [pick some first name] Hamermesh, and if I just send my bank account details to a particular large South African bank, they will wire my inheritance.

Q: *How will technical improvements in the ease of sending mass e-mails affect the amount of these requests for bank account details that you receive?*

1.15

My university held the "Party on the Plaza" yesterday, a version of its annual fun festival, featuring a rock-climbing wall, exhibits by many student groups, and lots of food. As I walked by, a student mentioned that there was "free" Ben & Jerry ice cream at one of the booths. I walked over, thinking I would get some, but there were at least twenty people in a line that was moving very slowly. There was no money cost of the ice cream; but its **opportunity cost**—the value of the time one would spend in line waiting—was substantial. I decided to forget about it; even though the ice cream cost no dollars, its **opportunity cost** was so large that it wasn't worth it for me. The ice cream wasn't really free.

> **Q:** *Why would students be more likely to stand in line than I would?*

1.16

At a party recently, one of my colleagues mentioned that his fourteen-year-old daughter was babysitting for her six- and three-year-old siblings, so her parents could be at the party. I asked how much they were paying the teenager, and he answered that she was not getting paid. He noted, however, that if his wife and he wanted the daughter to babysit, but she was called by someone else to babysit for pay, they would match the market rate that she would have received outside the house. My colleague is paying his daughter her **opportunity cost.** When she has an alternative babysitting job that pays, she receives a rate of pay at home equal to her opportunity cost—what she was offered for babysitting elsewhere. When she has no alternative job, she is again paid the opportunity cost of her time—which is then zero! Only an economist would do something like this.

> **Q:** *If you were in the daughter's position, would you settle for what you would be paid elsewhere? Are there economic reasons why you might be willing to settle for less, or to insist on—and get—your parents to pay more than others would pay for your babysitting services?*

1.17

The average human being will be substantially richer in fifty years, just as the average American today has a real income three times what it was in 1955. But the average human being will not have much more time in fifty years; and life expectancy has increased by only 10 percent in the U.S. since 1955, so for most people time has become relatively scarce compared to money. Not surprisingly, we feel more stressed for time than ever before—the **opportunity cost** of time has risen compared to the opportunity cost of goods. People with higher incomes usually express more time stress than those with lower incomes. It's not only that higher-income people typically work more hours per week; even those who don't work at all express greater feelings of being rushed than do poorer people. The reason is that it takes time to spend money and consume goods—you can't inject a vacation in Provence into your bloodstream—you have to go there, lie on the beach at St. Tropez, go to the Picasso museum in Antibes and tour the perfume factories of Grasse. So the next time you hear a wealthy person complaining about having no time, tell him or her that there's a simple alternative—give away money, perhaps even to you! Of course, a person who does that will then complain that his or her income is insufficient. Time or money is always relatively scarce!

Q: *Would you rather be rushed for time or find money scarce?*

1.18

In the long run, the increasing **opportunity cost** of people's time, as our wages rise, is one of the most important driving forces in economic behavior. Much of our racing around is a response to the increasing relative scarcity of time compared to income, as are efforts to introduce time-saving technology. A neat example of such an innovation is the combined urinal/television in the luxury hotel where I'm participating in a conference: Men can now perform a simple bodily function while catching up on the latest news. Women can now apply make-up while watching news or features. I don't expect to see this expensive innovation everywhere; but for the higher-wage people who frequent this hotel and whose time is quite valuable, it's sensible for the hotel's owners to make this investment. As incomes rise, are these screens the wave of the future?

Q: *What other innovations can you think of that have allowed people to save time by combining tasks? Does the opportunity cost of this multitasking diminish?*

1.19

I fell for a stupid story on the Web and turned off my home PC last night. The story said that Americans who leave computers on overnight are costing $2.8 billion per year. It ignores the cost of turning computers off—and having to turn them on again the next morning. Let's say that process takes 5 minutes per day, and one does it 250 days per year. That's 1,250 minutes, or more than 20 hours per person per year. Assume that the average computer-user's wage is $21/hour, and take the old estimate that time is valued at 1/3 of the wage. So each person's time per year turning his/her computer off and on is worth 20 × $7 = $140. Be conservative, and assume there are only 50 million U.S. computer users. That gives a cost of turning computers off/on of 50,000,000 × $140 = $7 billion—2.5 times the alleged savings from turning computers off. Even if people's time were valued at only $3/hour, less than half the **minimum wage,** leaving computers on would still make sense. This story is yet another example of environmental savings *über alles*—that saving $1 in environmental damage is worth much greater costs incurred along other dimensions. These stories assume explicitly or more usually implicitly that people's time has no value. But time has value—it has an **opportunity cost.** Stories like this and exhortations for environmental do-goodism hurt the environmental movement—because in the end people realize that heeding these exhortations would actually waste resources (even though some, like me, take a day to catch on!).

Q: *Suppose a person thinks that preserving the environment is worth more than simply the amount of savings on electricity. How would you then change the calculations in this vignette?*

1.20
A student was arrested while at a party where the underage participants were consuming a lot of alcohol. He was cited for a misdemeanor and was told by the judge that he faced a $200 fine. Afraid to ask his parents or the local loan shark for money, instead he asked the judge if he could serve jail time instead. The judge was amused and sent him to jail for one night. He had to spend time; but he figured that the **opportunity cost** of the night in jail was around $40, far below what he would have had to pay for the fine. So he figures that he saved $160 plus the embarrassment of facing his parents, plus he learned a lesson (in both life and economics!). He concludes, therefore, that sometimes crime does pay!

Q: *What would you do if you magically had two more hours per day? How would you spend the extra time? How would the things you buy change as a result of this time windfall?*

1.21

Service at our local post office is incredibly slow. On a normal day, I wait in line 15 to 20 minutes to mail a package or buy stamps. During the Christmas rush, the wait is typically 30 minutes or more. Last week, a Mail Boxes Etc. store opened up in the vacant space next door to the post office. What a great location decision! The post office is in a small strip mall. A coffee shop that had recently occupied the space was one of several stores that went bankrupt in quick succession, illustrating the relatively low **opportunity cost** of the space. Although apparently low in value for alternative uses, such as coffee shops, the space is quite valuable when used by a commercial mailer. I got tired of waiting in line at the post office, went next door, and mailed my packages in 2 minutes. I was willing to spend more money, and less of my valuable time, to accomplish the task of mailing out seasonal gifts. The clerk said that they had gotten a lot of business from people who saw the long lines at the post office and chose to save time by using their commercial services. My guess is that most of those people have jobs, and fairly high-paying ones at that.

> **Q:** *What are two other examples where a potential business location has a low opportunity cost, except in a particular specialized use that is made valuable because of something next door or in the neighborhood?*

1.22

Each semester after course grades were sent out, I used to be deluged with phone calls and e-mail from students asking why they got the grades they did (always below what they expected). The answer usually was that they messed up on the final exam. A late colleague suggested a way of reducing this harassment. He pointed out that the students' **opportunity cost** is low after exam week and stays low until classes start the next semester. To discourage students from calling and e-mailing, he said that he writes on the exam that no complaints about grades will be acknowledged until the second week of the next semester. At that time, students' opportunity cost of time is higher: They have better things to do, including attending their new classes. Only students who are deeply bothered by what they thought was unfair grading are willing to incur the high cost of inquiring. His suggestion has succeeded in sharply reducing the number of inquiries I receive.

Q: *How does this policy treat students differently by year in school (freshman, sophomore, etc.), by the number of courses they are taking, and in other ways?*

1.23

Very applied personnel economics. During an upcoming stay in Florida with the extended family, all six adults want to go out to a fancy dinner, leaving the six kids alone (since their parents say the older ones—boy 14; boy 13; girl 12; girl 11—can care for the little boys, ages 7 and 4). The older ones have a lot of successful babysitting experience; and their parents say they typically get paid. But what payment structure is both **efficient** (will induce careful babysitting) and **equitable**? One of the mothers suggested letting the two girls play, making the older boys the sitters, and paying only the boys. Hearing this, the 11-year-old said, "Not fair; and anyway, we girls are more responsible than the big boys." Another approach is to make all four big kids the sitters. I suggested this, with payments in proportion to their ages. The same grand-daughter, perhaps aware of federal law, argued for equal pay for equal work. OK; but the difficulty with putting all four big kids in charge and paying them equally may be that it diffuses responsibility and may not lead to sufficient care being taken. In the end, we paid all four bigger kids the same amount, but put the big boys in charge of the 7-year-old and the girls in charge of the 4-year-old. This seems like the right balance of efficiency and equity.

Q: *How would this situation be different if there were a set amount budgeted to spend on babysitting and the parents could only afford to pay two of the babysitters? What effect would competition in the labor market have on equity and efficiency?*

1.24

Flushed with excitement! "Potty parity" is in the news today. There's a report that more jurisdictions are adopting resolutions that require newly constructed public buildings to allocate more bathroom space to women than to men so as to equalize waiting times. As one woman waiting in a bathroom line put it, "The wait time for restrooms needs to be the same for both men and women." Implicitly the arguments stem from the desire for **equity**—that each person, on average, should wait the same amount of time as a matter of fairness. As economists, however, we know that different people's time has different value to society—a minute of Bill Gates's time is more valuable than mine; and he would be willing to pay more not to wait to use the bathroom than I would be willing to pay because his **opportunity cost** is higher. Does the same argument apply to gender potty parity? Would one be willing to argue on **efficiency** grounds that it is not unreasonable that women wait longer since their wages, the best indicator of the value of time, are lower than men's on average? I wouldn't make that argument; but it is not inconsistent with economic reasoning—with an argument for economic efficiency.

> **Q:** *If efficiency is important in this market, what should the time spent waiting to use the bathroom be in countries that are less wealthy than the U.S.? If you have traveled abroad, have you observed longer lines? What does this tell you?*

CHAPTER 2

Demand and Supply Curves

Demand

2.1

On a cold January day when our older son was five years old, he came into the house with an ice-covered rock, probably a small piece of cement. He asked me, "Daddy, would you buy this for 10 cents?" I said no, that was too much money for this particular rock. He then said, "Maybe you'll buy it for 5 cents." I said yes. Even though the rock was really ugly, I was pleased that our five-year-old son understood that **demand curves** slope downward and that he was willing to cut his price to sell his product.

> **Q:** *Offer to sell a much younger sibling, cousin, niece, or nephew ballpoint pens or CDs that you think might interest him or her. Start off with a high price and then work your way down. (This is what we call a Dutch auction.) See if you can trace out the equivalent of a downward-sloping demand curve.*

2.2

Another bad night's sleep! Perhaps that's because my wage is too high. Sleep takes time, and time has value—its **opportunity cost.** Instead of sleeping I could be working and earning a wage. A study of the economics of sleep a number of years ago showed that higher-wage people sleep less. Your wage is the price of sleep, and there is a downward-sloping **demand curve** for sleep. The demand curve shifts with other characteristics: Having young kids at home reduces the amount of sleep people get, especially women. Additional nonwage income—inheritances and gifts—has small positive effects on sleep time, and people say that if they had more hours in the day, extra sleep is one of the top three things they would do

17

with that extra time. Because time is scarce (there will always be only 24 hours in a day), the amount we sleep requires economic decision making.

    Q: *If your long-lost relative suddenly left you $1 million, would you sleep more or less? If somehow you were granted an extra two hours per day, how much extra per day would you sleep? What else would you do with the two hours?*

2.3

We lived in the northern U.S. most of our lives and used to love to go to the Caribbean in the winter. Since moving to Texas nine years ago, we have not gone at all. Today, an old friend from up north suggested a reunion with other old friends in the Virgin Islands next December. We'd like to see all of these friends, but we have no real interest in going to the Caribbean. Have our tastes for Caribbean vacations changed, thus shifting our **demand curve**? *No!* The good being demanded is not Caribbean vacations but rather the pleasure of being in a warm climate. We get that pleasure every winter living in Texas, so why travel 2,000 miles for still more of it? Tastes don't change in most cases if we properly define the good that is being demanded.

    Q: *Assume you believe that Caribbean vacations combine two goods: pleasure from warm weather and gorgeous beaches. What happens to the demand for a Caribbean vacation by someone living in Texas if the vacation combines both of these goods?*

2.4

When we got married in 1966 in Massachusetts, we had to take a blood test to make sure we weren't syphilitic (we weren't). In 1980, most states required such tests, but today only two do. Such tests essentially increase the price of getting married since they raise the time and money price of a marriage license. A new very neat study allows one to use the differential timing of the repeal of blood-test laws to infer what the **demand curve** for marriage licenses looks like as the implied price decreases. The paper shows that abolishing blood tests increased the number of marriage licenses issued by 6 percent, although half that change simply reflects people no longer crossing state lines to avoid the cost of the blood test. While no longer relevant today, one might think that raising the price of marriage licenses could have the beneficial effect of deterring spur-of-the-moment marriages. Of course, like so many restrictions, it might also have a negative unintended consequence—it might increase the number of out-of-wedlock births.

> **Q:** *As the time and money price of obtaining a marriage license decreased, the number of marriages increased. Considering that the marriage license is a relatively small expenditure compared with the other costs associated with getting married, what does this say about the responsive of the demand for marriage to changes in price?*

2.5

The hit movie of the week is *Breaking Dawn Part 2*, which several of my grandkids saw on opening night. A grandson reports that at the first showing there was a full 30 minutes of advertisements before the movie began. Since lots of people were waiting in line for hours, the theater owners figured that the theater would fill up immediately, implicitly **increasing the demand** for advertisements. That made the advertising time more valuable, so the theater responded by offering more ads. I would bet, too, that they charged the advertisers more per minute for the right to show their ads, so that having a captive audience increased price as well as quantity.

> **Q:** *If you had been one of those who had lined up for the movie, is there any way you could have avoided being deluged by these ads?*

2.6

Genesis 18:22-33 illustrates the Lord's demand curve for destroying sinners. He is about to go to Sodom and destroy the city, but Abraham asks Him if destruction would be justified if there were fifty righteous people in the city. The Lord says no; Abraham then lowers the price of destruction to forty-five righteous people, and the Lord says no; forty and again He says no. Abraham must realize that the Lord's **demand curve** for destroying sin (where the price is the number of righteous people also killed) is downward-sloping, so he lowers the price to thirty. Still no. Then twenty; still no. Finally, with ten righteous people the story ends with the Lord still refusing to destroy Sodom. By inference, only at a price below ten righteous people killed does the Lord's amount of destruction demanded rise above zero.

> **Q:** *Although we should not second-guess the Lord, how do you think His demand curve for destroying Sodom would look if He added in the destruction of Gomorrah?*

2.7

A news story mentioned the fact that the percentage of people cremated in the United States has risen from 3 percent to nearly 30 percent in the last quarter century. A spokesperson for the National Funeral Directors Association attributed this tremendous increase to the increased mobility of the American population: If you live far away from Grandpa and will not be visiting his grave, why not put him in an urn instead of in the ground? Does the rapid growth of cremation represent a shift in demand, as the spokesperson implies? Or does it instead represent people's substituting away from a product (burials) that has risen rapidly in price? It's difficult to tell: The quantity (of cremations) transacted can shift both because the demand has increased and because the price of its close **substitutes** has risen a lot. It is worth noting that no industry spokesperson is ever going to claim that a shift has occurred because consumers have responded to relative changes in price—to the rising price of burials. These people always argue that some factor beyond the industry members' control has caused the change. Price matters, but businesses don't want consumers to be reminded of that, *except* when a business cuts prices.

    Q: *If funeral directors got together and agreed to raise the price of a cremation to equal that of a burial, how would that affect the demand curve for cremations?*

2.8

The determinants of one's **demand** for a product are covered in every introductory course. Independent of prices, my income, and my general preferences, I also consider the cuteness of the product's name; a better name shifts my demand curve—**increases demand.** Even though I wasn't looking for a marinade, I bought a bottle of Soy Vay® hoisin garlic glaze. Not knowing anything about the quality of this product compared to its competitors, I figured, why not reward those who create a clever product or company name? I recently did the same thing in another context, by buying a six-pack of Arrogant Bastard® ale. In both cases, I have literally bought a package—the product and the name; and the package's quality is enhanced by the clever name.

    Q: *Can you think of other examples of cute product names that by themselves have increased your demand for some good? Or the opposite—stupid names that have decreased your demand?*

2.9

My wife and I have wine with almost every dinner at home. We prefer Australian wines because we have found European wines, especially Italian and French, to be high priced in Texas. We even drink an occasional good Texas wine (yes, there are some!). The high prices have meant that we go through a bottle in three dinners—hardly major drinkers! In Germany, we've been going through a bottle in two dinners only—a 50-percent increase in the quantity of wine consumed per night. I like to think it is due to substitution, to a move along the **demand curve,** as good European wines are incredibly inexpensive (I think) in Germany. For example, I bought a 2004 Barolo, one of the fanciest Italian wines I know, for €11 (only $15 these days), and I think it would have been twice as much at home. But is our increased consumption due to the drop in price; or are we consuming more because our taste for wine has increased due to the *joie de vivre* of the European ambiance? I believe it's the former—I don't believe tastes change much; but my dilemma illustrates a common problem in empirical economics (and life generally), separating **changes in amounts demanded** from **changes in demand.** And sadly, most non-economists will argue that behavior like mine results from taste changes; too few people think prices matter.

Q: *Draw a graph of the author's demand curve for wine. Show what happens when he moves along the curve as a result of the lower price of wine in Europe. Now suppose that the change in the amount of wine consumed is due to the fact that living in Europe and drinking wine are complements. How would this change the demand curve?*

2.10

I love to collect examples of bizarre pairs of goods that sellers or buyers apparently believe are **complements** or **substitutes.** Our local, now defunct Tower Records used to have condoms for sale at the check-out counter, presumably in the probably reasonable belief that condoms and rock music are complements in students' consumption. Near my apartment in Germany this summer, a funeral home has a casket in the window, with seashells on top, sand strewn around, and a seagull perched atop a cross. Do the owners really believe that customers will be consuming funerals and beach vacations together? I wonder. I disgust my introductory economics students by listing peanut butter and mayonnaise as complements since I used to make myself sandwiches of these two items.

Q: *Think of two amusingly bizarre real-world examples of complements or substitutes, the weirder the better.*

2.11

The house of one of my friends, an English professor, was listed on this week's Architectural Tour of Austin. People pay $10 to go through ten houses to admire the architecture. The artwork on his house's walls includes a number of paintings by his wife, an artist. He was dubious about the prospect, and the eventual reality, of 4,000 people traipsing through his house. What he had not realized was that these people represented a large rightward shift in the **demand curve** for his wife's paintings—the Tour was wonderful free advertising for her work. Indeed, she sold five paintings as a result of the Tour. The only problem, so he says, was that she did not realize that this increase in demand allowed her to raise prices, so she sold the works at her usual, pre-Tour prices.

Q: *How would you explain this* **change in demand** *for the paintings? Did the tastes of these 4,000 people change as a result of the architectural tour?*

Supply

2.12

Prof pilfers poop! I saw a story about an economics professor I know who has been arrested for stealing manure from a horse farmer in the Boston area. Ignoring all possible jokes about this (and there are many), the story illustrates a number of economic principles. First, one might wonder why the manure has any value—after all, is it scarce? Apparently it does have value, as the farmer is able to sell it for $35 a truckload. The value is determined in part by its **opportunity cost** since the farmer uses some of it to fertilize his own fields, thus saving on the cost of purchased fertilizer. When stopped by the farmer while trying to escape with the manure, the professor initially offered to pay $20 for it, and he then offered $40. The professor apparently realizes that the **supply curve** (even of manure) is upward sloping. Perhaps most interesting is that the farmer was smart enough to realize that the product has a commercial value—that it is scarce, and that the **equilibrium price** for horse manure is above zero.

Q: *Suppose the professor didn't mean to be dishonest and thought that he was doing the farmer a favor. What was he assuming about the farmer's value of fertilizer? What would be the equilibrium price if the fertilizer had no value to farmers?*

2.13

One of the students, a Russian émigré, tells me he left Russia to avoid being drafted into the army. I mentioned that I had heard young men can bribe someone with $100 to avoid being drafted. He said that's true, but for a bribe as low as $100 the exemption from service is offered by a low-level bureaucrat; and that exemption may not be honored by the people who decide whether you are drafted. To guarantee that you escape from the army, you need to bribe a high-level official whose exemption will be respected by everyone. That costs thousands of dollars. Apparently, the **supply curve** of exemptions from the army is upward sloping in the price of the bribe that must be paid.

Q: *You are driving in a poor country, are stopped on a traffic violation, and it is clear that the policeman would like a bribe. Would the bribe cost you more or less than in a similar situation in a richer country?*

2.14

As I do each year, I auctioned off candy (this year: Reese's Peanut Butter Cups) to my class. None were bought at a price above 50 cents; all twenty-three were sold at that price. As usual, a nice illustration of **downward-sloping demand** curves. I had kept one at the start, extolling its taste while eating half of it (and thus presumably causing an **increase in demand**). The other half fell off my lectern, and I stepped in it after returning to the front of the room. The first half-piece of candy was really tasty, and I was dying for another one. What to do? Aha—I started bidding to buy one from the students who had bought mine. At an offered price of 2 cents—nothing; 25 cents—nothing; 50 cents—nothing; $1—nothing. Finally, at $2 one student offered me a peanut butter cup. So because I stepped in it—literally—I got to illustrate **upward-sloping supply** curves, too.

> Q: *What are some other things I could have used in the auction that would have worked at least as well in illustrating downward-sloping demand? Which ones would I have had the same problem buying back? Which ones would have caused less of a problem?*

2.15

In the movie *Catch Me If You Can*, Leonardo DiCaprio winds up in a hotel room (in the 1960s) with a woman he discovers is a very high-priced call girl. She says, "You can have me for the night—just say the right price." He says "$300," and she throws a card at him and says, "Go fish!" He then says $500, getting the same answer, then $600, with the same result. He finally says $1,000, and she agrees. As with most activities, this transaction has an **upward-sloping supply curve.**

> Q: *Is $600 the opportunity cost of the call girl's time? Is $1,000? What does this story tell you about her opportunity cost?*

2.16

We've had some old unwanted gold jewelry lying around for a long time. With gold at $1,237 per ounce, we figured it was time to sell it. We are a living movement up the **supply curve** of gold. The local jeweler who bought the gold says we are hardly unique—but the pattern of supply has been interesting. There was little increase in **quantity supplied** until the price hit $1,000—then there was a flood. As price has risen still further, some additional amount has been supplied, but not too much. Apparently, potential suppliers were waiting for the price to hit $1,000; thereafter, only those who hadn't paid attention, like me, were left to enter the market.

> Q: *Draw the shape of this supply curve. What other items can you think of that may demonstrate similar patterns? Graph what this says about the shape of the supply curve.*

2.17

My Dutch friends tell me they read foreign (non-Dutch) novels that are translated into English rather than into Dutch. I know their English is very good, but their Dutch is clearly better. So, I ask, why read in English? The answer is simple: For example, take a book originally written in Swedish, like Stieg Larsson's wonderful *Girl with the Dragon Tattoo*. If somebody translates it into Dutch, the relatively small number of Dutch-speakers means that the market for the translation will be much smaller—and the royalties and profits smaller, too—than in the market for an English translation. These smaller returns attract translators who are not as good as those attracted into translating a book into English—the **supply curve** of translators is upward-sloping. My friends say they would rather read a good translation into a language they know well, but not perfectly, than a mediocre translation into their native language.

Q: *These Dutch readers' substitution to the English version also affects the demand for the Dutch version of the book. Draw the demand curve for the Dutch version and show how it shifts in the case where a better English version is available. How does this affect Dutch readers who are not bilingual?*

2.18

I've been mystified by the abundance of beauty parlors and barbershops in Germany, and by the low price they ask. At home, I pay $35 for a haircut by my wife's hairdresser (nearly $1/hair). In Germany, for an equal-quality haircut, I pay €13 ($17). Why so low a price, why so many shops? Apparently, haircuts used to be much more expensive—my Berlin colleague paid €15 (DM30) in 1994, and now he pays €8. Germany relaxed the rules on entry to the hairdressing trade, no longer requiring a master hairdresser in the shop. With the expansion of the EU, Polish hairdressers have entered the German market, shifting the **supply curve** far to the right and lowering the price drastically. Not surprisingly, the effect has been bigger in Berlin (near Poland) than in Bonn (far west in Germany). Who's been hurt by this price drop? Polish hairdressers are better off, as are German consumers. Young German hairdressers entered the field knowing full well what prices are, so they can't be worse off. The only losers are older German hairdressers, who expected high prices when they entered the field and have suffered a loss of earnings because loosened restrictions on entry into the market have reduced prices.

Q: *Would the entry of Polish barbers drive the earnings of German barbers to the same level as in Poland? Why or why not?*

Which Curve Shifts?

2.19

"The ethanol industry's growing appetite for corn has pushed prices for the grain to their highest levels in a decade amid a surge that agricultural experts say could lead farmers next spring to plant their largest corn crop in 60 years," goes a story on Yahoo.com. The **demand curve** for ethanol shifted rightward because of the huge increases in petroleum prices. That in turn has shifted the demand curve for corn, the input into ethanol, far to the right, too. The demand curve for ethanol has moved rightward up the **supply curve,** and, as the story notes, the rising price of corn is expected to increase the **amount supplied** as farmers increase their plantings next spring.

Q: *Draw the supply and demand graphs in the markets for petroleum, ethanol, and corn. Explain how they are related.*

2.20

A disaster has occurred in Germany: The staple drink—beer— is rising in price, and people may have to cut back the **quantity demanded.** The reason is that the price of barley, a major ingredient in the brew, has risen, and this has shifted the **supply curve** of beer to the left. I think the **shortage** is temporary—with higher prices for barley, more farmers will plant the crop. That should bring the price of this input back down, and after a year or two, beer prices should fall back more or less to their previous levels. Not much consolation for those wishing to imbibe now, but their pain will probably be short-lived (and, if they drink enough, they won't remember the pain anyway).

Q: *The same problem affects beer prices in France. Is the difficulty for French people likely to be as great as for German people?*

2.21

One of the silly things our grandchildren do each year at the beach is try to catch seagulls. This year, I asked the seven-year-old what he would do if he caught one. He said, "I would sell it for $20." I asked him what if nobody would buy it at that price, and he responded, "Then I would sell it for $1." Clearly, seven-year-olds understand the **law of demand.** The grandchildren have never caught a seagull and almost surely never will; but nevertheless, we were talking about how to catch one. My eighty-seven-year-old father told his great-grandchildren, "Lie flat and still on the beach, put some seagull food on your belly, and grab the seagull when he comes to eat it." It doesn't seem possible to increase the number of seagulls supplied by simply offering them *more* food—**moving up along the supply curve**—as there is always lots of seagull food on the beach. Dad's scheme to **shift the supply curve** of seagulls to the right thus seems the best way for the grandchildren to catch a seagull.

Q: *Would my Dad's scheme work better or worse if there were less garbage on the beach?*

CHAPTER 3

Demand and Supply— Quantity and Price in Unrestricted Markets

Single Markets

3.1

My younger brother is a professor of law and was formerly a partner in a large law firm. He specializes in corporate law and, not surprisingly, he informs me that he is increasingly turning down opportunities to advise law firms and corporations on legal matters. He mentioned the price he charges them, and I suggested the following: Raise the price! It's clear that the **demand** for his services in this kind of work exceeds the effort he is willing to **supply**. We know that in such cases of temporary **disequilibrium** the price should rise to equate the **quantity supplied** and the **quantity demanded**. So, even if he doesn't increase the amount of effort he supplies, at least his total earnings will rise as he rations his time more sensibly by charging a higher price.

Q: *Draw the supply and demand curves for this lawyer's time. Where is he currently producing? What will happen if he raises the price of his services?*

3.2

One of the students in my class is a saxophone player. Like all reed-instrument players, he buys a lot of reeds for his instrument. In 2001, bamboo trees in a large part of the world were infected with a virus that destroyed much of the bamboo crop. This change **shifted the supply curve** of bamboo to the left. This shift raised the price of bamboo, which is the major input into making reeds. As a result of this increase in the input price, the supply curve of reeds shifted leftward, too. The student noticed that the price of reeds skyrocketed. Being a smart young fellow, he wisely **decreased the amount of reeds he demanded** each month because they now were more expensive. He moved leftward along his **demand curve** for reeds.

> **Q:** *As anyone who lives in a warm climate (like Central Texas) knows, bamboo is a weed that grows quite rapidly. How long do you think it will be until the original equilibrium in this market is restored?*

3.3

My wife is helping with a local drive to get people to register to donate organs. We thought that she, as a cancer survivor, would not be allowed to register. Wrong. Anyone under age 85 can register as long as their cancer is not active and they do not have a systemic infection of any kind. The doctor who informed us said that this increases the potential **supply** of transplantable organs. If the **demand** is high enough, and the patients awaiting transplants sick enough, the doctors will use a donated organ even if the transplantation risk from the particular organ is substantial. Thus, while fortunately the price system is not used explicitly in the transplantable organ market, the choice to allow more people to register and to compare the demand to the increased supply suggests that economics is operating in this market even without prices.

> **Q:** *The sale of organs for transplantation is not allowed in the U.S. Should it be? What are the economic arguments in favor of this?*

3.4

In the James Bond movie *Goldfinger,* the main character, Auric Goldfinger, owns a huge horde of gold. The plot centers on his attempt to explode a nuclear device at Fort Knox, where the U.S. gold supply was housed at that time. He hatches this plot to irradiate the U.S. gold supply, rendering it valueless. His idea is that with the U.S. gold horde gone, the world **equilibrium price** of gold will rise. His wealth, which consists of the value of the gold he owns, will increase with no additional effort on his part.

> **Q:** *Analyze in a supply-demand graph the economics of Goldfinger's activities. What would happen in the market if,*

after Goldfinger's success, people decided that gold rings were not necessary mutual gifts to brides and grooms? [Extra credit, not economics-related: How long before the nuclear device was scheduled to explode did James Bond shut down its timer?]

3.5

My seven-year-old granddaughter called to tell me that she just lost her eighth tooth. I asked her how much the Tooth Fairy is paying these days, and she told me the price is $2. In 1950 when I was her age, I got 10 cents for a lost tooth. Even with inflation since 1950, my 10 cents is the equivalent of only 84 cents today, meaning that the Tooth Fairy is now paying more than twice as much after inflation as in 1950. The question is why? My guess is that the decline in the birth rate in the last forty years has reduced the number of little kids losing teeth, thus **decreasing the supply** of teeth. Assuming Tooth Fairies haven't changed their behavior, the **supply curve** has moved leftward and up the **demand curve,** reducing the number of teeth that Tooth Fairies buy and raising the price per tooth, as suggested by a comparison of the payouts my granddaughter and I received from the Tooth Fairy.

Q: *It is also the case that teeth today have fewer cavities and fewer metal fillings. If the Tooth Fairy doesn't like metal in teeth, how would that have changed the price that she is willing to pay for a tooth?*

3.6

In Dallas, all of the Jamba Juice outlets (which sell smoothies and related products) have placed a "Brrr Charge" on any smoothie containing oranges or orange juice. Apparently, there was a freeze in Florida, causing a **decrease in the supply** of oranges. This raised the price of oranges, a crucial input into orange smoothies, causing the supply of orange smoothies to shift leftward, too. The rise in the price of orange smoothies will in turn affect the demand in a closely related market—for banana smoothies. I would think that the **demand curve** for banana smoothies shifted outward, and Jamba Juice and similar stores are seeing more demand for substitutes for orange smoothies—and setting higher prices for those, too.

Q: *What do you think these changes will have done to the demand for "Slushies" at the 7-Eleven?*

3.7

A sign on the wall at a René Magritte exhibit noted, "Magritte repeatedly painted variants of his subjects, mostly to satisfy demand in the art market." Even artists are selling their products, just as businesses do. When the **demand** for their product increases, it calls forth an increase in the **amount supplied.** We also see this in popular literature, where a highly successful mystery writer winds up in a rut writing minor variations of an earlier hit. Sadly for us economists, this doesn't seem as easy to do—the premium is on originality and novelty; if today's demand called forth minor repetitions in what we supply, we soon wouldn't get the stuff published very well!

> Q: *This vignette makes clear the difference between creative markets in art or literature, and in scholarly economics. Why does this difference exist?*

3.8

If free to do so, markets tend toward an **equilibrium** where supply equals demand. That's even true for the market for dating, as shown in 1963's No. 1 hit song, "Surf City," by Jan and Dean. They sing, "We're going to Surf City, gonna have some fun, . . . Two girls for every boy." Two girls for every boy is not an equilibrium—it is a disequilibrium situation. There is a **shortage** of boys and a **surplus** of girls. Jan and Dean are going to Surf City because of the surplus of girls there. Their arrival will reduce the size of the surplus of girls and also reduce the shortage of boys. If enough other boys follow their lead, the market for dates in Surf City will be in equilibrium—the shortage and surplus will have been removed by the action of the market as people respond to the shortage of boys by "going to Surf City."

> Q: *If you have ever been to a mixer or a singles bar where there is an excess of members of one sex, why did this excess arise? What prevented the equilibrium, roughly equal numbers of men and women, from being reached?*

3.9

A joke book I own has the following story: A professor is fond of telling naughty stories, and a group of women in the class resolve to walk out the next time he does. The prof hears about this and two weeks later announces, "They say there is quite a **shortage** of prostitutes in France." The women immediately begin walking out, and the prof smiles broadly and says, "Ladies, the next plane doesn't leave until tomorrow afternoon." The prof's statement about the shortage makes it clear that it is a temporary excess of the **amount demanded** over the **amount supplied;** and his comment about the plane implies that the women's going to France will reduce the shortage and bring that market in France back to **equilibrium.**

Q: *At your university, there are some classes where there is a shortage of spaces for students wanting to take the class. How does the university remove the shortage? Does it get to equilibrium enrollment?*

3.10

A story in the *New York Times* discussed a problem in London: There has been a shortage of taxis on the streets in the evening and at night. There is no overall **shortage** of London cabs. The problem has been that drivers don't want to work evenings and nights. The solution: The city government has raised the regulated rates for evening-night cab fares to about 30 percent above daytime fares. This has encouraged a 20 percent increase in the number of drivers who are willing to switch from day work. Is this increase big enough? The fare increase will reduce the number of cab trips demanded, too. Unless the shortage was immense—more than 20 percent excess demand—we can expect the initial large increase in the supply of cabbies to be excessive. Passengers should have no trouble finding cabs, and cabbies will be complaining about insufficient demand.

Q: *Graph the situation in this market before and after the nighttime fares were raised. Show the new price in relation to the equilibrium in this market if the new fare is too high.*

3.11

How many zoos exhibit koalas? The answer is very few, which is really surprising since people love to look at these cuddly creatures—the **demand curve** for looking at koalas is far to the right. The reason is not that koalas are hard to breed in captivity. Rather, the **supply curve** of koalas on exhibit is so far to the left is because they are very fussy eaters and require the zoo to incur huge annual costs for food (the tips of certain eucalyptus leaves) to keep them alive. At an annual cost per koala of over $5,000, it's not surprising that zoos would rather exhibit less expensive animals. The **equilibrium** price of koala exhibits is so high that, even with the large demand, the equilibrium quantity is low.

> **Q:** *More generally, what does this tell you about the kinds of animals exhibited at zoos? What will allow zoos to have more diverse exhibits?*

3.12

A California junior college will be setting two levels of tuition for some of its classes. Many colleges set differential tuition based on in-state residence, level of class, or type of course. But this plan will explicitly set tuition differentially in order to fund additional offerings that would not otherwise be provided. Essentially, the college is moving up the **supply curve** of courses, recognizing the **demand** far exceeds supply at the current (very low) tuition level. The plan has generated an outcry among people bothered by pricing of education. But higher education requires resources, and if taxpayers refuse to pay taxes but insist on services, this seems like a perfectly reasonable way of meeting demand. I expect that, as in so many areas, California will once again lead the nation, this time into an expansion of additional differential pricing of course offerings in higher education.

> **Q:** *The vignette deals with economic efficiency. If instead you wanted to price courses based on equity, how would you do it? How would the outcomes—enrollments—differ from what is described above?*

3.13

All Christmas trees are imported into the Hawaiian Islands from the mainland U.S. Last year, sellers ordered too many trees. The **surplus** of trees caused the prices to be unusually low, and many trees were left unsold. This year, in reaction to last year's surplus, Hawaiian Christmas-tree sellers ordered many fewer trees. The result is that there is now a **shortage** of Christmas trees in Hawaii. The price of trees this week before Christmas has skyrocketed to $200 a tree, from the usual, presumably **equilibrium price** of $30 to $70 a tree. No doubt some potential buyers will be deterred by the high price, while others will cough up more money to purchase a tree than they had expected to spend. I would be happy to bet that next year the price of trees will be well below $200.

> **Q:** *Draw the* **supply** *and* **demand curves** *in the market for trees in Hawaii. Show in your graph the market last year. In the same graph, now describe this year's market.*

3.14

On the Web site http://www.intervivos.com/ the company offers "Premium services and top quality flowers. When words simply fail you . . .we'll help you get your message across. No matter HOW, WHEN and WHY—to your LOVED ONES—ANYWHERE under the sky. . . . (As expected, there will be price adjustment for Valentine's Day flora order, especially for roses. Please ask for quotation before delivery. Prices shown here are not applicable for Valentine season.)" The company clearly understands that there is a rightward **shift in the demand curve** for flowers around Valentine's Day, and that the shift is especially large for roses. The price it can charge—the **equilibrium** price—is much higher at that time of year than at other times, with the biggest increase in equilibrium price being for roses.

> **Q:** *Is the price premium for Valentine's Day roses likely to be larger or smaller than that for Valentine's Day chocolates? What happens to the supply and demand for these products after Valentine's Day?*

3.15

When I was a child, tickets for grandstand seats at Comiskey Park (where my team, the Chicago White Sox, used to play) cost the same regardless of who the opponent was (only seven possible opponents in those days), what time of day it was, or what day of the week it was. At a recent Minnesota Twins game, I learned that Major League Baseball has gotten smart, pricing differently depending on the identity of the opponent and the date and time of the game. For games in the same one-week period, a home-plate-view grandstand seat in Target Field ranges from $36 to $45, with a higher price for night games, weekend games, and most importantly, for more attractive opponents (sadly, the price is higher for the Red Sox than the White Sox, other things equal). Probably aided by Web technology, teams can do a better job of creating an **equilibrium** between

demand and the (fixed) **supply** of seats—although the current price range and the partly empty stadium in the game I saw (against the last-place Kansas City Royals) still doesn't seem great enough to eliminate a **surplus.**

Q: *My university cannot charge different prices for football games against highly competitive teams and for those against lower-quality teams. How do you think the market adjusts for this inability?*

Related Markets

3.16

The Economist of January 1, 2011 reports that the city of Shanghai has been **auctioning** car license plates. The average auction price recently was $6,900, truly remarkable considering the level of family incomes in China, and even in Shanghai. The number of plates given out in 2011 will be lowered further in an attempt to reduce gridlock and pollution (which my own experience several years ago in Shanghai suggests is of world-class caliber). This time, though, plates will be given away in a lottery. Why the substitution of a lottery for an auction? The State will be forgoing the auction revenue, which seems unfortunate. The article also notes the spillover of the limit on license plates to the **related market** for new cars. This will shift the **demand** for new cars leftward and reduce upward price pressure in that market.

Q: *What will this change do to the market for housing in the suburban Shanghai area? What will it do to land prices in central Shanghai?*

3.17

A television ad last night depicted a grocery store manager walking down an aisle, picking up a jar of Miracle Whip and saying, "Who marked the price as $1,000?!" He then notices two turkeys disguised as store workers busily marking more jars to sell at $1,000 each. The ad then shows somebody slathering Miracle Whip on a slice of bread, and the voiceover says, "Miracle Whip makes a better turkey sandwich." The turkeys in the ad understand simple economics. By raising the price of Miracle Whip, they hope to reduce the **amount demanded**. That reduction would in turn **shift the demand** for the **complement**—turkey for use in turkey sandwiches—to the left and result in fewer turkeys being slaughtered as inputs into turkey sandwiches. The turkeys know that the markets for Miracle Whip and turkey sandwiches are related.

Q: *On what other products in the store could the turkeys have altered prices in order to reduce the demand for their meat?*

3.18

An advertisement for financial advice in the *Toronto Globe and Mail* shows a naked couple in bed making love. (This ad probably would not appear in an American newspaper.) Below the picture is a small banner with a stylized news report saying, "Sheer Inc. recalls 100,000 condoms." On the right side of the picture are three graphs: The first shows the stock price of Sheer Inc. falling as it moves out the *x* axis over time. The second shows the stock price of Cupid Condom Inc., presumably a **substitute** for Sheer Inc., rising as it moves out the *x* axis. The final graph shows sales of maternity wear, also substitutes for condoms, rising as they move out the *x* axis.

Q: *If you were drawing up a revision of this advertisement, what two extra graphs depicting additional markets would you put on the right side of the picture? In other words, what are some other related goods that would also be affected by the Sheer Inc. recall?*

3.19

News of the Weird has a depressing economics story this week about food prices in the poorer sections of Port-au-Prince, Haiti, which is perhaps the poorest country in the western hemisphere. The price of rice, the staple product, has doubled in the last year. This increase naturally has residents looking for **substitutes** for rice. Apparently, in the past they have baked "dirt cookies" using salt and vegetable shortening along with clay from a nearby area. The clay has some nutrients in it, so it is not entirely filler. The problem, though, is that the **supply curve** of clay is not horizontal; so with this **increased demand** for the clay, its price has risen, too—by 40 percent during the same period. The dirt is no longer dirt-cheap!

Q: *Why did the price of clay increase only 40 percent when the price of rice doubled? What would you expect to happen to the price of clay if the price of vegetable shortening decreased?*

3.20

The U.S. government subsidizes cattle grazers to use federally owned lands (mostly in the West). The average price per month per animal unit is around $1.50. Private landowners charge around $11 per month per animal unit on their lands; the free-market price is around $11 per month. Does that mean that the **subsidy** is $9.50 per month? *No*—it's more than that. The federal subsidy induces cattle grazers to use federal lands. That shifts their demand away from private lands. The federal subsidy lowers the **equilibrium price** on private lands below what would prevail if there were no subsidy. In an unsubsidized market, demand for grazing private lands would be higher, resulting in an equilibrium price above $11.

Q: *Graph the market **supply** and **demand curves** for grazing on federal and private lands. Show the effect of the subsidy to grazing on federal lands on the prices observed in each market and then show what would happen if the subsidy were removed.*

3.21

The price of corn is the highest that it has been in many years. The reason is that corn is an input into ethanol, a **substitute** for gasoline. With the huge rise in the price of oil, the demand for ethanol has increased, **increasing the demand** for corn. The "problem," say some farmers, is that the rise in the price of corn, an input into production of cattle and other meat animals, will increase their costs, reducing their **supply.** We thus go from oil, to gasoline, to corn, to meat—illustrating very clearly how one price change ripples through other markets—how **general equilibrium** is re-established in a complex economy.

Q: *How will the general equilibrium change as the technology for hybrid and electric cars advances?*

3.22

My law-professor brother tells me of an unusual provision in last year's Dodd-Frank financial reform bill. It designates conflict minerals (gold, wolframite, and two others)—the mining of which yields profits that have financed wars in the Congo—and prohibits companies from using such minerals unless their provenance is appropriate, that is, unless they come from "compliant smelters." The problem is that the law applies only to corporations of a certain size, and not to small and unincorporated entities. The results are clear: The law **reduces demand** for conflict minerals, thus lowering their price and probably the revenue of the conflict country suppliers (probably minerals from the Congo). But it **raises demand** for other sources of the minerals from other countries, thus raising costs to companies that do business legitimately. My guess is that this was not the purpose of the act's authors.

Q: *How could the government change regulations so as to avoid the negative spillovers of this rule on the related market?*

3.23

Last week's horrific killings at the Ciudad Juarez drug treatment center were front-page news in Texas. The murders are partly the result of what happens in a market when restrictions on supply are imposed in a **related market.** It has become more difficult to ship drugs from Mexico to the U.S. because of increased border enforcement. This has **decreased supply** in the U.S., but increased supply in Mexico. The increased domestic competition in Mexico has pushed prices down there, resulting in a large increase in Mexican drug **addiction** and the violence associated with it. Sadly, I imagine that the new giant border fence will make shipping drugs to the U.S. even more difficult and result in still more addiction—and violence—in Mexico.

Q: *Draw the supply and demand curves for the U.S. drug market. How does the increased enforcement of drug laws affect this market? How would the U.S. and Mexican drug markets change if drugs and drug trafficking were legalized in the U.S.?*

3.24

Walking through the lobby of the San Diego Marriott Hotel, I see an empty wall with a bunch of chairs in front of it. The wall seems to have contained a bank of pay telephones, but they have been removed. Pay telephones are a **substitute** for cell phones. With the growth of cell phone usage, the **demand** for pay phones has surely dropped greatly. But why remove the phones? After all, they have already been set up, so they cannot be generating much further cost; and removing them costs money. In fact, there are substantial **opportunity costs** if the unused pay phones are left intact. First, each pay phone has a telephone number; and the growth of cell phones, fax lines, etc., has made phone numbers a scarce resource (witness the proliferation of area code designations needed to accommodate the explosive use of communication devices). Second, the space taken up by the bank of pay phones has some potential alternative uses—perhaps with chairs as an area for guests to converse, or for a cart selling muffins and coffee—that would enhance the value of the hotel. Removing the severely underused phones is a wise business decision.

Q: *There are still a lot of pay phones in airports and other places. Where would you expect to see pay phones still in place, and from what kinds of places would you expect to see them removed? Why?*

3.25

Every Saturday in a Jewish synagogue, a section out of the Five Books of Moses is read. Next weekend, the portion includes *Genesis* 41:1–36, dealing with Joseph's interpretation of Pharaoh's dream, in which Joseph tells Pharaoh to set aside one-fifth of the produce in the good years to tide the country over during the upcoming famine. This is a classic example of **speculation**: shifting supply from a time when supply is high to a time when it is low. The question is: Why one-fifth—why not more or less? Presumably, Joseph had some idea of how much of the stored grain would deteriorate, how bad the famine would be, and how the Pharaoh valued the current consumption of his subjects compared with their future consumption. He must have chosen one-fifth by accounting for all these factors since he was a pretty smart fellow.

Q: *Graph the supply-demand situations in the good years and the bad years. Then show how Joseph's suggestion affects the markets in the two different times. Now show how the amount Joseph asked the Pharaoh to set aside will change if Joseph believes that a plague of rats might infest the stored grain. How would it change if Joseph believed that Egypt would have an influx of foreign purchasers (like his brothers) during the time of famine? Graph both cases.*

3.26

Students apparently consume mass quantities of the performance-enhancing drug Adderall during exam time. Normally, the price is $3 for 10 mg, but it rises during exam week to at least $5. One student reports that in his suburban Dallas hometown drug dealers, realizing this price variation, **speculated** by buying up large supplies of the drug at $3 and dumping them on the market during exam time, hoping to sell at $5. They didn't realize that this large **increase in supply** would cause the price to drop below $5 during exam week. Indeed, so many dealers engaged in speculation that there was a **surplus** at the usual **equilibrium price** of $3. Students were able to buy the drug for only $2, as dealers sold off their excess supply. One imagines that the dealers were less enthusiastic about speculation the next year, and that the exam-week price stayed above $3.

> **Q:** *Suppose that word gets around to the drug dealers that the equilibrium price for Adderall is $7 in a nearby suburb. What would you expect to happen in each market?*

3.27

In the movie *In Bruges,* Colin Farrell's character is in a hotel room in Bruges with a pair of prostitutes. He asks one where she's from, and the woman says she's from Amsterdam. Farrell says there are a lot of prostitutes in Amsterdam and asks her why she came to Bruges. She answers that the fact that there are a lot prostitutes in Amsterdam is exactly the problem—she can get a better price in Bruges. The woman clearly understands the nature of **arbitrage**—she is taking her services from a market where the price is low to one where it is higher. Presumably, if enough others realize this, the **supply curve** in Amsterdam will shift to the left, the supply curve in Bruges will shift to the right, and prices in the two cities will be equalized.

> **Q:** *What if the prostitutes have a preference for sleeping with Colin Farrell lookalikes, of which there are many in Bruges? How will this affect the equilibria in the two markets?*

CHAPTER 4

Demand and Supply—Quantity and Price in Restricted Markets

Price Ceilings

4.1

Charles Clotfelter's book, *Big-Time Sports in American Universities*, (2011) offers examples of a number of schools that have great teams in one major sport, for example football, and mediocre teams in another, say basketball. For their mediocre team, the arena is often half-empty, even though the ticket price is quite reasonable. There is **excess supply**. For the powerhouse team, the ticket price is also reasonable—but at that price there is a huge **excess demand** for seats. The price is an effective **price ceiling**. How to remove the **shortage** and **equilibrate** the market? Simple: At one school, the price of a pair of season tickets is $1,000; to be eligible to pay this amount, though, you must make an annual "charitable gift" of $7,000 to the university. Presumably, this contribution is sufficient to get supply and demand to the **equilibrium** price. I suppose it is more desirable for the university to earn the **revenue** than to have speculators profit by purchasing the tickets and then re-selling them at the market price—although I would bet some season ticket-holders do scalp tickets on games that they can't attend.

Q: *How might the school change its pricing scheme to remove the excess supply for the less popular sport?*

4.2

The Cirque du Soleil show "O" is a permanent installation in the Bellagio Hotel in Las Vegas and is in tremendous demand. The highest face price for a ticket is $125, but they are unobtainable: The free-market (scalpers') price is $250, far above the **price ceiling** of $125. Tickets are also allocated outside the free market—a certain number are bought up by the major casinos very early and are given away "for free" to the casino's high rollers. For these people the price of the ticket is not zero, though: The dollar price is zero; but these people generate enough extra profit for the casino that the total price to the high rollers (the majority of whom lose money when gambling) is probably at least $250.

Q: *Why doesn't the casino just charge $250 per ticket? Why doesn't it charge the high rollers $250 and take a little bit smaller profit on each gamble?*

4.3

Last month, I was told that there were many doses of the annual flu vaccine available. I was lucky enough to get one. Last week, half the vaccine supply was declared contaminated, and suddenly there is a **shortage:** Many more people want the vaccine that can currently obtain it. Not surprisingly, the moment that this large **decrease in supply** was announced many people rushed to their doctors and health clinics to obtain the inoculation. Some wholesalers of the vaccine have been trying to charge clinics $150 per dose (for which they paid only $8.50). Since letting price rise to let supply equal demand is generally not considered appropriate, the health providers have instead chosen to limit the vaccine to the elderly and to young children—they are **rationing** the vaccine to overcome the shortage rather than letting it be rationed by price increases.

Q: *Who would be the most likely to receive the vaccine if health providers chose to let it be rationed by price increases? Which groups do you think would have the highest willingness to pay?*

4.4

Maastricht University requires most business and economics students to spend one of their six semesters at another university. Students choose from over a hundred schools covering six continents (no exchanges with Antarctica!). The number of available slots varies across schools; unsurprisingly, some schools are over-, others under-subscribed. How to solve these problems of **shortage** and **surplus**? Simple: The university rations by student GPA, with positions in the queue for each school allocated on the basis of GPA.

This year, the greatest excess demand was for Sciences Po in Paris—the three slots were filled by students in the top 20 percent of their class. Other cases of excess demand this year were Simon Fraser University (post-Winter Olympics publicity) and, as in every year, the University of California campuses. Is rationing by GPA sensible? To me, it seems both fair and incentive compatible; it gives students an incentive to perform well here, and the more desirable campuses get the better students.

> **Q:** *Can you think of a system that allocates the exchange places in any ways that would make the business major at Maastricht even better? Can you think of a fairer system?*

4.5

There's a **shortage** of sperm in Britain! Apparently, the U.K. needs donations for about 4,000 women per year; about 500 sperm donors per year are required, while only 300 are currently registered. Things were fine until 2005, when a law was enacted allowing children of sperm donors the right to discover the identity of their father when they reached age 18. Simultaneously, the number of women who could use the same donor's sperm was limited further. The first change scared off a lot of potential donors, shifting the **supply curve** of sperm to the left, while the second change caused the **demand curve** for individual donors to shift to the right. Because there is no price that might help the market reach **equilibrium,** the country has been forced to search elsewhere for donated sperm. The shortage is getting worse, with some women who want babies not having them, others resorting to imported sperm. The simultaneous restrictions have made both potential mothers and some donors who might have been willing to donate unable or unwilling to participate. The potential solutions are clear—either loosen the restriction on the number of women that can be inseminated by one donor's sperm (the Dutch have a limit of 25 women per donor); pay for sperm, as in the U.S. and Spain; and/or reinstitute donor anonymity.

> **Q:** *The vignette lists three possible solutions to this shortage. Which do you prefer, and why?*

4.6

The state of Texas, like an increasing number of others, puts a dollar-amount cap on jury awards in lawsuits. Recently, some lawmakers have proposed exempting lawsuits against nursing homes so that there would be no cap on the amounts for which plaintiffs and their attorneys could sue. The **price ceiling** on lawsuits in the rest of the market—the limit on the amount that plaintiffs and their attorneys, who supply lawsuits, could receive—would affect the related market, lawsuits against nursing homes. It would increase the supply of lawsuits against nursing homes, as the attorneys, seeking more clients, encourage people who feel aggrieved against the homes to file more suits. The net result would be more lawsuits against nursing homes. Although the current bill reduces jury awards in total in the whole state, the exemption would increase total jury awards against nursing homes.

Q: *Why would the lawmakers want to exempt nursing homes from this ceiling while at the same time being willing to impose a ceiling on lawsuits against doctors and hospitals?*

Price Floors

4.7

My visiting eighty-three-year-old mother told the assembled family one of the oldest economics jokes under the sun. A lady went into a butcher shop and asked, "How much is the ground beef?" "It's $2.95 a pound," responded the butcher. "That's outrageous," said the lady. "The other butcher shop in town advertises it for $1.79 a pound." "Yes," said the butcher, "and I have it even cheaper than that when I also don't have it in stock." Telling customers that an item is priced very low when in fact none is in stock may be a good way of getting them into the store, but it will leave them unhappy because their **demand** exceeds the storekeeper's available **supply**.

Q: *Think about the market for labor instead of the market for ground beef. What does this joke tell you about the effect of the demand for low-skilled labor on proposals to set the* **minimum wage** *in the U.S. at $10.10 per hour?*

4.8

In Belarus the government doesn't allow trading of its ruble outside a narrow price range, which greatly overvalues the ruble—there is a **price floor** on the ruble compared to euros or dollars. Because of the floor, currency trading has dried up—who would want to sell foreign currencies for grossly overpriced Belarusian rubles? A friend of one of my students has a Web site designed to overcome rigidities in this market, www.prokopovi.ch, a sort of Craigslist for currency. People specify amounts they are willing to buy or sell, agree to trade at some price and arrange a meeting place (often one of the empty currency-trading booths!). When they meet, the trade nominally occurs at the official price floor, making the transaction nominally legal; but the person selling rubles makes extra payments to the buyer to lower the price sufficiently so that the trade actually takes place at the **equilibrium price.** This is one more way in which technology helps markets circumvent imperfections and rigidities.

> **Q:** *If the Belarusian government increases penalties for these illegal trades, what will that do to the price at which the trades take place? Show this in a supply-demand graph.*

4.9

A friend attended a speech by the nation's leading advocate of a universal living wage. This idea is essentially a **minimum wage** on steroids: The minimum amount payable would be much higher than the current minimum wage; and some versions of the proposal mandate minimum benefits, as well. The effects of this higher **price floor** on labor markets are in the same direction as those of a minimum wage: By reducing the amount of low-skilled labor demanded and creating a **surplus** of low-skilled workers at the required higher wage, it will reduce employment of low-skilled workers. The only difference between the universal living wage and the current minimum wage is that its negative effects will be bigger. Because the minimum is at a higher level, it will affect the market for many more workers.

> **Q:** *I think we need a living wage for professors—no professor should be paid less than $100,000 per year at any college or university in the country. Currently, only a very few schools even pay that much on average. What would be the effect at your school if my wishes were legislated nationwide?*

4.10

During much of the semester, my four weekly office hours are nearly empty. The students who show up get a lot of individualized attention: There is a **surplus** in the market for my office hours. In the week before each midterm, however, my office hours are jammed, with long lines of students seeking help and being urged to finish quickly: There is a **shortage** of office hours. What can be done to solve the peak-load problem, in which the supply is fixed but the demand varies greatly over the semester? Unless I spend thirty hours in the office during each midterm week, I will be unable to satisfy all the students. The best solution is advertising to shift demand from peak times to slack times. Early in the semester, the students are told about this problem. The clever ones shift their visits to the usually slack times and hope to benefit more from their time in my office. It helps, but there is still a shortage right before exams and a surplus most of the time.

> **Q:** *Economists believe in using prices to eliminate disequilibriums in markets. If the professor could charge the students for office-hour visits, do you have any suggestions on how prices might be used to remove or at least reduce this problem? Are there any other nonmonetary incentives that the professor might use?*

4.11

In the movie *Stealing Harvard*, one main character goes into a convenience store and buys four six-packs of beer. He then walks out to the car where two teenagers have been waiting and sells a six-pack to these underage kids for $20. His friend hears about this and is outraged that he would charge so much for a six-pack. He justifies his actions saying, "One way or another, they were going to get drunk. They might have to drink mouthwash," so he views himself as increasing economic well-being by selling them the beer that they otherwise couldn't buy. In some sense, he is. The government has imposed a ban on drinking by minors, essentially the equivalent of a **price floor** of infinity. By supplying the beer at $20, he is helping society remove the rigidity of that price floor and getting consumers (the teenagers, in this case) the product at a price they are willing to pay.

> **Q:** *Instead of outlawing sales of beer to minors and implicitly setting a price of infinity, why doesn't the government just put a special high tax on liquor sales to minors? That way those minors who wish to consume alcohol could do so, although at a higher price.*

Quantity Restrictions

4.12

One of my favorite souvenirs in my office is a set of my grandpa's leftover gasoline ration coupons from World War II. These coupons, which allowed U.S. drivers to purchase gasoline during the war years, accompanied money in the transaction for this product. You needed a coupon and enough money to buy a gallon of gasoline. By issuing coupons the federal government both guaranteed that civilians had access to a fixed **supply** of gasoline and ensured that civilians in war-essential jobs had the opportunity to buy more than other civilians could. The system did not work badly, so my parents tell me, but would it work as well today? Actually, if the coupons could be traded, it probably would work better now. Markets, aided by computerized trading, would quickly spring up, and the coupons would very quickly wind up in the hands of those citizens who value them most at the margin rather than those who were fortunate enough to receive them. But if that were true, why give out the coupons in the first place? Why not just let the free market determine who gets the gasoline?

Q: *What are the differences between what would happen in a free market and what would happen if tradable coupons were used?*

4.13

In a recent Harry Hole mystery novel, *The Leopard*, Jo Nesbø (an economist as well as a novelist) has Harry ask someone, "Where would you go to get it (a particular anesthetic) now?" and is answered, "Ex-Soviet states. Or Africa. . . .The producer sells it at bargain-basement prices since the European ban, so it ends up in poor countries." When rich countries **ban** something, they increase its **supply** to poor countries that refuse to ban it. Prices are lowered to consumers there. Rich countries' safety is enhanced, poor countries' worsened, with the only consolation that consumers in poor countries become able to obtain the harmful substance at a lower price.

Q: *Think of another example of a banned substance that nonetheless is consumed. How much higher do you think its price is compared to what it would be if there were no ban?*

4.14

In response to the rising rate of obesity among students, the principal of Austin High School ordered candy removed from vending machines in the school. The candy was replaced by granola bars and tuna kits. This **ban** on candy sales quickly led to a market in illegal candy, smuggled into the school by enterprising students. The ban created an artificial **shortage** of candy, and the price of regular-sized (but outlawed) candy bars quickly rose to $1.50, about twice the price in vending machines elsewhere. One student reports that he was making $50 per day selling candy to other students. The principal has now realized that, although the ban did reduce the consumption of candy, it also meant that the students who wanted candy were paying more. She was also bothered by the creation of the "illegal" candy market. She has ordered the vending machines to be stocked with candy again, although only candy that meets the state's minimum nutritional standards will be sold from the machines.

> **Q:** *Will the principal's actions solve the problem? Or will a market in illegal, non-nutritious candy arise?*

CHAPTER 5

*T*he Consumer— *Elasticities and Incentives*

Elasticity of Demand

5.1

I often do a survey of my students to see if their demand for places at the university responds to prices. The price of places at the university is the tuition charged. I offer students the possibility of zero tuition increase for next year, a 5-percent increase for next year, and a 10 percent increase. Each student is then asked whether he or she will return next year. I recently got the following results: For a 5-percent tuition increase the number of students returning would decrease by 2.2 percent, implying a **price elasticity of demand** equaling 0.44. For a 10-percent tuition increase, however, the number returning would fall by 11.8 percent, implying an elasticity of 1.18. The **demand curve** is surely downward sloping. Not only does the number of places demanded decline as tuition rises; the responsiveness of demand—the price elasticity of demand—is greater in percentage terms when the university tries to raise tuition by higher amounts. That's not surprising: **Substitutes** that suddenly become slightly cheaper don't affect behavior proportionately as much as substitutes that suddenly become relatively a lot cheaper.

> **Q:** *Ask yourself the same question. List tuition increases for your school for next year and ask how many of you and your friends are planning to return. Are your freshman friends more or less likely to return than your friends who are juniors?*

5.2

Yesterday's *New York Times* talked about the efficacy of fuel taxes in reducing gasoline consumption, with a very neat graph depicting gas taxes and consumption for driving per capita in many rich countries. The U.S. tax is $0.50; the German tax is $3.50. We consume 1,500 gallons per capita; they consume 500. Assume without the gas tax that the price would be $3.50 in both countries, so the U.S. price is $4, the German price $7. This allows computing a **price elasticity of demand** of ([1,500 − 500]/1,000) / ([$7 − $4]/$5.50) = 1.83. The German-U.S. comparison suggests the demand for gasoline is highly **elastic**. This is the biggest number I've ever seen for the elasticity of demand for this product. It is probably an overestimate, but it does suggest that raising our low gasoline tax might be a good way to reduce oil imports since the quantity demanded appears to be very responsive to price increases.

Q: *How do you think the introduction of increasing numbers of all-electric vehicles will affect this demand elasticity?*

5.3

During class, a number of students were amused when they thought I had made an obscene gesture while pointing to something on the overhead. I hadn't, but it reminded me of a story. In spring 2000, I was taking a taxi from a conference center in rural Bavaria, Germany, to the Munich airport. Another driver did something really stupid, and I told the taxi driver that in the U.S. I would have given the driver an obscene gesture. He said he would, too, but there's a fine of 500 deutschmarks (about $240) in Bavaria for doing that. I asked if there were other fines, and he mentioned a fine of 300 deutschmarks for giving a certain other obscene gesture. The questions are: (1) Do these fines reduce the number of gestures given (do people move up the **demand curve** as the price rises)? (2) To what extent are different gestures **substitutes** whose consumption depends on the relative prices (the fines)? (3) More generally, what is the **price elasticity of demand** for giving obscene gestures?

Q: *How elastic do you think your own behavior would be in response to a difference in fines for different gestures? If the chance that you might be caught increases, what happens to your price elasticity of demand for giving obscene gestures?*

5.4

A student gives swim lessons at the local YMCA. One summer, the Y charged $40 and enrolled 1,000 kids. The next summer, the managers decided to raise the fee to $50, and only 400 swimmers enrolled. The managers of the Y should have thought about the **price elasticity of demand** for lessons. Calculating it out, one gets: $(400 - 1{,}000)/(700)/(50 - 40)/(45) = 3.86$. If the managers had realized how high the elasticity of demand for their product is, they might have avoided a half-empty pool.

> **Q:** *This seems like a very high elasticity. Give some reasons why it might have been this big.*

5.5

My nephew has switched to making art glass full-time, and I think his work is gorgeous. His problem, though, is what price to charge. Among other things, he blows gorgeous candlesticks, which he thought of selling for $70 a pair. I say he should charge $250 a pair. He says no because he thinks he can sell many more at the lower price. He assumes it takes one hour of his time to blow a pair after he's done the first pair. So I guess his decision depends on the **opportunity cost** of his time and the **elasticity of demand** for his product. There is a set of combinations of the demand elasticity and his opportunity cost that should make him indifferent between the high and low prices, with a higher opportunity cost requiring a higher demand elasticity.

> **Q:** *If you were in his position, what price would you charge? Why?*

5.6

Elasticity in the real world—sort of. The managers of a scholarly journal that I edit were thinking of raising the subscription prices. We used to charge individuals $32 for four issues per year, and charge libraries $52 for four issues. The managers proposed raising the prices to $45 and $75. My feeling was that these increases were too small, especially since the prices of **substitutes** (scholarly journals of a quality similar to ours) were much higher. I suggested that we charge $50 and $85, respectively. I believe that is more sensible since I feel that the demand is quite **inelastic** over this price range, so that with a larger price increase our **total revenue** would rise further. Apparently the managers agreed, and we raised our prices by the larger amount. Next year, our revenue rose, suggesting that my guess about the **elasticity of demand** was correct.

> **Q:** *Why do you think the journal charges different prices to libraries? Do individuals have a higher or lower elasticity of demand than libraries?*

5.7

Flying coach on the plane home from Europe last weekend, I had to have a glass of wine; so I paid $6, being hit by the airlines' revenue-increasing pay-by-the-piece policy. I asked a flight attendant when the airline would start pricing the use of the toilet, got a laugh, but no answer. Today's *USA Today* has a front-page poll asking people, "Would you fly on airlines that charge for access to the restroom?" Most respondents said no, but I bet that people wouldn't let this bother them, wouldn't alter their flight plans and would pay for use of the john. Pricing the bathroom would reduce the **quantity demanded**—some people would wait and race off the plane to the airport bathrooms (unless airports started charging also). But I would think that the demand for using a plane's bathrooms is fairly **inelastic** so that, except on short flights, behavior wouldn't change very much. Of course, if airlines starting charging for bathroom use, that would affect a **related market**—their sales of drinks since drinks and bathroom use are **complements.** So perhaps charging for bathroom use is not a good idea—airlines' revenue might even drop!

> **Q:** *It seems like the demand for use of public restrooms in general is fairly inelastic—when you gotta go, you gotta go. Why, then, are most public restrooms in the U.S. free of charge?*

5.8

On the television show *The Apprentice,* the Synergy and Gold Rush teams were competing to increase sales of their P'Eatzza sandwich. Selling these sandwiches at one for $4, and two for $6, Synergy increased revenues by 997 percent. Selling these sandwiches at one for $8 and two for $9, Gold Rush only increased **revenue** by 608 percent. After Gold Rush lost, their team leader, Leslie, claimed, "If we would have lowered the price by $1, we would have lost by a bigger margin." Clearly, she was wrong: Looking at her sales and those of Synergy, it must be true that the **price elasticity of demand** is far above one—the demand is highly **elastic.** Synergy made more revenue by selling P'Eatzzas for a lower price. Because she had underestimated the price elasticity of P'Eatzzas, Leslie was fired by Donald Trump.

> **Q:** *How might Synergy have made even more money, given what the vignette implies about the price elasticity?*

5.9

A student reported that her six-year-old sister employed the following trick on her when they were little. When the then eight-year-old student came home from school, the younger sister blocked the kitchen entry with a sign saying, "50-cent entry fee." Mom wasn't around and the student was hungry, so she paid the little brat 50 cents. The little sister, realizing that the **demand curve** for entering the kitchen was especially **inelastic** at suppertime, decided to hold up a sign saying "$1 entry fee" at suppertime. Fortunately, the parents were around that time, and my student's complaints to the government (Daddy) caused the free market to disappear: Daddy imposed a 1-cent **price ceiling** on entry to the kitchen. I hope to have the younger sister in class in two years, but I sure am glad she wasn't *my* younger sister!

> **Q:** *What does this tell you about the ability of a private seller to impose an effective price ceiling?*

Income Elasticity

5.10

The easiest example to use to understand elasticity is the behavior of the Cookie Monster on *Sesame Street*. As nearly every American under the age of thirty-five knows, the Cookie Monster eats only cookies. Assume that his income is $100 per week and that the price of a cookie is $1. If the price doubles, he cuts his consumption in half; the amount that he spends on cookies stays constant at $100. This means that Cookie Monster's **price elasticity of demand** for cookies is exactly 1. His demand is **unit-elastic.** If the price is $1 and his weekly income doubles to $200, he doubles the number of cookies he buys. That means that Cookie Monster's **income elasticity of demand** for cookies is +1. For him, cookies are neither a **luxury** nor a **necessity** but are on the very thin border in between.

> **Q:** *The Cookie Monster is having a makeover for the new television season: In order to combat rising child obesity, the producers of Sesame Street are having "Cookie" add other foods to his diet. His new song will be "A cookie is a sometime thing." What does this do to his income elasticity of demand? His price elasticity of demand?*

5.11

A story in the press today notes that the price of rat meat in Cambodia has quadrupled, even as the overall inflation rate is "only" 37 percent. Consumers are **substituting** away from higher-priced meats (beef is still four times as expensive as rat), increasing the demand for rat meat. How can this be if the relative price of rat has risen? Rat meat is almost surely an **inferior good.** As inflation accelerates and erodes people's real incomes, they switch to cheaper alternatives. Cambodian consumers are fortunate that the price of rat meat hasn't risen even more. There has been flooding in the Mekong Delta, forcing rats to higher ground and making them easier to catch—an **increased supply.** Not surprisingly, the rise in price has raised the return to rat-catching, so more kids are entering the labor market for rat-catchers and offering rat meat to the market.

Q: *What would have happened in the market for rat meat if, instead of the flood, there had been a drought?*

5.12

I asked my ophthalmologist how his business was doing in the recession, and he said it was stable. He noted, however, that his colleagues who specialize in Lasik surgery had seen a 60-percent drop in business. Clearly, Lasik, not being reimbursed by most insurance plans, can be postponed in times when incomes drop—at least in the short run it is a **luxury good.** We also know that plastic surgery is another luxury good. Other medical procedures may even be **inferior goods** in the short run: A report noted that there had been a rise in vasectomies in the U.K. Apparently, some couples, fearing that their incomes may be permanently lower, wish to minimize the chance of having another child for whom it will be difficult to provide.

Q: *Which types of medical procedures are more likely to be luxury goods? Are there any others you can think of that are inferior goods? How would you classify still more medical procedures?*

5.13

A story in *The Economist* reports on recent coal-mine disasters in China. It notes that the number of deaths in Chinese coal mines has been declining sharply in recent years, even though the amount of production has been rising rapidly. This parallels the tremendous decline in deaths on the job in the U.S. from the early 20th century and the recent rapid decline in industrial deaths. These declines should not be a surprise to economists: Of all goods, I would think that life is a **superior good**—its **income elasticity** is positive and probably pretty high. As living standards rise, societies are willing to spend resources on being more careful. Workers will not put up with primitive safety standards when they value their lives more, and they are willing to give up a bit of extra pay to have their employers invest a bit more in their safety while at work.

> **Q:** *What does this behavior lead you to expect about trends in injuries on the job? How about in spending on health?*

5.14

After a particularly sumptuous dinner with a great choice of wines, my wife pointed out to me that there seem to be many more types of wine available now than when we were dating in the mid-1960s. She's right—and it is partly a reflection of the growth of per-capita wine consumption in the U.S. But it is also a reflection of the positive **income elasticity of demand** for variety. As we get richer, we not only substitute toward higher-quality goods—we demand more diversity in what we consume and what we do. As another, less tasty example, the number of varieties of lettuce available today is amazing; when I was a kid, we got iceberg lettuce—there was nothing else. Variety is a **superior** good.

> **Q:** *In what product areas have you seen an increase in the variety available in the past few years? How has the internet increased consumer welfare with regard to variety?*

Incentives

5.15

On its Web site, the university makes available the distribution of the course grades each professor gives out. One of my clever young colleagues knows this and says that he likes to give out a lot of A's and a lot of F's. This encourages the students he hopes will take his courses while discouraging the students he doesn't want. Students who might normally be B students think they can get an A and sign up. Students who are C or D students believe that they have a much higher than usual chance of getting an F and stay away from his courses. His grade distribution thus allows students to voluntarily sort themselves in a way that maximizes the quality of the students taking his class.

> Q: *Ask yourself and your friends: Would you respond to this information the way my colleague believes students do?*

5.16

The City of Austin offers airport parking in three tiers, from garage ($20/day), to close-in surface ($10/day), to distant surface ($7/day). Frequent parkers accumulate points entitling them to free parking days. The **incentives** for redeeming the points are bizarre:

Garage	2,500 points
Close-In	2,500 points
Long Term	2,500 points

The "price" of a free parking day is the same for the very desirable garage, where I never park if I have to pay dollars, as for the close-in surface parking (where I park for money if staying for fewer than five days) as for the distant surface (where I park only if staying more than four days). Seeing this, we will redeem our 10,000 points for four days in the garage—parking for "free" elsewhere makes no sense. If the airlines would only charge the same number of frequent-flyer miles for a trip to Australia as they do for a trip to New York, I would be even better off!

> Q: *Does it make sense for me to pay for parking in the close-in lot only if I'm staying for less than five days, or would it be more sensible to park there always?*

5.17

What can the University do about people who are in their last semester of teaching because they are on a terminal contract? Other than pride, self-respect or a desire to help the students, why should the instructor put any effort into teaching? This lack of incentives— this **endgame problem**—arises often in universities. Fortunately, the University does have an incentive to offer, namely withholding letters of recommendation or even threatening to go out of its way to send negative recommendations about the instructor. This threat should provide sufficient motivation. But what can the University do about old professors in their last semester of teaching before retirement? The threat of a negative recommendation letter has no force—the professor may never look for another job. The only thing that keeps the old professor from goofing off is his/her self-respect and pride in teaching—there can be no current or future monetary **incentive** to put for the effort the job requires.

Q: *Think of other situations where monetary incentives are not effective. What social structures and non-monetary incentives are in place to enforce socially constructive behavior?*

5.18

A student was in my office hours yesterday and asked a very specific question. I gave a sheepish look, and she asked why I was looking that way. I hemmed and hawed, then blurted out that I had a question on that exact point on today's quiz. I said I was worried that she would tell other students about this. She said she had an **incentive** not to tell, since to some extent I might be grading on the curve. I said with 500 students in the class, her inference wasn't correct—she has an incentive to tell five friends and help them without appreciably affecting the grading scale in the course. BUT—she would have to swear them to silence, or tell them only right before class, otherwise they might talk to five of their friends, etc. Enough students might then get the question correct to wipe out the advantage arising from her little bit of advanced knowledge about the quiz.

Q: *What are her incentives if I don't grade on the curve but just base the grade on the percent of correct answers?*

5.19

The dean of our liberal arts college wants to get more of the 500 faculty members to submit proposals to foundations and governments to obtain funding for their research. If you submit a proposal, he will give you a grant of $2,000 to be used for academic travel, book purchases, computers, and the like. This incentive is designed to get faculty members to do something they otherwise would not do; it raises the returns to submitting a grant proposal. The dean's idea has two problems. The obvious one is how to police the proposals: What's to prevent me from submitting a slipshod proposal that has no chance of outside funding so that I can get the dean's $2,000? The bigger problem—one that is inherent in any **subsidy**—is how he can avoid subsidizing proposals that would have been written anyway. How can he subsidize only the marginal proposals and avoid giving the $2,000 grants to faculty members who already had planned to seek funding? He can't; his only hope is that the elasticity of supply of proposals is sufficiently high that very many faculty members who had been just below the margin where they would apply for grants are induced to write proposals.

Q: *Draw a* supply curve *of proposals where the dean's subsidy will create a lot of new proposals. Draw one where his subsidy will not have much effect.*

5.20

My wife overheard a conversation between two young women she knows. One of them, who is very wealthy, was telling the other that she had decided to have permanent eyeliner put on—essentially a tattoo around her eyes—since it would save her lots of time applying eyeliner each day. The woman does not work for pay, and she does not have many skills that would get her a high wage should she seek work. So why is she trying to save time—to substitute the expensive procedure of the permanent eyeliner for her time spent applying temporary eyeliner? Where is the incentive? The answer is that the opportunity cost of her time is high, even though she doesn't work—she is so wealthy that she can use the time that she might otherwise spend applying eyeliner in more enjoyable pursuits, such as tennis and yoga. It is worth her while to spend money to get more leisure for less time in caring for her person.

Q: *How would her behavior change if she also had a high-paying job?*

5.21

The hotel I'm staying at in New Zealand has three ways for me to do my e-mail/check the Internet: For $0.68 per minute, up to $33 per day maximum, I can use my laptop and a cable modem in my room; for $10 for one-half hour, I can use wireless and my laptop in the lobby; or for $1 for each 10 minutes, I can use the hotel's hard-wired computers in the lobby. So many choices, so many incentives to think about! Typically, my e-mailing takes no more than 20 minutes, so the hotel's computers are a pretty good deal, and I've been using them. The problem is, however, that I can't download attachments on them; so I've also used—very hurriedly—the option of my laptop in my room at $0.68/minute. The $10-per-half-hour option is always inferior to one of the other choices, and I haven't been using it.

Q: *If you were the hotel owner, would you stick with this pricing scheme? Do you think it is a good idea to give people incentives to use the hotel computers rather than their laptops?*

5.22

We toured St. Basil's, the Orthodox cathedral near Red Square, Moscow, which is probably the most familiar sight in Russia. On the wall in one of the chapels was a description stating that Czar Ivan the Terrible, who had commissioned building it, thought the cathedral was so beautiful that he had the architect blinded so that he could never again create something as beautiful. Ivan was clearly not a nice guy—but he also wasn't a very good economist. The next time he needed a builder, the (remaining sighted) architects had tremendous incentives to do good, but not great, jobs, lest they too be blinded. By blinding the architect, Ivan ensured that he would never get any buildings as magnificent as St. Basil's.

Q: *How would Ivan's incentives to put out the eyes of architects differ early versus late in his reign?*

5.23

A senior scheduled to graduate this term is failing a course. He decides to download a term paper and turn it in as his own work. Since his prior record is clean, the university's most severe punishment if they catch him cheating is to fail him, so the student is clearly optimizing his situation in light of the **incentives** he faces. If he cheats and is not caught, he passes the course and graduates. If he doesn't cheat, his complete lack of knowledge of the course's material means that he will surely fail and not graduate. Cheating and getting caught leaves him no worse off than he would be if he doesn't cheat (ignoring any moral qualms he should have), and he at least has a chance of getting away with it and graduating.

Q: *What could the university do to alter the incentives facing graduating seniors to make the less moral ones behave better?*

5.24

We have just spent 4 hours hiking up a mountain in the magnificent archaeological site of Petra, Jordan, and are completely exhausted. We decide that, rather than walk the 3 kilometers back to the main path to the entrance, we would get a ride back from one of the many camel drivers trying to sell their services. I ask how much it costs, and the guy tells me it is 25 Jordanian dinars (about $35) per person. But, he says, it is only 7 dinars to go more than halfway to the entrance. We bargain, and I get him down to 5 dinars for the more-than-halfway ride. But I wonder why it costs so much less than half to go more than halfway. The reason becomes apparent once we get off the camels and begin walking the rest of the way. The camel ride was over sand, while the rest of the route is concrete and paving stones. Sand is easy on the camel's feet, but the concrete surface is difficult for the camel and his driver. This strange pricing mechanism provides the customer **incentives** to take only the partial ride; and with it the camel driver is setting a price equal to the true costs of providing the different services.

> **Q:** *Would anybody even take the full ride all the way to the entrance? What does the high price tell you about the* **price elasticity of demand** *of those who would ride all the way?*

5.25

I came back to Berlin from lecturing in Hamburg this morning by high-speed train. Regrettably, the train was quite late: Because there was a dead body on the main-line track, it had to divert to a slower route. If a *Deutsche Bahn* train is more than 60 minutes late, the conductor gives each passenger a short form to fill out, mail in, and get a 25-percent refund. Not bad, but my students tell me that *Deutsche Bahn* understands the **incentives,** so one sees a lot of trains that are late by between 50 and 59 minutes. It is nice to observe the *Bahn* responding economically; but it's also nice to get a refund when they can't quite respond to this kink in the incentive structure.

> **Q:** *Make a graph with minutes late on the horizontal axis and amounts reimbursed to customers on the vertical axis. Graph what you think the amounts paid back to customers over the year look like.*

CHAPTER 6

*T*he Consumer— How to Choose

Utility

6.1

Utility is funny. I lived perfectly well for years without a cell phone and without a Kindle (using land phones and dragging books in suitcases), and right after I got them, I did not feel all that much happier. At this point, though, if they were taken away, I'd feel much worse. There's an asymmetry or ratcheting effect on happiness, at least in the short run, which keeps raising our so-called needs for goods once we have gotten used to them. Our utility depends not only on what we are currently consuming, but also on what we are accustomed to consuming.

> **Q:** *What new goods can't you live without? If one of them were taken away, would you feel worse? Would you continue to feel worse for years, or would your negative feelings diminish?*

6.2

A few days ago, I appeared on NPR *Morning Edition* talking about Monopoly (the game, not the market form). Until then, I hadn't thought much about the economics of the game (which I played very often as a child, with our sons and for the past five years with our grandchildren). Monopoly teaches us some useful economic lessons: 1) The very first event illustrates the diversity of people's **utility** functions: I like the "Top Hat" piece, but others may prefer the racing car or the Scotty dog. 2) With only $1,500 to start, you can't buy everything you land on. This requires constrained utility maximization. (I never buy railroads or utilities early in the game.) 3) You need to maximize your utility over time since you should retain money to build houses and keep enough money to avoid bankruptcy if you land on other players' properties before they land on yours.

Q: Think about the limited resources in your life. How are you rationing these resources to maximize your own utility over time?

6.3

Several years ago, an economist asked undergraduates to place values on gifts received from various people. Gifts from girlfriends or boyfriends were valued at almost $1 per $1 price of the gift, and presents from parents at somewhat less. Relative to the students' valuations, presents from grandparents had the least value per $1 the grandparents actually spent on the presents. It's possible that the source of the gift matters: A present from a girlfriend or boyfriend is valued more than the identical present from one's grandparents. An economist would say, though, that girlfriends and boyfriends know your **utility** function best, while grandparents are almost clueless about what does or does not make you happy.

Q: If you had been one of the student participants in the study discussed here, how would you value a typical present costing $100 from your parents, your aunt Sadie, your boyfriend or girlfriend, and your grandmother?

6.4

The owners of a local shopping mall have made use of the Rolling Stones song (see Vignette 1.1) in an advertisement. Their billboard claims, "You can't always get what you want. But you can give them what they want—every time," and then has a big picture of a gift card usable at all the stores in the mall. Their claim is correct if "they want" to shop at one of the stores in the mall. In that case, the dollars on the gift card are worth one dollar each—they are equivalent to money. But if the value of the card exceeds the value of what the recipient would buy in the mall anyway, the card's value to the recipient falls short of what the donor paid for the card. In that case, the recipient's **utility** would be higher if the donor just gave him or her the money and didn't bother with the card.

Q: Think about the last birthday or holiday presents you received. Would your utility have been higher if you had received the cash value of your presents, or were the presents the utility-maximizing choice?

6.5

My oldest grandson will be thirteen years old in thirteen months. We made a bet on whether he would be as tall or taller than me (5'9"), noting that he's already 5'5-1/2". If he is, we agreed that I have to pay him $20. Then he thought and said, "But that can't come out of my *bar mitzvah* present at that time—it has to be on top of what you would give me anyway." The grandson clearly understands a basic idea in consumer behavior: If somebody is given a quantity less than s/he would otherwise buy, all that will happen is complete **substitution** away from buying that amount. If I give you three loaves of bread free, and you would have used your own money to buy fifteen loaves, in general you'll buy twelve, use the savings to expand purchases of everything—including perhaps, but just perhaps, a slice of bread. My grandson's problem is how to ensure I don't cheat him out of his present—but as a grandpa, I can't cheat him.

Q: *If the grandson isn't sure whether to trust his grandpa, should he collect his bar mitzvah present before or after reporting his height?*

6.6

I got an invitation to give a speech at a conference in southern France next June. I had to decline since we've planned a week with the extended family on the New Jersey Shore (the only week the entire family is available). The man who invited me said, "Southern France would not have been a bad place to spend this holiday." Even though we love the Jersey Shore, he's right—the relative **utility** from the French week would be higher; and if the price of each were the same, we'd be off to France. The prices aren't equal—it would cost over $1,000 extra for each of twelve people to do the French week; and it would take a lot more travel time. Too bad—we'll stick with the New Jersey week, a sensible and still very enjoyable economic decision in the face of income, price, and time-constrained behavior.

Q: *How would my decision have differed if I had an annual income of $1 million? Think carefully on this one!*

6.7

A colleague asked me today if I have any exciting trips scheduled, and I said, "Yes, I am giving some lectures at the University of North Dakota next week." He said, "Didn't you go to Europe last month, and isn't that more exciting than North Dakota?" I said,

"Yes I did, and no, North Dakota is more exciting to me." The reason is that I've been to Europe more than sixty times—the **marginal utility** of another trip to Europe is low; but I've never been to North Dakota, and that is the only state I've not visited. So even though the **total utility** of all my trips to Europe is huge, the marginal utility of my first trip to North Dakota exceeds the marginal utility of the sixty-first European trip!

> **Q:** *Are there examples in your own life where something new that is not obviously exciting to others is worth more to you than something apparently more interesting, but that you have done many times before?*

6.8

I was lucky enough to read the story, "Murmel, Murmel, Murmel," in *Munschworks 2* by kids' author Robert Munsch, to four grandkids. In the story, five-year-old Robin finds a baby in a hole in a sandbox. She begins looking for someone to care for the child. She asks a woman, who answers, "Heavens no, I already have a baby." She asks an old lady, who says, "I already have seventeen cats [presumably babies and cats are **substitutes**]." She then asks another woman, who responds, "Heavens no, I have seventeen jobs, lots of money and no time [illustrating the **opportunity cost** of having kids]." She asks a man, who, when told the baby will not wash his car and can't be sold for lots of money [babies today are mostly consumption items, not used for production], also says no. She finally asks a truck driver, who sees the baby, happily takes it, and walks off, leaving his truck. Robin says, "Wait, you forgot your truck." He says, "I already have seventeen trucks. What I need is a baby." The **marginal utility** of the seventeenth truck was very low for him; the marginal utility of the first baby was very high.

> **Q:** *What is something you have lots of and that costs the same as something you don't have? Why don't you switch?*

6.9

It's a difficult decision for an opera lover like me: I must choose between going to see a performance of *La Boheme*, my favorite opera, which I have seen live seven times before, and going to see a performance of *Nabucco*, which I have never seen live but don't like anywhere nearly so much as *Boheme*. What to do? The answer is to apply economic analysis and think about the **marginal utility** of the two choices. While the marginal utility of the first live performance of *Boheme* would be higher than that of the first live performance of *Nabucco*, this would be my eighth. As much as I love *Boheme*, the marginal utility of the eighth live performance is less than that of seeing the other opera. So I go to *Nabucco* and am not disappointed—the singing is glorious, the staging imaginative, and I have a great seat to enjoy it in!

Q: *What if I have the same choice next week—which one do you think would be more sensible,* Boheme *or* Nabucco?

6.10

The Big Texan Steak Ranch and Opry in Amarillo, Texas, offers the following deal: "Eat The Big Texan's famous 72 oz. steak dinner with all the trimmings (shrimp cocktail, salad, roll, butter, and baked potato) in one hour and it's FREE! Almost 35,000 people have tried and 5,500 have succeeded." But you must eat it all—you can't eat part and throw the rest away. Let's say you really only want to eat a smaller amount, say only 64 ounces, and that eating the remaining 8 ounces makes you worse off (feelings of bloat and even nausea). The marginal utility of the last 8 ounces is actually negative. It might still be sensible to eat the whole thing if the loss in utility from eating the last 8 ounces is smaller than the gain in utility that results when you save the cost of buying the steak dinner because you ate it all. With this unusual pricing scheme it could pay to keep on consuming even though the **marginal utility** is less than zero, if that is the only way you can get the pleasure of the first 64 ounces.

Q: *Give two examples of "all-or-nothing" deals that you have seen. Have you bought them, why or why not?*

6.11

We took two of our grandchildren to the Schlitterbahn, a very extensive water park about one hour away from Austin. I spent the morning going on various rides with my nine-year-old granddaughter—and standing in lines with her, too. We spent 10 minutes lining up to go on the Black Knight, but then had to spend 60 minutes in line to go on the Wolfpack. We debated whether waiting the 60 minutes for the Wolfpack was worth it. The time spent waiting is like a **price,** so the first trip on the Wolfpack was six times as "expensive" as each of the second through seventh rides down the Black Knight would have been. So, was the **marginal**

utility of the first Wolfpack trip equal to the marginal utility of the second Knight trip, plus that of the third, fourth, fifth, sixth, and seventh trips? My guess is that the marginal utility of additional Knight trips after the third one that day is probably zero. Moreover, judging by my granddaughter's expression of sheer delight once we started down the Wolfpack, the marginal utility of the first Wolfpack trip exceeded all the extra utility that would have been generated by six additional Knight trips. We made the right choice!

Q: *Imagine there was a third ride with an 80-minute wait. Under what conditions would that be more attractive than either the first Wolfpack ride or the six additional Black Knight rides?*

6.12

Texas and some other states are dotted with sheds selling fireworks on a seasonal basis (before New Year's Day and before July 4). Many of them offer, "Buy one, get five free." Why don't they just cut the price from, for example, $6 per item to $1 per item and sell them one at a time? Would their **revenue** be the same if they did? I assume not, or they would do that. There are several reasons why their behavior might make sense. First, and most important, this gimmick lowers the price of each of the second through sixth firecrackers to zero. Since the cost of each extra firecracker is zero, you will be willing to spend more in total than you would if each were priced at the same positive amount. If the fireworks seller is clever, the total cost of the six exactly equals the sum of what you would have been willing to pay for the first plus the second plus the third, and so on. This is similar to the pricing of ski lifts, "all you can eat" buffets, and other such deals. In all these cases, the seller is hoping, by charging the equivalent of a fixed fee for purchasing the goods or services, to get the buyer to spend more. In economists' jargon, the seller is hoping to extract the entire **consumer surplus** from the buyers, to obtain **revenue** equal to the entire area under each buyer's **demand curve** for the product.

Q: *What might lead a seller to offer "Buy one, get five free," as opposed to offering "Buy one, get ten free"?*

6.13

We went to the local spa—a collection of swimming pools, saunas, steam baths, etc. The pricing structure was extremely clever and created just the right **incentives** for us consumers. The price is €10.90 for two hours, and a fixed additional amount of €4 to use the saunas. The price of an extra hour is only €2, and you can stay for 19 hours for only €2 more. Seems like a great deal! In fact, we stayed exactly two hours. After one hour, we were still enjoying ourselves greatly. While the third and subsequent hours are a bargain, and there are tremendous monetary incentives to go beyond two hours, at that point we both looked like prunes, were completely relaxed and exhausted, and left. **Diminishing marginal utility** had long ago set in. Assuming we are typical customers, this **two-part tariff**—essentially a fixed entry fee and a very low price for additional usage—maximizes the company's profits. It is typical of places like this where people get tired of consuming after some period of time. The firm presumably sets the fixed entry fee at an amount that eats up most of the **consumer surplus.**

> **Q:** *Would we be better off if the spa simply charged a flat fee per hour? Would spa profits go up or down?*

6.14

In my room at the Sheraton Boston Hotel a sign says, "Reward yourself with a $5 voucher at participating food . . . outlets for each night you decline housekeeping services." My **consumer surplus** from not having my room cleaned and the bed made actually exceeds the $5: I would pay a little bit extra not to have the cleaning people in my room since I wouldn't have to worry about packing things up to hide them, nor about the cleaning people mistakenly throwing something away. So I take the deal. One friend here says this isn't worth it to him—he likes having his room cleaned up each morning. This illustrates how crucial individual tastes are to determining the surplus we gain from transactions—and the choices we make, or don't.

> **Q:** *So if my consumer surplus is so large, why is the hotel willing to give me $5 in vouchers rather than, for example, only $2?*

6.15

My wife made me give my twelve-year-old suit to charity, so I had to get a new one. Men's Wearhouse had some nice outfits, and I was willing to pay a lot for a good suit. Top-of-the-line models were available for $600, and they were on sale: "Buy one, get one free." I was going to buy one even without the sale, and $600 was about what I wanted to spend. But I have almost no use for the "free" suit—I derive little **consumer surplus** even from a "free" second new suit. I asked if I could get half-price on the one suit, but the manager said no. I hope I am typical—that when confronted with "buy one, get one free" deals generally most people rationally prefer half-price on each item. But I wonder if that is really the case. Thinking quickly, my wife said, let's take the second suit anyway. She called our older son on her cell phone, as we knew he was shopping for a suit, and he said he was interested. The store has a branch where he lives, so we are taking the suit to him next week when we visit. He will take it into the store and exchange it at no cost to himself for the suit he wants. While I would have derived perhaps $50 of **consumer surplus** from the "free" second suit, a suit's value to him is at least $300; and with the pick of the store, he'll buy a fancier suit. Giving up a suit worth $50 to me, I confer at least six times the amount of surplus on him and get even more pleasure than that myself since I will enjoy seeing him wearing the best possible outfit. So I converted the nearly worthless (to me) second suit into something of value to me!

Q: *How do you think my behavior would differ if, instead of this being Men's Wearhouse, it had been a locally owned store with only the shop in my town?*

6.16

In the movie *Pretty Woman*, Richard Gere and Julia Roberts are bargaining over the price of her "services" for a week. They settle on a price of $3,000. She informs him that she would have stayed for $2,000—implicitly she obtains a **producer surplus** of $1,000, the excess of what she receives over the lowest price for which she would have provided the services. Richard Gere then goes on to say that he would have paid her $4,000. He is getting $1,000 in **consumer surplus**—the price he has to pay is $1,000 less than the highest amount he was willing to pay.

Q: *What is the consumer surplus if Richard Gere had been willing to pay only $3,500? Would the movie have been made if he had been willing to pay only $2,500?*

6.17

I went to buy a glorious Montecristo cigar at the local liquor store. The price on the label was $9.99, and I was happy to purchase it at that price. The cashier rings it up, though, at $5.99. I tell him that the sticker said $9.99, and he says, "Well, given how honest you were, I'm charging you only $8.99." Fine with me. Especially fine because I was willing to buy it at $9.99, so I must be getting at least $1 of **consumer surplus** at a price of $8.99. My honesty, and the cashier's concession, means that the **producer surplus** becomes $1 less. His loss exactly equals my gain; but presumably he still gets some producer surplus, or he wouldn't be offering the cigar to me at just $8.99.

> **Q:** *Knowing that I was willing to pay $9.99, why did the cashier give me a dollar of that price?*

Voting, Addiction, Altruism, and Risk

6.18

My Ph.D. student is agonizing over which of several jobs to accept. He has two offers so far, School A and School B. He tells me that he unquestionably would prefer School A to School B, but he wants to wait to reject School B until he hears whether he will be getting an offer from School C, which is his top choice. Is he being rational? No! If he prefers A to B, having C as an extra choice should not affect that preference ranking. Economists and social theorists call this notion the **independence of irrelevant alternatives.** The student was very upset when I called him "irrational" (probably the worst thing you can say to an economist) and began trying to explain how his reasoning was sensible. In the end, though, he laughed and admitted that he wasn't being very rational. But he still refuses to say no to School B until he finds out about School C.

> **Q:** *What if School C is preferred to School B but not to School A? Would waiting on School C make more or less sense than it did in the vignette? Would it be rational?*

6.19

Self-control mechanisms restrict one's choices, which you would think might reduce utility; but they raise lifetime **utility** by helping to overcome **addiction.** One of my favorites is brushing my teeth several hours before bedtime. Since I don't want to brush twice, this device helps me resist late-evening snacking and thus reduces weight gain. Another addiction is workaholism; but even workaholics may excuse themselves from some work if it isn't paid. The question is: How to avoid part of one's pay, and thus the urge to work, without forgoing pay entirely? Many older academics arrange deals that allow them to be paid part-, usually half-time, and teach only one semester. Not only does this provide a self-control device that might discourage some work; it also enhances flexibility and variety, something that is important to most people.

Q: *Some law firms do the opposite of this: They encourage the workaholic effect by paying extremely high salaries but then expecting employees to work 80-hour weeks. How does this policy affect the overall utility of the lawyers working at these firms?*

6.20

Marginal utility diminishes, but not always very rapidly. My four-year-old granddaughter has been going down the waterslide into the pool at the beach house we are renting, and she shows no signs of getting tired of it (even though my wife and I are very tired of watching her). She must have gone down the slide thirty times in a row. Finally, and fortunately, she decides she is finished, suggesting that the marginal utility has diminished and some other activity (being read to) is now more appealing. My question is: Is going down the waterslide **addictive** for her? Will she do it more times tomorrow? The answer turns out to be no—she goes down the waterslide a lot each day, but her interest seems to diminish across the days. I infer that watersliding into a swimming pool is not addictive for a four-year-old.

Q: *Are there any things that you see little kids do that are addictive, where they do more and more on each separate day, or week?*

6.21

60 Minutes had a story about snus, smokeless tobacco that is not messy and that might be a **substitute** for cigarettes. An anti-tobacco activist talked at length about how it might worsen tobacco's hazards by **addicting** more people to nicotine and leading to more smoking. This is a standard problem whenever the damage from undertaking a risky activity is reduced: Offer a life raft and more people will jump off a sinking ship. Many will be saved, but some will drown off the life raft. Mandatory seat belts do this—lives are saved, but people drive faster and more accidents occur. Sex education does this—there are fewer pregnancies per sexual encounter, but more sexual encounters are undertaken. Unemployment insurance does this—it is a life raft for working, but it attracts people into the workforce who are more likely than others to be unemployed. I'll bet that snus, like the others, will reduce the total damages of the risky behavior, although more people will engage in the behavior because they expect that its costs are lower.

Q: *Have you ever been more inclined to engage in a risky behavior because it became safer?*

6.22

My nine-year-old granddaughter announced, "I feel very sorry for my friend Olivia." "Why?" my son asks her. "Because I will be away and won't be able to attend her birthday party." This struck me as a typical child's self-centered behavior. But another way of looking at it is that it is the epitome of **altruism:** Most young kids view themselves as the center, or near the center of the universe. That being so, their absence from an event honoring somebody else will in their minds detract from the other person's enjoyment so that my granddaughter's sympathy for Olivia can be viewed as charitable. We economists have lots of trouble describing what constitutes true altruistic behavior, and in that light my granddaughter's pronouncement doesn't look so bad. Of course, if she were 13 and made this comment, I would be pretty convinced that her grandmother, others and I had succeeded in spoiling her!

Q: *Can you think of any examples of pure altruism? What seemingly altruistic behaviors are actually selfish, and vice versa?*

6.23

Defibrillators (machines designed to restore heart rhythm during a heart attack) are dropping in price so rapidly that they will soon be affordable by individuals for home use. Some doctors applaud this development. Others are concerned that people, knowing that the defibrillators provide some protection, will reduce their efforts to stay healthy and engage in more risky behavior. Of course, that's true: Whenever you are provided insurance, you take more risks. The question is: What will be the net effect? On this general issue, there is a lot of guidance. For example, one study examined the impact of sex education. It showed that it does increase the amount of teenage sexual activity but does not affect the rate of teen pregnancy. A similar thing probably will happen with home defibrillators: People will take a little bit less care, but the net effect will be that heart attack deaths at home decline.

Q: *Can you infer from this example what the likely effect of laws requiring the use of seat belts might be on driving speeds and deaths in automobile accidents?*

6.24

The old saying, "A bird in the hand is worth two in the bush" is a fairly profound statement about risk and people's attitudes toward risk. If people don't care about risk at all, the saying that the **utility** from one bird in the hand equals the utility from two birds in the bush must mean that the chance of catching a bird is .5 (50 percent) since the expected catch is one bird. But if people don't like risk (are **risk-averse**), the chance of catching a bird has to be higher than .5: The only way that one in the hand equals two in the bush, if you don't like risk, can be if the expected number of birds caught is more than one bird. We think that most people are risk-averse. The best evidence for this assumption is that risky investments must yield higher returns if they are to attract investors. This old proverb must be implying that the chance of catching a bird in the bush is greater than 50 percent. How much greater depends on how much you dislike risk, how risk-averse you are.

Q: *Most of us do not catch birds. But there are other activities where we can get all or nothing or something in between; for example, an A or a C in a course, as opposed to a B. Which would you rather have: a 50 percent chance at an A and a 50 percent chance at a C or the certainty of getting a B?*

6.25

You shouldn't buy the extended warranties on electronics and other goods that places like Best Buy are pushing when you purchase their products (unless you think you have an unusual tendency to buy lemons, are remarkably hard on the products you purchase, or are extremely **risk-averse**). But what about deals offered by our plumber, or our HVAC firm, which for a lump sum give you a discount on future purchases? This adds a new dimension, in that we are guaranteed priority scheduling on any repairs. Unlike an extended warranty, this deal allows us to economize on our time when we need repairs. On purely monetary grounds, it probably doesn't pay for itself; but figuring the **opportunity cost** of my time or my wife's at one-third our wage, the time saved more than justifies joining the "Ben Franklin Society" for the plumber, or the Silver Medallion Society with the HVAC firm. I would bet that those people who buy these additional services are disproportionately high-wage earners; but who's buying extended warranties?

Q: *Web sites such as Groupon allow you to pay a smaller amount now for services to be received in the future (such as pay $10 and receive $20 worth of food at a restaurant). How is that similar to the plumber/HVAC discount? How do they affect consumer utility?*

6.26

Several students claimed in class that our university would give you straight-A grades for the semester if your roommate died. I said I doubted this claim for two reasons. First, it creates a **moral hazard**—you are more likely to engage in behavior that would kill your roommate; you might even kill him or her yourself. Second, it will generate **adverse selection**—people will be more likely to want to room with the dying or those in bad health. Given these difficulties (and the absurdity of the story), I am 99.99 percent sure that this is a local urban legend. A similar, equally implausible student urban legend at UT Austin is that you receive free tuition for the rest of your college career if you are injured by a university-owned vehicle. I don't see any adverse-selection problem here, but it sure creates a moral hazard!

Q: *What is the moral hazard in the case of university-owned vehicles? How would students' behavior change?*

6.27

A pair of students cheated on my final exam—the probability they had so many identical answers on the multiple-choice exam is infinitesimal. If I pursue them, it takes me time, and there's no assurance they will be found guilty. If I don't, I'll feel badly about giving them an undeserved grade. Even for fairly **risk-averse** students, cheating seems like a good idea. I doubt that most cheating is caught; and unless the penalty is very severe (expulsion) and/or the students' costs of contesting the accusation are high, and both are very well publicized, the **incentive** to cheat for students with weak consciences seems overpowering. To salve my own conscience, I do report them; but it turns out to have been a waste of my time—the university says I can't prove they cheated. So the students may be risk-averse, but their little gamble paid off.

Q: *If you were one of these students and had suffered no penalty for cheating in this case, how would your behavior differ in the next class you take? Why?*

6.28

For many years in my giant introductory class, I gave two midterms and a final (plus several quizzes). The midterms counted 20 percent each, as did the total grade on all the quizzes, and the final counted 40 percent. Since the hassle of make-up exams for midterms would be immense, I automatically dropped the lowest midterm or half the final score for everybody, whether or not they missed a midterm. Great solution, but the students could never figure out how well they were doing in the course. Two years ago, I got tired of complaints about the grading uncertainty and decided to drop the midterm only if they missed it, and then weigh the other midterm and the quizzes 25 percent each and the final 50 percent. This removed uncertainty; but it gave students who had done very well on the first midterm an **incentive** to stay home during the second midterm. And, in fact, a lot of students who had done surprisingly well on the first midterm failed to take the second. What to do? The answer is to rely on the students' **risk aversion:** If they miss a midterm, I now keep all the other grade weights the same—20 percent each on the midterm they took and their quizzes; but I count the final exam as 60 percent of the total grade. This worked very well—many fewer students are now missing the second midterm since they do not want to put so much weight on the final exam.

Q: *Are there any situations where, having done well on the first midterm, you would choose to skip the second midterm in light of my new grading scheme?*

Tips on Hunting for Economics Everywhere in Part I

1. Look at your own behavior and your friends' and family's behavior when you buy things or undertake a new activity. How does scarcity affect that behavior?
2. Consider what you give up when you choose something else. What is the true opportunity cost of the choice—what are the trade-offs being made?
3. Look at the choices society makes when the government spends tax dollars. What is being obtained, and what is it worth? What is forgone when the choice is made?
4. Look for cases where the government or another outside force restricts the ability of prices to equate supply and demand in a market. Also, look for cases where governments limit the quantity available.
5. Look at how people change their behavior when the actual or implicit price of an activity or good changes. Are the responses large or small?
6. Consider how purchases change as income changes. How do these differences in purchases vary among people with different characteristics? How do people's choices change as their circumstances change?
7. Look at your own behavior as it reflects the satisfaction you get from different activities. Is it rational in terms of your objectives? Does it reflect diminishing marginal utility and a balancing of marginal utilities and prices?
8. What does behavior imply about attitudes toward risk? What does it show about altruism? Do you have any of what economists would define as addictions?

PART II

*P*roduction, Cost, and Markets

CHAPTER 7

Production and Cost

Production and Technology

7.1

We did a kayak/hike/swim tour with Kayak Wailua, a tour guide company in Kauai, Hawaii, mainly because our guidebook said it was as good as other tours and less expensive. I think the book was correct, so I asked the guide: "How can you guys charge a lower price and still survive?" He answered that they are larger (because they have more permits for river trips), enabling the owner to do his own booking directly, thus saving expenses. Fine; but implicitly, the **opportunity cost** of his time must be less that the cost of contracting out, or he is not **profit-maximizing.** If he is profit-maximizing, then implicitly he has taken advantage of **economies of scale** in this "industry," while his competitors haven't. If that is so, I would expect some consolidation among his competitors as they understand the role of those economies of scale.

> **Q:** *The vignette mentions scale economies in booking tours. Are there any other scale economies that you can think of in this business?*

7.2

One of my young colleagues has a planning problem. He is teaching two sections of introductory economics, and he has two teaching assistants to help out. He intends to assign one teaching assistant to one section, one to the other. He is giving the same exams to both sections. I suggest to him that this is a bad idea for several reasons, and that he should have one teaching assistant handle all the grading for both sections on one midterm, and the other assistant handle all the grading on the other midterm. The reason is that there are substantial **economies of scale** in grading a question, so my proposal would save the TAs' time, making them happier. Also, it would be fairer (the quality of the teaching output will be higher) to the students if one person graded the same questions for all of the students. Otherwise, those students who happen to be in the section with the nastier assistant will be disadvantaged.

Q: *Does my suggestion generate any additional costs to the TAs? As a student, which method of assigning TAs to grading would you prefer?*

7.3

We tend to think of recent **technological change** as a complex process involving huge amounts of **capital** and **labor** (large numbers of researchers and developers). Yet the Winter Olympics should remind us that it is still possible to improve output with a little thought, luck and experimentation. Consider cross-country skiing. It is now standard for skiers to "skate," as that enhances speed; yet nobody was doing that when I learned the sport thirty years ago. Similarly, no ski jumper would have spread his skis at an angle thirty years ago, yet today forming one's skis into a wing is standard. Further afield, stomach ulcers were treated in many ways, until a lone Australian researcher showed they are caused by bacteria.

Q: *How many other examples are there of major improvements in an activity that result from a single individual's insight?*

7.4

The eight windows in my office extend about 12 feet up from the floor, so I'm not surprised when the window cleaner hauls a ladder in and climbs up to wash them. I leave for a few minutes, come back, and there's a different cleaner washing the lower four windows. I ask one cleaner why they divide the labor, and he has no answer. Does having two workers raise the **average product**? It could, but I don't see why, since this cleaner tells me that he always does the ladder work and high windows. Does having a colleague reduce boredom and perhaps raise productivity? Perhaps they take turns driving the truck from place to place? Overall, this seems to be a strange way of organizing production.

Q: *What if the windows were only 6 feet high—would it make sense to organize production differently?*

7.5

February 14—I received a forwarded e-mail today listing twenty-two supposedly clever pickup lines by economists for Valentine's Day. One is "More of you is always better." This makes good sense in the context of production: If you love someone, more of that person should be better. The **marginal product** should always be positive. Another line on this list is "There is no **diminishing marginal productivity** with you." It's really hard to believe that there is never diminishing marginal productivity, even with one's spouse or lover. Eventually, even the greatest romance can benefit from a (brief) respite, a bit of time apart.

> **Q:** *Economists are famous for being brutally frank. If you have a really strong relationship, and only if that is true, try explaining the economics in this vignette to the person you are involved with.*

7.6

I left a stack of handouts containing a problem set by the classroom door today. Each student was supposed to pick one up on their way into class. The problem was that in the last 3 minutes before the start of class, the line of students waiting to pick up the handouts and walk through the entryway to the classroom was getting longer and longer. I had a brilliant idea—make two piles—and I did that. More students per minute were able to pick up the handout and walk into the classroom. With the addition of more of the variable input (piles of handouts) the output (students walking into class) increased. But despite my doubling the number of stacks, the number of students walking into class each minute didn't double. The reason is that there was a fixed input—the size of the entryway into the room. If I had added a third pile the output might have increased further, but not by very much. Even in distributing handouts before class, the principle of **diminishing marginal productivity** (of number of stacks of handouts) seems to work, caused by the existence of a related input whose quantity is not changed.

> **Q:** *What would be the marginal product of making a tenth pile of handouts if I already had nine? Is it possible that it is negative (in terms of the output; that is, the number of students picking up the handout each minute)? If so, what should I do?*

7.7

Just before class, my economics major students were laughing at a conversation they overheard between the instructor of the previous class and one of her students. The student said, "I really need a good grade in this class 'cause my GPA has to be high for me to get into grad school." My students were laughing because the grade in that particular class could not have had much of an effect on the senior's GPA. The student (it wasn't an economics class, thank goodness) did not distinguish **marginal** from **average.** The same thing happens among my intro students at least once a year. Someone tells me that unless he or she gets a B in my class, his or her GPA will be so low that he or she will be thrown out of the university. These students also don't seem to know marginal from average. Their average is low because of their previous bad grades. The marginal grade—what they get in my class—is not going to affect their GPAs very much.

> **Q:** *Calculate your grade in this class so far and assume that it will be your course grade. What will happen to your GPA after this class? Compare that with this class's grade (the marginal grade).*

7.8

Over the years, razor manufacturers have added more and more blades to razors. I started shaving in 1958 with a single-blade razor, switched to a double-blade around 1985, and to a triple-blade in 2004. Recently, I got a free sample of a four-blade razor. The question, though, is: What is the **marginal product** of an additional blade, where we define the marginal product in terms of quality of shave and avoidance of pain from cutting oneself? We can safely assume that the first blade is highly productive—without it there would be no shave! Successive blades add successively less to shaving quality—there is **diminishing marginal productivity.** Indeed, after a certain number of blades the additional blade may have zero or negative marginal product—it adds nothing, and it might even increase the risk of cutting oneself while shaving. In fact, I found this to be true with the four-blade razor, which I threw away after just two uses.

> **Q:** *If my behavior is typical, why do companies promote razors with more and more blades?*

7.9

There was an announcement today that the Netherlands is opening a new, high-tech prison. Prisoners will be in dorm-suite like cells holding six people, and they will be in charge of their own cleaning, cooking, and washing. The will be monitored by video surveillance mechanisms at all times; and there will even be microphones that will relay sounds to a central monitoring system that warns guards when prisoners are angry or fighting. The prisoners will be less regimented directly, but that's not the reason for building the prison. Rather, the **average variable cost** will only be $25 per prisoner instead of $170. The prison **substitutes** capital for the increasingly expensive labor time of guards and others.

Q: *How will the fixed costs associated with this prison compare with those of a traditional prison? How does this relate to the number of prisoners that can be incarcerated?*

Cost Minimization/Profit Maximization

7.10

I was waiting in line at the local post office. In this post office, you take a number and get called by the clerk when the number comes up on a screen in the main room. In addition to two clerks in the main room there is a third clerk in a little office on the side. He can't see the screen, so whenever he finishes with a customer, he walks out, looks at the screen, and calls a number. He did this three times in the 10 minutes that I waited, taking about 15 seconds each time he walked out and back. I figure he must do this about sixty times a day, taking a total of 15 minutes walking back and forth. That means he spends at least 50 hours a year wasting the U.S. Postal Service's time this way. If he earns $20 per hour, he is wasting $1,000 per year. It's not his fault, but for no more than $500 the Postal Service could install an extension screen in his little office. Spending this little bit of capital would enhance this clerk's productivity. The **marginal product** of this investment good surely would exceed its price.

Q: *What if he did this only twenty times a day? Would it pay the U.S. Postal Service to install the extension screen then?*

7.11

When I visited the casinos in Las Vegas in the mid-1980s, there were large numbers of people working there whose job it was to walk through aisles around the gaming machines (slot machines, poker machines, etc.) making change for people (so they could shove more nickels, dimes, and quarters into the machines). On my visit in 2002, these people had almost disappeared. The reason is simple: The machines are now able to accept paper money and can distinguish ones, fives, tens, twenties, fifties, and even one-hundred-dollar bills. This technical change has sharply reduced the demand for the unskilled workers who used to offer change. With labor costs rising, the casinos have **substituted** a technology that relies more on capital and less on labor.

Q: *There is a third input in this industry—real estate—the space that the machines occupy. As the gains to being located on the Strip in Las Vegas have increased, what do you expect has happened to the number of machines per square foot of space?*

7.12

Every morning, the bedspread has to be put back on our king-sized bed. How to do this involves a **choice of technology**—in this case between two different methods of accomplishing the task of making the bed. Method A involves my wife or I doing it alone; with Method B, we do it together. With Method A, the person has to walk from one side of the bed to the other twice to pull up the spread partway on each side; with Method B, we each stand on a side of the bed and pull the spread up together. The total labor in Method B is less. Since it requires less labor, and since we value each of our labor the same, Method B is the economically efficient technology in this case. Only if we decided that my wife's time is much more valuable than mine, or that my time is much more valuable than hers, would it pay to choose Method A.

Q: *Let's say that it takes us 3 minutes if one of us makes the bed alone, but takes 1 minute if we use Method B and do it together. How much more valuable than mine would my wife's time have to be to make it worthwhile to have me do the job alone? How does your answer change if she and I derive some pleasure from making the bed together?*

7.13

The parking meter has been almost unchanged since I started driving in 1959—one meter per space, put your money in the slot. In my driving in Northern Europe, I never see parking meters—I buy a piece of paper at a parking automat (typically one per block) and put it on my dashboard. Why the difference? I assume that available technologies are the same on both sides of the Atlantic, so it must be that the lower wage in the U.S. of the low-skilled meter collectors leads us to choose individual meters—to choose a **labor-intensive technology.** Lo and behold—as of last month, no more meters in downtown Austin. Instead, we have spiffy European-style kiosks, which take credit cards or cash, and which dispense parking slips for your dashboard. Why the change? I think it's because the price of the kiosks has fallen steadily, while even low-skilled wages continue to rise, to the point where the European-style technology is now cost-effective.

> **Q:** *Even the European parking technology requires a person to check each car to make sure payment has been made. Can you think of an invention that would act as a substitute for all the labor inputs?*

7.14

My wife and I bumped into each other while both trying to prepare breakfast. That's reminiscent of the saying "Too many cooks spoil the broth." Why should that be true? After all, if each cook's **marginal product** is positive, the broth has to be getting better and better as more cooks are added. Implicitly, the proverb states that at some point the marginal product of an extra cook becomes negative, and if still more cooks are added, the quality of the broth gets worse and worse until it is spoiled. No **profit-maximizing** firm would ever get to this point, though: As soon as a cook's marginal product fell below what his or her wage was, the firm would stop hiring. Even when cooks are "free," as in your own kitchen, the proverb is correct in implying that no cook should ever be allowed to have a negative marginal product.

> **Q:** *Have you ever worked in an office or plant where total product seemed to decline when certain workers were present? Have you ever had roommates (or siblings) whose "help" on a task appeared to lower total output?*

7.15

A study examined the determinants of the grades of students in Economics I. The authors had data on each student's grade in the course, his or her SAT score, the number of hours per week spent studying economics, and the number of hours spent in class. This research viewed the student as a "factory," generating a grade in the course with inputs of ability (or at least SAT score) and time (spent in the two uses, studying and attending class). If each hour of the day is equally valuable and students are rational, the productivity of the last hour studying should be the same as the productivity of the last hour going to class. This didn't happen: Among the men, the last hour of class was much more productive than the last hour they studied. They could have improved their grades with no more work by studying a bit less and attending class a bit more. The women's results showed the opposite. The **marginal product** of class attendance was zero for them: Their grades would have been just as high if they hadn't gone to class quite as often. A heartwarming additional finding was that while higher SAT scores did raise the grades, the effect of a low SAT score could be offset by a few extra hours of study each week.

Q: *If completing more homework assignments also raises your economics grade, what should be your rule about the effect on your grade of an extra hour spent doing homework assignments compared with an extra hour spent studying or going to class?*

7.16
In Luxembourg City, one building—the so-called *Ilot Gastronomique*—houses five quite different-themed restaurants, all owned by the same person. Having them all in the same location seems confusing to me as a customer, and it means that the owner is competing with himself for customers among passers-by. I thus assume that having them all together reduces **total revenue;** but presumably, it also reduces **total costs,** perhaps both **fixed costs** and **variable costs,** because of economies of scale.

Q: *How does it reduce these costs? Give specific examples of fixed costs, and of variable costs, that this arrangement would affect.*

7.17
I finally watched the Johnny Depp version of *Charlie and the Chocolate Factory* yesterday with several grandsons. At one point, the narrator, explaining why Charlie's father is out of work, says that with all the sales of chocolate bars there are more cavities, more

toothpaste sold, and with the profits the toothpaste makers (Charlie's father's employer) have put in a lot of machinery. Presumably, the company is making more toothpaste; but there is no necessary reason to use more capital and less labor. **Substitution** would occur if labor became relatively more expensive; but that hasn't happened. It must be the case (in the movie) that the technology for producing toothpaste is such that it is much, much cheaper to produce large amounts of toothpaste with fewer workers, and much more capital, than are used to produce small amounts.

Q: *Draw a curve for the marginal product of capital in the toothpaste industry.*

7.18

Rachel, one of my students, operates a pie bakery in the summers. She buys all the inputs herself (blueberries, flour, etc.), employs a paid helper, and counts all those as her costs. She sells the pies and obtains **revenue** from the sales. She tells me that she made a profit of $200 a week, where she defined profit as these revenues minus these costs. I told her that she is calculating accounting profits, not **economic profits.** She is not including the **opportunity cost** of her time in total costs, and she needs to do that to decide whether to stay in business. If her opportunity cost is less than $200 per week, her economic profits are positive, and she should stay in business. If her opportunity cost is more than $200 per week, she should leave the business if the money is all that matters because her economic profits are negative—she would make more by getting a paid job (at above $200 a week). If she loves baking and loves the smell of pies, though, she might stay open, even if her economic profits are negative.

Q: *Do you expect that Rachel will still be running this small-scale pie business after she graduates with her degree in finance?*

7.19

In "The Boxer," Paul Simon wrote and sang, "Still a man hears what he wants to hear and disregards the rest." In economics, we call this bounded rationality: Consumers maximize utility and producers maximize profits, but it doesn't pay them to process all the information that constantly assaults them. A firm will not make every little change that would be required if it responded to each change in its costs or technology. This is not just a matter of avoiding costly adjustments of production to short-run changes. Instead, these limits arise because it doesn't pay firms to obtain and analyze all the information that might be relevant to decision making. Instead, a **profit-maximizing** firm will devote its resources to analyzing the information that the managers believe is most important to making profits. The rest will be disregarded.

> **Q:** *Consider the nearest McDonald's. List changes that you think would cause it to alter its methods of operation. List others that would change its costs but that it might not pay attention to.*

CHAPTER 8

The Firm in the Short Run— Fixed and Variable Costs

How Much to Produce

8.1

We just revisited the Dutch spa we visited last year. Its policies provide a chance to watch a company testing the market, trying to find the best mix of pricing and output to maximize **profits.** Last year, dress rules were identical on all days—bathing suits always required in the pool area, always prohibited in the saunas. This is currently true on most days, but on two days a month suits are required everywhere, and on one day a month they are allowed nowhere. I hope that management will be experimenting with other arrangements, trying to find the best mixture. If so, the pattern next year will tell me more about what the consumers' preferences are for the mix of services offered.

> **Q:** *What if only 10 percent of all potential customers would ever like to wear bathing suits? Does the experiment that the spa has undertaken make sense in that case?*

8.2

In the movie *Fight Club*, Edward Norton's character tells a fellow airplane passenger that he works as a "recall coordinator" for an automobile company and that the job is simple: "Multiply the size of the out-of-court settlement of a lawsuit times the number of cars times the probability of an accident. If less than [some level of cost] *x*, no recall." This expected value calculation is a good **profit-maximizing** strategy for a (heartless) car company if it doesn't care about risk. If it does, the policy leads to too few recalls: It ignores the chance that one big, although unlikely, lawsuit will bankrupt the company. It also ignores the possibility that enough bad publicity will lead consumers to demand fewer cars, costing the company **revenue** and reduced profits.

Q: *Do you think that a small company would be more or less likely than a large company to be concerned about the kind of risk described here? Why or why not?*

8.3

Tomorrow is the big football game between the University of Texas in Austin and the University of Oklahoma. As always, the game will be played in Dallas, which is halfway between the schools. For many years, the Oklahoma Boosters Club of Austin, Texas, has rented a billboard over the freeway in Austin for a few days and posted a huge sign making fun of the Texas team. The new owner of the billboard faces a business decision now, as the Oklahoma Boosters want to rent it again: Should he let them rent it, which would bring in some **revenue** and make use of the billboard, which would otherwise remain vacant (no revenue); or should he tell them no? The billboard represents a **fixed cost**—he paid for building it and for renting the land on which it stands. His **total variable cost** is tiny—pasting a large piece of paper on the billboard, much smaller than the **total revenue** he will receive from the Oklahoma Boosters. It seems like an easy decision—rent out the space and increase profits. The owner is not doing it, however, because he is thinking about longer-run profits: "I hate to turn down business, but . . . I don't need to give people [Texas fans, who provide most of his business] reasons not to do business with me."

Q: *If the man also owns billboards in Dallas, how and why might his decision about putting anti-University of Texas ads on his boards there differ from his decision about the billboard in Austin?*

8.4

One of the teaching assistants from last semester's class came by my office to ask me to write a recommendation for an internship he is seeking. I said I'd be happy to do so. He then asked would it be okay if he used my name for other internships or jobs he might seek. I said, "Of course: The marginal effort required for additional recommendations is almost zero once I've written the first recommendation." He seemed a bit surprised by my reaction, but the

marginal cost of writing more recommendations for the same student is tiny since I have an electronic version of the letter on file. (The gain to him in terms of potential jobs is the same for each additional letter I write.)

> **Q:** *I always tell students to bring all recommendation requests to me at one time. How are the costs to me different compared with what they would be if I handled them one at a time?*

8.5

A student who did very well in my principles class last semester came by to ask about other classes to take. After he received the usual advice, including an offer to steer him to the better teachers of economics, he flatteringly (and naively) asked if I teach all the courses in the curriculum. I chuckled and said no, of course not. The reason, I told him, is that teaching a course requires incurring large **fixed costs** of generating lecture materials and organizing notes. For that reason, I, like professors at every college and university, try to repeat courses as much as possible. By doing that, we can spread the fixed cost of generating the course over as many units of output (number of times teaching the class) as possible.

> **Q:** *Given my response, if you were a professor and had to teach four courses per semester, would you rather be in a faculty with five economics professors or one with forty economics professors? As a student, how do you think the quality of teaching differs if each professor is responsible for teaching all the courses in the curriculum, compared with a situation like the one I described in my response to the student?*

8.6

Blackboard has a wonderful business providing online services to institutions of higher education and also to a lot of K–12 districts. I use it to communicate with my students, and I provide running totals of grades in my principles class through Blackboard's eGradebook. Each university pays a price based on the number of students in the university—not on actual use. Graduate students are charged at half the price of undergrads; and the price per undergrad decreases as the size of the university increases. (Indeed, if a whole university system, such as the University of California or the University of Texas systems, negotiates as one, the price per student is even lower.) Graduate classes are less likely to use Blackboard—I have never used it for a graduate class—and there are substantial **fixed costs** in setting up a Blackboard system on a campus or set of campuses. This pricing system thus reflects the high **average cost** and low **marginal cost** of constructing and maintaining a Blackboard system.

> **Q:** *If your campus has Blackboard, find out how much the college pays for it, and also try to discover the amount of use it receives.*

8.7

The local electric company is offering me a "free" fancy thermostat, one that is programmable for different times of day and different days of the week. In return, I have to agree to let them turn off the air conditioning for up to 10 minutes each half hour between 4 PM and 8 PM on the hottest summer days. Why are they offering this deal? The **short-run marginal cost** of producing electricity is very low—most times the power plants are underused. They are fully used only at times of peak demand, including dinnertime. At those times the **marginal cost** of producing electricity becomes huge, prompting power companies to buy expensive power from elsewhere or even to propose building new plants. If it can get consumers to cut back at these peak times, its **long-run average cost** will be reduced by a lot, and it will make greater profits.

> **Q:** *How can the same idea be applied to tolls on local highways?*

8.8

McDonald's has reintroduced its McRib offering. Consisting of meat that at one point belonged to a pig, it is now on yet another farewell tour, its sixth since 2004. (Actually, the first three were called "Farewell Tour," the last three have been called "Reintroduction.") An article on the Web site TheAwl.com points out that the reintroductions of this unusual product have all coincided with downturns in the price of pork. This seems reasonable to me: McDonald's assumes there is some best **price** for the McRib and compares it to the **marginal cost,** exactly as in our introductory textbooks. When the marginal cost drops sufficiently (and presumably the price of pork is an important part of **variable cost**), back comes the McRib.

> **Q:** *Are there any **fixed costs** that McDonald's needs to consider when deciding whether or not to reintroduce the McRib?*

8.9

My son visited the Walt Disney World complex and pointed out the methods used to spread demand across time. Coupons for 30% discounts on restaurant food purchased before noon or between 3 PM and 4:30 PM are available. Merchandise coupons for 20% discounts are given for use between 9 AM and noon. Both coupons are offered to **shift demand** rightward at non-peak times. Why do this? Disney trains its workers extensively so that to a large extent labor costs are **fixed costs**. To spread those costs—to maximize labor productivity—it makes sense to reduce the peak demand for labor. Spreading these costs also has the virtue of reducing the negative impact on Disney's reputation in the labor market that would accompany layoffs that might occur if demand were more variable. An additional virtue is that spreading customer demand helps the park's reputation with consumers and allows them to spend less time in line—leaving them time to spend more money!

> **Q:** *What other businesses use time-dependent pricing? Do you think it is effective in raising profits?*

8.10

A café sells a three-egg omelet for $7.99, and a six-egg omelet breakfast for $9.99. It will let two people split the six-egg omelet, and even let the two people order one slice each of different kinds of toast with the shared omelet. Is this pricing strategy crazy? Perhaps, but unless each person would order a three-egg omelet otherwise and pay $15.98, perhaps not. The **marginal cost** of making the six-egg omelet is really just the three eggs, which cost much less than $2. The good deal on the shared six-egg omelet induces a couple to split it, and stuff themselves, rather than split a three-egg omelet, which my wife and I often do. The **incentives** provided by this pricing decision may actually raise the café's **profits**.

> **Q:** *Why doesn't the café also allow couples to split the three-egg omelet and allow them to buy different kinds of toast with it?*

8.11

The guy on the elliptical trainer next to me at 5:30 AM asked whether I have teaching assistants (TAs) in my large micro principles class. I said yes (and thought about how the production process requires my labor and TA labor—we're the human inputs into production). Between gulps for air he then asked, "How many TAs?" I am typically offered five TAs to help with the 500 students in the class. The problem is that the **marginal products** of the fourth and fifth TAs are low. They're low both because of the way I organize my grading and exams and because the last two TAs assigned to me are typically new and inexperienced graduate students. On the cost side, I don't pay any money for the TAs, but the more TAs I have, the more time and effort I must spend coordinating their activities and supervising them. Worse still, the required effort rises very rapidly as the number of TAs rises. So with declining **marginal "revenue"** and rising **marginal "cost,"** I don't want all five TAs. I just thank the department chairman and tell him that three good TAs are enough to do the job just fine.

> **Q:** *In many universities, a "head TA" supervises an army of TAs for the professor who does the lecturing. As a student, how do you feel about this? Is this a gain in the "output" of the course? Does it result in improved learning for you, the student?*

The Firm's Shut-Down Point

8.12

Our local movie house in suburban London charges £11.90 ($18) for a regular ticket, and even seniors (ages 60+) pay £8.90 ($13.50). But there is a special deal for seniors: Every Tuesday the theater presents a recent movie (e.g., *Lincoln* was showing in May 2013) and charges only £3 ($4.60). Moreover, you get "free tea, coffee and biscuits!" How can they make money off this, or is it just **altruism** by the theater owners? The reason may be that showing the movie in the morning has no impact on the theater's cost of renting it from the distributor. The only **variable costs** are the wages of the one or two workers who sell the tickets and make the eats. The **fixed costs**—of the movie rental, the theater, the heating, and the electricity are irrelevant for the owner's decision. I should think that, if they can sell even twenty tickets, they will increase their **profits.**

> **Q:** *Why does the theater offer this deal only to seniors? After all, if they offered it to more people, wouldn't they make more profit on Tuesdays?*

8.13

The entire city was essentially shut down for the past two days because of an ice storm. (Texans aren't used to driving on icy roads; the roads aren't well de-iced; and the hills make driving especially hazardous.) A local restaurateur, whose business was open yesterday, said, "With the low cost of being here, anything we make is fine." Now that cannot be entirely true. If he sells one Coke in 8 hours, surely the **revenue** will be less than the **variable cost** of operating the business. (If nothing else, the **opportunity cost** of his time for a day is probably more than the revenue from one Coke.) But his point is important: He has to pay the rent and most utilities anyway (the **fixed cost**), so all he needs to do is cover variable cost.

Q: *How would his decision be affected if his fixed costs were even higher?*

8.14

The Bourbon Outfitter in Lexington, Kentucky sells souvenirs and paraphernalia related to bourbon distilling and drinking. Its only physical retail outlet is a kiosk in a shopping mall; and its selling season is the Christmas shopping period. Its difficulty is that the mall will only rent kiosk space in three-month intervals—the kiosk is a **fixed cost** to The Outfitter. The Outfitter has the following solution: It rents the kiosk from November through January, and opens on November 1, sufficient time before Black Friday to make an impression on shoppers. It stays open until New Year's Day and then closes down. The owner tells me that this is a **profit-maximizing** policy: It has already incurred the fixed cost of renting the kiosk for January, and the **variable cost** of remaining open after New Year's Day exceeds the revenue it will earn after New Year's Day.

Q: *Think of three other examples where a company shuts down for a long period of time because it expects its variable costs of remaining open to exceed its revenues.*

8.15

It's a Sunday evening in June, in the tourist section of Moscow, Russia, not far from Red Square. It's 9 PM and still quite light out at this very far northern latitude. Amazingly enough, the stores, such as Burberry, Cerruti, and others that cater to tourists and rich Russians, are open. This seems to make no sense—how much are they going to sell at this time of day, and on Sunday? In fact, it makes a lot of sense. Most of the costs of operating the store are **fixed costs**—the land, the inventory, etc. The only **variable cost** is labor and power, both of which are relatively inexpensive in today's Russia, especially compared with the price of land in downtown Moscow and with the prices of the goods sold in these stores. That being the case, the stores don't have to sell much at this time of day to cover their variable costs and make additional profits.

Q: *Okay, so why don't these stores stay open 24 hours a day?*

8.16

Universities offer summer school classes for a variety of reasons. I hope when my university offers a class in the summer that the people doing the planning are thinking economically. The university has a fixed plant that will sit idle if it is not used in the summer. So, the university shouldn't worry about the **fixed cost** of the buildings, but **variable costs** are still important. The professor's salary and fringe benefits are extra costs that wouldn't be incurred if he or she were not teaching the course. The building must be cooled (no small issue in Texas in August), and lighting must be provided. Also, the extra cost of registering the students for the summer must be considered. If the tuition payments of the students who signed up for a summer class don't cover these variable costs, the university should think carefully about whether to offer the course. If it offers the course for a tuition that doesn't even cover variable cost, the university is choosing to subsidize students to attend summer school.

Q: *Say the professor's salary and benefits for teaching the course are $5,000, the extra electricity for air-conditioning and lighting costs $500, and the extra cost of registering the students in the class is $50. How much tuition* **revenue** *must be received to justify offering the course? Given what tuition charges per course are at your college or university, how many students need to sign up for the course to make it worthwhile for your school to offer it?*

8.17

I either do a long-distance run or work out in the gym, and I try to avoid doing the same thing two days in a row. This morning, I went to the gym at 5:30 AM, but it wasn't open yet (even though it was scheduled to be open by then). I stood in line for 10 minutes, and it still hadn't opened. Should I wait around or go home and go for a run? Remembering lectures about the firm in the short run, I realized that **fixed cost** (the time I had already spent) shouldn't matter. I assumed that it would be awhile before the gym opened, and since I had neither run nor been to the gym yesterday, and had only a limited time left to exercise, I left the line and went home for a run.

Q: *How should my reaction (or yours if you were in this situation) differ if I had exercised every day for the previous three days? What if I had been unable to exercise for a week? Why the difference?*

8.18

A lot of the musical events my wife and I go to are on workdays. By the time the shows start, usually at 8 PM, we're pretty tired after a full day's work. By the intermission we say to ourselves, "Why stay for the second half? We've gotten a lot of enjoyment already, the marginal enjoyment is small, and we're exhausted." Nonetheless, most times we stay. You would think we would realize that the prior purchase of the ticket as a **fixed cost** that shouldn't matter to us, yet it does. This is quite common behavior. While businesses may think only about the dollars in their marginal decisions, people have more than just dollars in their utility functions. Having already spent the money, we have a mental commitment to the entire show and will stay even though a simple marginal consideration that looks only at future costs (in this case, our increasingly valuable time) and benefits (the remainder of the show) would lead us to go home at intermission.

Q: *Why even buy the ticket, knowing that it is likely we will be ready to leave at intermission yet will feel we have to stay?*

8.19

On New Year's Eve we went to a very long movie that was boring right from the start—and continued to be boring. We had planned to see a movie then go out partying. After one hour we were ready to give up on the movie and leave the theater, having wasted our money on the $7 tickets. Being an economist, I said: "Let's wait, it's almost over. Our tickets are a **fixed cost,** but the remaining **variable cost** must be tiny since the movie can't last more than 45 minutes more." After another 45 minutes we debated leaving and again decided that the remaining variable cost—the time left in the movie—had to be small. This happened two more times, resulting in our enduring three-and-a-half hours of boredom. We hadn't ignored the nature of fixed cost. Rather, we kept on underestimating the size of the variable costs (of staying longer in the theater). We weren't irrational, just badly informed about the length of the movie.

> **Q:** *What if we had known how long the movie was right from the start and had paid $20 for the movie tickets? What should we have done after one hour?*

8.20

Wine Spectator had a feature on Nicolás Catena, who received its Distinguished Service Award for 2012. His online biography states, "One year, Domingo [Nicolás' father] realized that it would cost him more to harvest than to leave the fruit on the vines. He asked his twenty-two year old son Nicolás, a recent PhD graduate in economics, what to do about such a dilemma. Nicolás advised him not to harvest." You don't need a Ph.D. to see the sense of Nicolás's advice—if price is too low to cover **average variable cost,** shut down. Sadly, "Domingo could not follow his son's advice with a clear conscience and picked anyway." No doubt the family vineyard lost even more money than if Domingo had listened to his son.

> **Q:** *Once the grapes were picked, would it make sense for the vineyard simply to throw them away? Or should they make them into wine and market them?*

8.21

Texas has been the home of the boom in emu ranching. In the late 1980s and early 1990s there was a speculative boom in emus, the Australian equivalent of ostriches. Prices for eggs and chicks skyrocketed as ranchers foresaw that emus might replace cattle as a cash crop. Unfortunately, while a small market for emu burgers was created, the price of a breeding pair of emus had fallen by the late 1990s from $4,500 to $20. The supply of emus was huge, and there was little demand. What is an emu rancher to do? The **variable cost** of raising an emu to slaughter weight—the cost of feeding the emu—was more than the price of a mature bird. Not surprisingly, smart farmers simply released their emus into the wilds of Texas. The local paper headlined, "Abandoned emus run amok on Texas roads," and several of the flightless birds wound up being hit by cars at night on rural roads.

> **Q:** *How high would the price of adult emus have to be to lead farmers to raise chicks to maturity?*

8.22

The city of Austin recently began marketing bottled water under its own special label. The water is just tap water that the city pays to have taken by truck to Dallas (nearly 200 miles away), bottled, and then shipped back to be marketed in Austin. The **average total cost** of a case of 24 bottles is $8.90, while the city sells a case for only $6. It thus loses $2.90 on each case that it sells. The city has decided to stop marketing the water. Is this a wise decision? It probably is: It is hard to believe that **average fixed cost** is as high as $2.90 a case—the major costs appear to variable and arise from the bottling, shipping, and distribution of the water. **Average variable cost** is almost certainly above $6, meaning that the city is losing money on every case it sells. What's amazing is not that the city is stopping production; it is that, knowing the price and cost structure, it ever got into the business in the first place.

> **Q:** *Let's say the average fixed cost currently is $2? How should the city's decision about whether to stay in the bottled water business be affected if it could get fixed cost down to $1 per case?*

8.23

Luke 13:6–9 recognizes **opportunity cost, fixed cost,** and **variable cost:** "A certain man had a fig tree . . . and said unto the dresser of his vineyard, Behold, these three years I come seeking fruit on this fig tree, and find none: cut it down; why cumbereth it the ground? And he answering said unto him, Lord, let it alone this year also, till I shall dig about it, and dung it; and if it bear fruit, well; and if not, then after that thou shalt cut it down." The dresser realizes that the fixed cost (the three barren years) that annoy the owner have gone by. He also knows that the land has a positive opportunity cost—another tree can be planted there. He believes, though, that incurring a bit more variable cost (the digging and dunging) might have a high **marginal product** (lots of figs) and that this **marginal cost** is worth paying, but only for one year. After a year, he assumes that the marginal cost of another year of dunging and digging is not going to make the tree more productive, and the tree should be cut down.

> **Q:** *How would the dresser of the vineyard have responded if the fig tree had been barren for nine years? Why might his answer have been different even though both three years and nine years of barrenness would represent fixed cost?*

8.24

Most of the snow cone stands in Austin close in mid-October, once the days of 90-plus degrees have disappeared and the demand for snow cones becomes small. At that point it doesn't pay a company to incur the **variable costs** of keeping the stands in operation. But the company that has shut down still has the **fixed cost** of renting the stand that is sitting idle. One of the owners has a solution: He has switched the snow cone stand to a taco stand! The demand for tacos is higher in the winter in Austin than in the summer, so the owner can spread the fixed costs of the stand over more months, thus lowering the **average total cost** for the year and making higher profits. This is a clever way of handling the problem of seasonal variations in demand for a product.

> **Q:** *List two businesses that you know of that close down in the winter. How could each of them adapt itself to a different product that could be marketed in winter so the owner could spread the fixed cost?*

8.25

We just returned from four days hiking in Big Bend National Park, driving the 500 miles home today along I-10. A number of oil rigs were pumping vigorously along the highway. When we took the same road six years ago, the wells were there, but the rigs were not pumping. This is no surprise at all: In 2002 the price of crude oil was less than $30 per barrel; today, it is more than $100 per barrel. The 2002 price of $30 probably did not exceed the **marginal cost** of pumping oil out of these wells, which probably are not among the most efficient in the world. At today's price, every barrel pumped yields a profit—price exceeds marginal cost and probably **average total cost,** so profit-maximizing rig owners have re-activated these old wells. This is a standard response in a competitive industry—as the product price rises, suppliers move up the short-run **supply curve.**

> **Q:** *As the cost of pumping the oil out rises, what do you expect to observe even if oil prices stay very high?*

*F*irms and Competitive
Markets in the Long Run

Equilibrium

9.1

We're going to a Thai restaurant near our apartment in Germany. I asked a long-time resident how it is, and she said it's brand new. It was a Texas barbecue (!) joint for a few months, and something else before that. Why the turnover? Of course, being unable to cover **variable costs** matters generally as always; but the German government apparently gives small business an **incentive** to open up, and an incentive to close quickly if it cannot cover those costs. Certain taxes are waived if the business is small, but only for a short period of time; thereafter, the tax break phases out. Thus, the risks of opening a new business are reduced; and, if it is not very successful, the tax break provides an incentive to close it down within the time period necessary to escape these taxes. I have grave doubts about this policy and about subsidizing small business generally: If there are **economies of scale** naturally, why should the government try to offset them? And it's hard to imagine that there are too few new small businesses—that people are so unwilling to take risks that the government should offer subsidies. I see no good economic rationale for these policies; but they are widespread in Germany—and in the U.S., too.

Q: *If you want to subsidize small businesses but don't like this German scheme, what other policies can you propose that would accomplish this task?*

9.2

The economics editor of a major commercial textbook publisher mentioned a very interesting problem facing his company. They sell an increasing share of their books internationally. The profit on those books is much lower than the profit on domestic sales. Competing textbooks that are printed abroad are of much lower quality, with inferior paper and fewer colors. To compete with these books when it sells to international wholesalers, his company must charge a low price. He then mentioned a problem in a related market: The used-textbook market in the U.S. has been growing. He and his colleagues believe this has occurred partly because international buyers buy up used copies of the low-priced textbooks that originally were sold abroad. They then ship them back to the U.S., where they are resold at the high price in the U.S. market for used books. The original publisher finds the market for new books in the U.S. undercut but has made only very low profits from the international market. The solution, he claimed only half-jokingly, is a textbook that self-destructs after one use. Only that way can low **average-cost** products be excluded from the market.

Q: *If this editor's analysis is correct and the market for new U.S. textbooks here is trimmed, what does this behavior do to the amount that publishers are willing to pay to textbook authors? What will happen to the supply of new textbooks?*

9.3

In the movie *American Gangster,* Denzel Washington's character is an innovative entrepreneur, essentially the Wal-Mart of the heroin trade. As he says, "My . . . [heroin] is twice as good for half as much." He buys direct from the growers and imports directly, eliminating the middleman and cutting costs. The Mafia is very upset with him because he is undercutting their sales by lowering his prices to reflect his lower **average total cost.** He still makes huge **profits;** but because his costs are so much lower, he is selling for less (and selling a purer form of heroin, too). Not surprisingly, after he is arrested and his operations are shut down, the Mafia leaders appear quite happy about the end of this efficient competitor.

Q: *What would the equilibrium price be if Denzel were suddenly allowed to import heroin from Afghanistan, as well as from the sources he uses in the movie?*

9.4

There have been a number of stories recently about instant "dates," a "market" in which single women are seated at a long table and single men sit down for a 3-minute date with a woman. At the end of the 3 minutes, each party makes a note of whether he or she would be interested in seeing the other again. The men then move on to the next woman, and so on, so that each person meets roughly thirty new people in a single evening. Dating can be viewed as the information-gathering activity in the competitive market for spouses. It's a way that we can find out about other people and how well they match us and we match them. It is very time consuming at a period of life when the value of time is increasing rapidly. The instant date reduces the time costs of gathering information and makes the dating market work more efficiently. It may be a bit crude, but it is hard to argue that the instant date is any more crude than singles bars, and it is much more efficient.

> **Q:** *Another market uses the same idea but has 8-minute dates. What are the relative advantages and disadvantages of using the 3-minute instant date market compared with the 8-minute instant date market? Which do you think is preferable?*

9.5

We spent the weekend in Las Vegas, going to two Cirque du Soleil shows, taking two hikes in the desert and, of course, gambling. We wanted to play roulette, but the table minimum bets are $10, too steep for us, and we were also hesitant about getting the etiquette correct. Fortunately for small-timers like us, a technological improvement has solved both problems. Several of the casinos have installed "Rapid-Roulette" machines: A small roulette wheel is attached to a console operated by a single worker. Each player has a console on which to place bets electronically, with a minimum bet of only $2.50. The action goes much more quickly than at a regular wheel since the operator doesn't need to check the placement of chips or move them around after each spin. (The player's console automatically registers his/her total money after each spin.) The casino can operate on lower minimum bets and still cover **average total cost** because more players can be accommodated and more spins per hour can be made than on a regular roulette table. Also, a different, lower-class kind of player (like us) can be attracted to a game that before had not been accessible to them.

> **Q:** *Many of the games at Las Vegas casinos have a variety of tables offering different minimum bets. What would you expect is the*

*difference in fixed and variable costs between a blackjack table with
a $3 minimum and one with a $100 minimum?*

9.6

The Barbie doll has long been one of the premier toys in America
and even beyond. The price has been very high. (We recently purchased Cowgirl Barbie for my granddaughter for $37.75.) This
has created large profits for Barbie's manufacturer, Mattel, Inc.
Given the cost of production and marketing, the prices have always seemed unusually high—much higher than could be sustainable in the long run in a competitive market. In the past few
years, the prices of Barbie dolls have fallen tremendously. Other
manufacturers are now making dolls that are the same size as
Barbie, so they can wear Barbie's clothes. Apparently, the main
attraction of the doll is not the Barbie face, but the ability to dress
Barbie up. This new competition has caused the prices of Barbie
to plummet—now you can buy some Barbie dolls for as little as
$9.99. Competition has driven the price down much closer to
long-run average cost.

Q: *Why might it have taken so long before companies entered
the market and reduced Mattel's economic profits on Barbie dolls?*

9.7

A student describes her efforts in the lemonade-stand industry in
her neighborhood when she was little. She and her friends opened
up lemonade stands on various blocks in the area, doing a good
business because the only **fixed costs** were the table, jar and stir-
ring spoons, and the only **variable costs** were the cups, ice, lemonade (and their time, which as eight-year-olds they didn't value
very highly). Julie, their former friend, opened up her own stand,
with an advertised "secret ingredient." Despite charging 50 percent
more, Julie stole all the business for a while. Customers later discovered they could get the same satisfaction as with Julie's lemonade by buying slushies at the local 7-Eleven store. Julie was forced
to cut her price and, to continue being profitable, she had to stop
using the expensive ingredient. My student and her friends were
back in business, making **normal profits,** as the market settled into
a long-run (for the summer) **equilibrium.**

Q: *How do the lemonade market and the slushie market
interact in this example? Suppose that the equilibrium price*

of slushie doubled. Would Julie be able to reintroduce her special lemonade?

9.8

A friend of mine reported on gasoline prices on a trip he just took from Austin to Port Aransas, a resort on the Gulf Mexico coast. Right now gas is $2.43 per gallon in Austin. He said that it got progressively cheaper as they got closer to the coast. He figures this is because the oil refineries are closer and transportation costs are thus lower. With a lower **average total cost,** he thought that competition would force prices to be lower. This makes sense to me. BUT—he noticed that the lowest price of all was in Port Aransas itself, which is an isolated town on an island that is in fact farther from the refineries than the inland towns he passed through. So why was gas so cheap ($2.08 per gallon) there? I had no easy answer on this one; but perhaps there was a local price war going on when he was there, with the few local gas stations competing in a frenzy for the available business, temporarily selling at unusually low prices.

> **Q:** *If it is the case that the low price was due to a price war between gas stations in Port Aransas, what would you expect to see happen in this market in the long run? What would happen if another gas station opened in Port Aransas?*

9.9

Casinos operated by Indian tribes have expanded tremendously nationwide in the last twenty years, with some turning into billion-dollar businesses. More recently, profit-making casinos have expanded beyond Nevada and Atlantic City to a number of southern states. The Indian casinos are not liable to federal regulations on wages and working conditions. This gives them a competitive advantage over other casinos since they can operate with lower labor costs and thus lower **long-run average cost.** The only way the other casinos can survive is by offering inferior payouts (retaining more of the money that is wagered) and hoping that not all their potential customers are lost to the Indian casinos.

> **Q:** *One state has both Indian and non-Indian casinos; another state has only non-Indian casinos. In which state are the non-Indian casinos more likely to survive?*

The Role of Market Size

9.10

In 1776, Adam Smith wrote in *The Wealth of Nations*, "The division of labor is limited by the extent of the market." One implication is that the bigger the market, the more room for specialized products. The applicability of this statement to a big city such as Austin, Texas, was made clear this morning. A pickup truck had a sign advertising "We Scoop Poop," and saying that it belonged to Dog Duty, Inc. The company offers to scoop things up from your lawn for $9 weekly for up to two dogs. This kind of specialized service couldn't exist in a smaller town because there wouldn't be enough business to occupy the sellers of the service on a full-time basis. But in a big town, the **market demand curve** is far enough to the right—and enough people are willing to pay the high price necessary to get someone to perform this fairly unpleasant task for them—that the company can survive and even prosper.

> **Q:** *Why might this company be able to offer its services at a lower price than a company that combines this service with lawn mowing or landscaping?*

9.11

Marginal decisions to increase the net of revenue–costs arise in non-profit organizations as much as in companies. The designers of a recent book, Peter Leeson's *The Invisible Hook* (2009), recognized this in picking a cover. The dust jacket features a wooden background (a plank?), onto which a transparent hook has been laminated—thus a semi-visible hook! Pretty cute, but the lamination adds to **total variable cost.** So why do it? Presumably, the publisher believes that this design will make the book stand out from others and sell more copies. **Total revenue** will rise, perhaps by more than the increase in variable cost. If so, this was a wise business decision; if not, at least it's an innovation that will help make the publisher more visible in the publishing world.

> **Q:** *Do you think this book has many substitutes, or few? How will altering the product lead to an increase in total revenue?*

9.12

I'm chatting with the proprietor of a small chain of coffee shops in Montana. She tells me that Starbucks just can't make the variety of coffees that she can, particularly those that involve lighter-roasted beans. Apparently, the huge chain uses immense roasters (3,500 pounds at a time) that are not well suited to lighter beans. The **economies of scale** generated in using these roasters make possible substantial profits, but they do not allow roasting small amounts that, she says, are essential for light roasting. I don't know the technology of coffee roasting; but if she is correct, perhaps Starbucks will wind up like the beer giants, Miller and Anheuser-Busch, having large shares of the popular market, with substantial room left for local brands and micro-roasters.

> **Q:** *Can you think of other industries where there are a few huge firms and lots of little ones with specialized market niches? How are the reasons for their existence the same or different from those that characterize the coffee shop or beer markets?*

9.13

What's an efficient size for a church or synagogue? If there were **economies of scale** throughout, with all the Baptists in a big Texas city such as Austin, we'd see just one giant Baptist church. With 15,000 Jews in Austin, we'd see just one big synagogue. But we don't: There are many churches in each denomination, as well as many synagogues. As the city has expanded, more and more different kinds of Baptist churches, Jewish synagogues, and other churches have been organized. It's not just that each one serves a local area. People drive a long way to the church or synagogue of their choice, even when another one is closer. They like the peculiarities of a leader's ministry, the type of service, and even the particular social interactions of a congregation. With one big house of worship, these choices would be lost. Statistical studies of the **long-run average cost** curves of churches suggest that this is true: There are economies of scale up to some size, but as the church or synagogue begins growing beyond a certain size, **diseconomies of scale** set in—it becomes less efficient.

> **Q:** *What would cause there to be diseconomies of scale in churches and synagogues? List some of the cost and production factors that limit the growth of an individual church or synagogue?*

CHAPTER 10

Competitive Markets— Responses to Shocks

Changes in Technology and Costs

10.1

We watched the Ben Stiller comedy *Zoolander* last night. While its humor is delightfully sophomoric, the premise of the movie is economic: Zoolander is brainwashed to assassinate the prime minister of Malaysia because the latter has proposed doubling the **minimum wage** and thus raising **average total cost** for the Western apparel companies that are located there. The villain (the Will Ferrell character) says that if other developing countries do this, his company will be put out of business. The writers of the movie apparently understand that in a competitive industry higher costs will cause firms to go out of business. Implicitly, they also understand that raising the minimum wage, a **price floor,** will reduce employment.

> **Q:** *What would happen to prices of apparel if the assassination plot fails? What about consumer well-being?*

10.2

It is very annoying when I am in some sparsely populated area and my cell phone cannot get any reception. The reason is that there are no cell phone towers in such areas because at a price of about $250,000 per tower it doesn't pay the providers of cell-phone service to build a tower with so few customers. Only with sufficient **economies of scale** is such service potentially profitable. A company is proposing to launch large hot-air balloons carrying the transmission equipment necessary to provide the service. A huge area could be covered by just a few balloons floating across it

100,000 feet up in the air; and the balloons are so inexpensive that a continuous series of launches would keep a large area covered and do so at much lower cost than fixed-location cell towers. Essentially, this new technology would lower the **long-run average cost curve** for cellular service over a range of output at which average costs are currently prohibitive.

Q: *Draw a graph of the average fixed cost and average variable cost for traditional cell phone towers and the new hot air balloons. Which technology has higher fixed costs? Which has higher variable costs?*

10.3

A recent story discusses how the airlines are lobbying to rescind a new provision requiring commercial pilots to obtain 1,500 hours of flight training before they are certified (a Congressional response to a fatal crash). The companies believe that this will cause pilots' wages to rise (to pay for the increased training costs the pilots must incur), causing **average total cost** to increase, increasing industry price and reducing output and profits. But there are winners: Flight schools would see an **increase in demand,** as pilot trainees stay enrolled longer; and, most important, the consumer who values safety a lot would be safer, at the cost of higher-priced air tickets. No doubt the airlines would welcome a return to the good old days, when almost all pilots were former military men whose training costs were paid by taxpayers, which represented a huge indirect subsidy to the airlines.

Q: *In the old days, when the military provided lots of retired pilots who sought commercial airline jobs, who was paying for the training?*

10.4

I taped a video on the costs of traffic accidents for DefensiveDriving. com. This new company is licensed to provide online instruction in safe driving for people who wish to avoid paying traffic tickets and reduce the penalty points on their drivers' licenses. Until its inception, bad drivers had to attend classes in person. They bore the cost of the time spent driving to and from the defensive driving school and doing so at possibly inconvenient times. Also, the providers had to rent space large enough to accommodate their "students." The new technology has thus both lowered the **average total cost** of providing the service and has made it more attractive to "students." Not surprisingly, business for the new online company is booming—it can undercut its live competitors.

Q: *Why isn't Web-based college education replacing in-person college education as rapidly as it is in this example?*

10.5

A student mentioned her family's business, a small pet store. Her parents emigrated from Korea in the early 1980s and started this store in Houston. The business prospered for a while, but in the 1990s things started to go badly. The reason is that a PetSmart outlet opened nearby. PetSmart and one or two other pet superstore chains expanded tremendously during that period. **Economies of scale** in inventory storage and purchasing have increased the efficient scale for production in the retail pet industry. This happened many years ago in the grocery business and in some other retailing, but is recent in this industry. My student's parents are the unfortunate victims of a change in technology that has changed the **competitive equilibrium.**

Q: *Draw the* **long-run average cost** *curves describing this industry in the early 1980s. Then show how they changed in the 1990s.*

10.6

Many illegal immigrants from Mexico pay *coyotes*—people who arrange for their illegal crossing into the U.S. The prices *coyotes* charge vary along the border and over time. We would expect that where the *coyotes'* work is more difficult—more dangerous and a greater chance of being caught—their price will be higher. The major danger to *coyotes* is posed by the U.S. Border Patrol. So in this **perfectly competitive** market, when/where costs are higher—when and where there are more Border Patrol agents per mile along the border—*coyotes* must pass on these costs in higher prices. That is just what we see: One recent study showed that each doubling of the number of agents per mile of border increased the prices *coyotes* charge by 20 to 50 percent.

Q: *Why did doubling the number of agents only increase the price by 20 to 50 percent? What other expenses does a coyote incur besides avoiding border patrol?*

10.7

Denmark is the leading exporter of pork products in Europe. In the early 1980s the typical Danish pig farmer produced 200 pigs per year. Presumably, the farmers of the time were efficient—they were operating at the minimum of the **long-run average cost curve** given the technology of the 1980s. That scale of operation wouldn't be competitive today. Technology has changed so that today's Danish pig farmer produces more than 1,500 porkers per year—the minimum of the long-run average cost curve has shifted far to the right. **Economies of scale** now cover a much broader range of production in this industry than they did in the 1980s so that, as the theory of **perfect competition** suggests, pig farms needed to become larger to survive.

> **Q:** *Draw the long-run average cost curve for the early 1980s and for now. What do you think has happened to the number of pig farmers in Denmark, and why?*

10.8

I'm taking a shower in my hotel room after my morning run and notice that the shower curtain is a curved rod that bows outward from the tub area (as opposed to a straight rod that is more common). I've seen these several times at newer or remodeled hotels. This is an extremely clever **technological change,** one that has major implications for costs and prices. The new rods do a much better job of allowing the shower curtain to prevent water from spilling over onto the bathroom floor. As such, there is less cleaning to be done by the hotel's staff each day, and less likelihood that water may leak through the floor and cause damage to paint and plaster on floors below. This should reduce the demand for hotel workers, both skilled and unskilled, thus lowering labor costs. Prices in **long-run equilibrium** in this **competitive** industry should be lower than they would otherwise be, as companies that fail to pass the cost savings on to consumers will be undercut by competitors. In the end, the consumer—the hotel-goer—will benefit from the new technology.

> **Q:** *Hotels also give customers the option to re-use their towels in order to save water. What effect does this have on wages and prices in the hotel industry?*

10.9

There is a large surplus of luxury housing in China—lots of fancy, but empty, houses. In a speculative binge, builders—believing that a new upper class would want such housing—have been constructing luxury villas. How can the market get so far out of kilter? How can this temporary departure from **equilibrium** exist? The reason is that the Chinese government has offered builders abundant cheap credit, allowing them to borrow in order to build the housing. And construction labor is relatively inexpensive, as is the land on which the housing has been built. This increase in supply has not led builders to cut the prices they are asking; but it seems likely that competition will force them to reduce prices to fill up the large, unutilized stock of luxury housing.

Q: *Graph the cost curve of a typical producer, and in a supply and demand graph, show the current state of the market.*

10.10

An Australian friend mentioned that her high-school-aged daughter's choir raised $60,000 over a one-year period to finance an international performing trip. They did this by going around to sheep farms in the area, asking farmers if they could shovel sheep poop into bags, then selling the bags to suburbanites as garden fertilizer at $10 per bag. Implicitly, the kids made substantial **economic profits.** The problem is that they won't be able to repeat the fundraiser: The farmers have realized that the poop is valuable and are now charging people who want to collect it. The profits in this **perfectly competitive** market will disappear, now that **average cost** has increased. I expect that farmers will soon be charging enough for shoveling privileges that the returns to shoveling will just about equal the **opportunity cost** of the kids' time, which probably isn't very high.

Q: *If you were advising this choir, what would you advise them to do to raise money by staying in the fertilizer business?*

10.11

Checking out of the local supermarket yesterday, my wife was thanked for bagging her own groceries. She then realized that in the U.S. supermarkets have baggers while the local supermarkets that we shopped at in Germany and the Netherlands did not. We would pay for the groceries, and then race to bag them ourselves while the next customer's purchases were scanned. Why the difference? One possibility is **cost-based**—the low-wage labor of baggers is relatively cheaper in the U.S., so the equilibrium leads to bagging being provided (and a higher price for groceries, other things equal). Another is **demand-based**—the average customer is in more of a rush in the U.S., perhaps because his or her value of time is higher.

> **Q:** *Which do you think causes the equilibrium to be different in Europe and the U.S.: Is it the U.S.'s lower cost of unskilled labor or its more rushed pace of life?*

10.12

I usually travel to Germany late in May. One of the special treats while I'm there is asparagus: with hollandaise sauce as an appetizer, in large clumps as a main course, and once even as asparagus ice cream. These are not the typical green stalks we see in the U.S., but white asparagus. This seasonal delicacy is picked by farm workers who come from Poland. With Poland having now joined the European Union, the Polish workers must be provided numerous employee benefits that they had not previously received. This rise in input costs has shifted **short-run average cost** and **marginal cost** upward, and not surprisingly in this competitive industry, price has risen—my asparagus treats are much more expensive than they were last year. To avoid this short-run increase becoming an increase in **long-run average cost,** German farm owners are trying to find substitutes for the Polish workers. The problem is that, while Bulgarians, Romanians, and others might be less expensive, since they are not yet covered by EU labor restrictions, they are much less skilled than the Poles. Input **substitution** does not seem very likely: The increased costs will persist in the long run, so that asparagus prices will be higher for the foreseeable future. The only question is how **inelastic** is consumers' demand for the product—will the cost-induced increase in price lead to **decreases in the quantity demanded** and a decline in industry output?

> **Q:** *What will the rise in input costs do to asparagus farmers' profits if we assume that consumers' demand for asparagus is completely inelastic?*

10.13

Jiminy Peak in western Massachusetts was a famous ski area, always in the weather news in Boston in the 1950s. Like most ski resorts, it was only open for a few months each year. Today, it's not year-round, but does operate for 9 months: In warmer weather it features the usual amusements for kids, plus (this adult's favorite) a 3,500-foot ground slide that snakes among the ski runs. Why didn't this happen earlier, given that the new arrangement helps spread the **fixed costs** (if nothing else, the **opportunity cost** of the land) of the site? Probably technological improvements—this kind of slide did not exist in this form in the 1950s; also, with much richer families and easier highway access, the **superior good** summer fun is now in greater demand.

> **Q:** *Are there other similar businesses that used to be open only in one season and that have now expanded to several? Can you explain what has caused their expansion to multiple seasons?*

Shifts in Industry Demand

10.14

I drove by a drive-in movie theater today—and of course, it was long-since closed. There were nearly 5,000 drive-in theaters in the U.S. in the 1950s. Today, there are fewer than 1,000. Why? This is a case where the **average cost curve** rose a lot, while average cost in competing industries fell relatively. The land the drive-ins were built on became more valuable; drive-ins take a lot of land, while movie multiplexes take much less land per customer. The drive-ins were also hit by a **leftward shift in the demand curve.** Hearing the movie through a speaker hanging on the window of your car wasn't so bad when the sound in movie theaters wasn't so good, either; but it couldn't compete against Dolby and THX Surround sound. Finally, as any suburban teenager in the 1950s knew, drive-ins were attractive on dates for other reasons; and with looser attitudes in the 1960s, the demand for drive-in movies declined, too.

> **Q:** *There are a number of drive-through stores that sell beer that had been gasoline stations until the 1970s, when the price of gasoline skyrocketed. How is this switch analogous to that described here? What use can be made of old drive-in movie sites?*

10.15

The headline in *The Onion* of October 6, 2011, states "Boardwalk Con Men Hit Hard By Sharp Decrease in Chumps." According to the story, the weak economy has reduced people's willingness to be swindled—the **demand** for being swindled has shifted left.

It's gotten tough for swindlers, with one complaining, "In a stagnant economy like this, I can't get no one interested in the same old grift." Not surprisingly, in this **competitive** industry (presumably entry/exit into/out of swindling is fairly easy), it is likely that some swindlers will leave the industry. The story notes that, unless the economy improves, many will ". . . pull up stakes and take it down to Florida, where the chumps are a dime a dozen." That exit should restore **normal profits** for the swindlers who remain on the boardwalk.

Q: *Graph the markets for being swindled up North and, implicit in this story, in Florida.*

10.16

A story on the Web today talks about the "problems" of coffinmakers in Malawi caused by improved health programs that have lowered death rates from AIDS. The **demand curve** for coffins has shifted leftward so that fewer carpenters are making coffins in the specialized "coffin street" of the capital city of Lilongwe. Instead, as in any **perfectly competitive** industry when market demand decreases, they have left the industry and have shifted to making a close substitute—wood furniture. I bet it didn't take them long to switch to furniture-making—they have the skills needed and have very little capital that is specific to coffin-making—in the case this re-establishment of long-run **equilibrium** in the coffin industry occurred quickly.

Q: *Draw the market demand and supply curves for coffins, and show how they change with the decline in the death rate from AIDS. What happens in a graph showing the cost curves of a typical surviving firm?*

10.17

When I've tried to schedule our window cleaners, they have always been able to come within two days. Despite the still-slow economy, the first available appointment is in three weeks. "Why?" I ask. The owner says that during the worst of the recession his firm had enough clients to survive, but barely; smaller, less efficient companies died off. Now that **demand** for cleaning has increased, his own customers are coming back; and the customers of the now-defunct companies are hiring him too, so he's swamped with business. Recessions kill off inefficient firms; but at least in this case, those that survive come out stronger than before. I can't resist noting that some macroeconomists refer to this phenomenon as "the cleansing effect of recessions," especially apropos in this case!

Q: *Compare the surviving window cleaning firm to its former competitors. What characteristics would you expect the recession-proof company to have?*

10.18

As of May 1, it is illegal for foreigners to buy soft drugs in the Netherlands. This new constraint is especially important in Maastricht, which lies only 20 miles from the larger German city of Aachen and only 60 miles from Brussels, Belgium. Before May 1, foreign "drug tourists" flocked to the fourteen "coffee houses" in the city, paying €3 or so for a joint and lighting up (since this activity is illegal in neighboring countries). In protest against the law, all fourteen houses have closed. While the law restricts industry **demand,** I doubt that it means the industry's complete demise. I expect **competition** will lead some of the houses to reopen, while others will be closed permanently. The industry will be smaller—fewer firms serving fewer customers. And since I see no reason for **average cost** to change, surviving firms will look very much as they do now— small shops, each with the same size crowd as before.

Q: *Why are there many small "coffee shops" instead of one big one? Graph what you think is the* **long-run average cost** *curve for a typical firm in this industry.*

10.19

The government of Thailand is trying to regulate its "entertainment" industry, which is notorious throughout Asia for massage parlors, nightclubs, and other venues. It has proposed limiting the hours in which these establishments can be open. The government's proposal is equivalent to a reduction in demand in a **perfectly competitive industry.** No doubt the owners are correct when they argue that the proposals would reduce employment by causing large numbers of establishments to close. Whenever demand drops in such an industry, some incumbents are forced to close, and the **equilibrium price** of the "commodity" is driven down. The government has responded to the operators' complaints by modifying its proposal, making the restrictions applicable only to new establishments. This amounts to a tax on new establishments—raising their costs relative to incumbents—and is essentially a method of protecting existing firms. It makes entry into the industry more difficult and will reduce the rate at which existing firms that are least efficient are forced to leave the industry. Rather than being a proposal designed to protect consumers—to clean up this industry—the regulations have become a method of aiding operators who were lucky enough to get into the business earlier.

Q: *What will happen to the price that existing operators will be able to charge for their services?*

10.20

The local camera store and photo-finishing outlet has closed and has posted a sign urging customers to go to its central location instead. This is a fairly common phenomenon now, as the growth of digital cameras and high-quality color printers has reduced the demand for commercial photo finishing. Grocery stores and drugstores that have photo-finishing sections may be closing those sections, too. The question is what this decline in demand will do to the **competitive equilibrium** quantity of camera stores. Will they close, or will the shift help them out compared with nonspecialty stores that have done photo finishing? The eventual location of the most efficient scale of operation in the photography business as a result of the digitization of photography is not clear at this point.

Q: *How will these changes affect the* **long-run average cost** *curves facing firms that still do photo finishing? How will they affect the price of this service?*

10.21

The Los Angeles City Council may require condoms in porn movies produced in the city limits (http://news.yahoo.com/porn-industry-mulls-leaving-la-condoms-required-095300909.html). How will this affect the market? Whether companies stay in LA or leave, costs will rise (condom costs if they stay, the costs of relocation, loss of agglomeration economies, if they move outside the city limits). Even if costs do rise, will that matter to producers? I imagine product demand is fairly **inelastic,** and they can easily pass the cost increase onto consumers. But even if costs were unaffected, consumer **demand** might shift far leftward if producers remained in LA since customers may not wish to view protected sex. Industry members lobbied strongly against the bill—perhaps because they feared the direct drop in demand rather than the cost increase.

Q: *What would happen in this industry if the U.S. Congress passed a law like that being proposed for Los Angeles only?*

10.22

The first commercial egg bank—which will store unfertilized human ova—will open. Why didn't this industry exist before? Demand and costs. Demand has increased. A growing number of women in their mid-thirties are purposely childless but may want to have a child later on. The technology for operating the bank has been available for a while, but **long-run average cost** has been declining. The conjunction of these two events has given rise to this new industry. Shocks to demand or cost change the **equilibrium price,** quantity, and number and size of firms in an existing industry, but they also can call into being a new industry—or they can kill off an existing industry (for example, the buggy-whip industry).

Q: *List two other completely new industries that have come into existence during your lifetime. List two others that have disappeared during your lifetime.*

CHAPTER 11

Efficiency and Well-Being

11.1

We have 10 days with the extended family in a large rented house near a beach. The problem is that we don't have the house for the first day and instead have a motel reservation. My wife talks with the owner about checking in to the house, and the owner says check-in is easy since the house won't be occupied the day before we arrive. My wife, always a quick-thinker, asks if we can have it that first day. The owner says yes, and offers to split the surplus evenly. **Producer surplus** and **consumer surplus** are both received. Is it a **Pareto improvement,** though? Yes, if the owner and we are the only relevant agents; no, if one adds in the owners of the motel that now may have several vacant rooms that night.

> **Q:** *Expanding beyond the owner, us, and local motels, are there any other people whose well-being might be affected by this transaction?*

11.2

This season the University of Texas at Austin's football team is scheduled or has already played against such athletic powerhouses as the University of Louisiana—Monroe (59-20) and the University of Texas—El Paso (64-7). Most other top-flight teams are also scheduled against Division I schools that they are likely to wallop. Why? Very simple—a team must win six games to qualify for a post-season bowl game; and scheduling a few teams that are nearly certain to be beaten makes the post-season minimum requirement much more easily attainable. We ease ourselves into qualifying for the post-season; athletic programs at the smaller schools make substantial sums of money playing against a top-level team; and their fans probably enjoy seeing the big-name team play against their men. How about UT fans? Seeing your team destroy another, while not desirable in every game, probably makes UT fans happy if it occurs a few times each season. This schedule represents a **Pareto improvement** with every agent better off.

Q: *Why doesn't the University of Texas schedule every game against teams that are easy to beat? Can you think of any further Pareto improvements to the schedule?*

11.3

At breakfast at our hotel in Chongqing, China, five Western (probably American) couples walked in, each carrying a roughly one-year-old, very cute little Chinese girl. My guess is that each couple is probably in the process of adopting a little girl since the couples seem to be in their late thirties, and I know that adoptions like this are a fairly common practice. I feel somewhat bothered by this—it just doesn't seem right to me; but as an economist how can I complain? The adopting parents are better off since they have chosen to adopt. While I may object to Chinese parents' preferences for sons and the Chinese government's policies trying to limit family size, given those restrictions the birth parents have made a choice that is best for them; and given those restrictions, the little girls are probably better off, too. So, this does seem like a **Pareto improvement.** But, as one of my students points out in class, what if the American parents would have otherwise adopted an American child, who now goes unadopted? If we include American babies in the group we consider, as we should, this practice can no longer be viewed as a Pareto improvement.

Q: *This is a very difficult moral question. What do you think—is this a Pareto improvement or not?*

11.4

My wife has recently been buying cheese and having small cheese-and-cracker snacks as part of her Zone diet. She views the cheese as hers, not to be touched by me. The difficulty with that is that her cheese quickly disappears because I'm a cheese addict. If there is a half-pound of Gruyère or Emmenthal in the fridge, I'm likely to eat a quarter-pound between lunch and dinner. I just can't help myself, even though I know it is not good for me. Can we improve the family's well-being? If my wife was not **altruistic** toward me, a **Pareto improvement** would be possible only if she could find some other food that she enjoyed as much, that provided an equally attractive dietary snack to her, and that I didn't find addictive. Failing that, she might, out of altruism, be willing to buy a snack she didn't like as much as a way of imposing controls on my **addiction.** The best solution, as she points out, would be to cure my addiction; but I've tried and failed many times, and the only hope is to keep good cheese out of the house.

Q: *Are we at a* **Pareto** optimum *or not?*

11.5

Before class a student asked, "Can you pass out the problem set assignments far ahead of time? I like to have them before I begin to read the chapters." I asked other students if they wanted them early, and no one said yes. I then asked the other students if they would object to having them way ahead of time. No one objected. Therefore, the only person left in "society" who might be affected by this change is me, the instructor. Since I have the assignments ready two weeks before they are due, it doesn't hurt me to give them out early. The young woman who asked for the problem sets will be helped, and nobody will be hurt if I hand them out early. This is clearly a **Pareto improvement,** so I will start doing it.

Q: *Suppose I took a vote and a majority, but not all of the students, voted in favor of handing out the problem sets early, but some voted no. Would it then represent a Pareto improvement if I handed them out early?*

11.6

I write all my papers, letters, and exams using the typeface Times New Roman. As a lunch-table discussion pointed out, the university insists on certain typefaces that are dyslexia friendly, particularly Arial, Trebuchet, and Verdana. It costs me or any other faculty member nothing to use one of these typefaces on exams; non-dyslexic students are not harmed by them, and dyslexic students are better off. Henceforth, no more Times New Roman on tests—mine will all be in Arial. A clear **Pareto improvement.**

Q: *Can you think of other changes professors might make that would be Pareto-improving?*

11.7

Students' first-draft papers are due in two weeks. I'll mark them, hand them back, and give the students a chance to improve the paper before handing it in for a final grade. One student timidly asks me, "Could I turn mine in a few days early? Would you mind marking it early, so I could have more time for the revision?" I say of course not: My **marginal utility** of grading papers diminishes rapidly with each paper graded in a day, so I'm happy to have her paper alone. Is this a **Pareto improvement**? Yes—the only other people involved are the other students in the class, and there's no reason why our little deal would affect their grades or the attention their papers will get. They're no worse off, and she and I are better off.

Q: *How would your answer change if I grade on a strict curve, giving a fixed percentage of A's, B's, etc.?*

11.8

We are flying with the younger son and his family (four kids), from Dallas to Maui. My wife and I booked and paid for seats for everyone, including the nine-month-old; but when we get on the plane the little guy just wants to sit on his mama's lap the whole time. Just then they announce that the airplane is oversold, so my son races to the front of the plane and offers up the baby's seat. Some lucky fellow gets to take the trip to Maui; my wife and I get $800. I think this is a **Pareto improvement**—all of us Hamermeshes are certainly better off. One might argue, though, that the people next to my daughter-in-law may be worse off if the baby doesn't sleep much during the flight—so maybe it isn't a Pareto improvement.

Q: *If you've ever been at an airport when they announce they are oversold and are seeking volunteers to give up their seats in exchange for money, what are the characteristics of the people who volunteer—age and apparent occupations, in particular?*

11.9

We parked our car at the Austin airport for six days, and my brother then picked it up to use during his three-day visit to my mother. He left it in airport parking when he flew off three days later, a few hours before we returned. This exchange was a clear **Pareto improvement:** He avoided the cost of renting a car, but he saved me three days of charges for parking ($30). I can't think of anyone who was made worse off by this exchange, and BOTH of us were made better off. My mother commented how **altruistic** I was to let him use the car; but, as is so often the case, my motive might just as well been pure selfishness.

Q: *If I wanted to be mercenary, how much could I have charged my brother for using the car? If he wanted to be mercenary, how much could he have asked me to pay for the privilege of a lower cost of parking?*

11.10

A senior professor at another university, one of his department's top researchers and best teachers, asked the department chairman for a temporary, one-course teaching reduction for this fall semester. The chairman refused but offered a terminal three-year appointment that included this reduction for all three years, at the same salary as if this professor taught a full load each year. The professor accepted the deal, as he desperately wanted the teaching reduction this fall, figuring he could get a teaching job elsewhere after three years. But he tells me he would have been happier teaching a full load in the next two years and would rather not have to search for a job in two years. He is worse off. The department and university are worse off since they lose his courses in each of the next two years, and thereafter will not get the benefit of his teaching or his research and publication luster; and students are worse off, too. Could this be the opposite of a **Pareto improvement**—a Pareto deterioration—a new economic phrase denoting a change in which at least one person is worse off, nobody better off?

> **Q:** *Is there any way in which this deal doesn't make everyone worse off? Can you rationalize the department chairman's behavior?*

CHAPTER 12

Monopoly and Monopolistic Competition

Monopoly

12.1

Whenever I stay at a hotel I vow not to buy anything from the mini-bar. The prices are outrageously high, often twice as much as the same price I would pay at the bar downstairs. Yet occasionally I succumb and buy a beer for $5 or a bottle of water for $3 at 11 PM. Why do the hotels charge so much, given that it surely doesn't cost the hotel that much to stock the drinks in your room? The answer is that they have a **monopoly,** not over the product itself, but over the products at the particular time and place. At 11 PM, having gotten undressed and not wanting to go out again, buying the drink from the mini-bar is the only way you can satisfy your demand. With demand that locally **inelastic,** the hotel can charge a very high price and still maximize profits. Similar behavior is exhibited by airlines, which are now charging $6 for a beer in economy class. There are no alternatives to buying from the flight attendant if you want a beer during the flight. With demand that inelastic, the price can be jacked up very high.

Q: *Why don't airlines allow you to bring beer onto a plane?*

12.2

Uncle Booger (www.unclebooger.com) manufactures a patented item, the Bumper Dumper. This device attaches by a hitch to the rear of a vehicle for use when the outdoorsman is far away from toilet facilities. You just stop the car in an isolated location and use the Dumper. Uncle Booger has a **monopoly** on this device. But like any monopoly, the price Uncle can charge is limited by the potential for competition from **substitutes.** In this case, Uncle charges "only" $69.95, as the great outdoors itself provides a substitute that is readily usable by the less than fastidious camper.

> **Q:** *What do you predict will happen to the price of the Bumper Dumper when its patent runs out? Would you expect to see competition in the market for this product?*

12.3

We inherited several art works, including a Rembrandt etching— a portrait of an old man. Is it worth anything? An art appraiser/detective hunted down its story. The print itself is new—pulled on highest-quality paper in the 1990s from Rembrandt's original plate. Apparently, no prints were made in most of the 20th century. In the 1990s, the plate's owner pulled a small number, but none since, and none are planned. The owner has a **monopoly** on the plate and understands revenue maximization (there are essentially no **variable costs**): Pull just enough prints to have sufficient quantity to drive the **price elasticity of demand** to unity, but no more than that. Not only does his strategy gain him the most revenue, but it keeps the price of our print up in case we decide to sell it. This is a rare case where I benefit from monopoly!

> **Q:** *So if I benefit, who loses from the fact that the prints are monopolized?*

12.4

The City of Houston has contracted with towing companies and given each company the sole right to do all towing on a pre-assigned section of highway. The purpose of granting these **monopolies** is to make sure that broken-down vehicles are removed quickly so that the highway does not become congested because of an accident or even a flat tire. Indeed, the towing companies are required to remove vehicles with 6 minutes of a police report that a vehicle is stalled. If these provisions are enforced, the city will have created a series of monopolies whose service quality is **regulated.** But what about their pricing? With monopoly power (albeit only over a small section of road), the companies, which are freed of competition, can charge substantially higher prices. There has already been an outcry about prices; and I expect that the city will either change its policy or be pressured into regulating (and limiting) prices as well as the quality of service.

Q: *So if monopoly on these services causes problems, why not allow competition in providing the services?*

12.5

More than 25 percent of trade between the U.S. and Canada goes over the Ambassador Bridge between Detroit and Windsor, Ontario. The bridge, built in 1929, has since 1979 been owned by one individual. He also owns duty-free stores and sells gasoline that escapes taxes. The bridge isn't quite a **monopoly**—there is also a tunnel; but the bridge is more convenient for a lot of traffic. The state of Michigan has a constitutional amendment on the ballot requiring that any new bridge be approved by voters before state money is spent on it. Perhaps unsurprisingly, the bridge owner is funding a large advertising campaign supporting the amendment. No monopolist likes to have the stream of monopoly **profits** diminished, which a new bridge would surely do. His political advertising is a smart move for him—a good way to ensure a continuing flow of profits. Whether it's good for Michigan, for U.S.-Canada trade, and the well-being of the average North American consumer is questionable.

Q: *How does the increased security post-9/11 affect the monopolist's profits on this bridge?*

12.6

According to a story in the local media, the City of College Station Texas, home of Texas A&M University, will be marketing a section of its cemetery for A&M graduates. Although other schools have them, this is the first university-related cemetery in Texas. The price of a plot is $2,000 compared with $950 in the regular section. Residents will have an opportunity to be near their fellow Aggies forever—and will also have a chance to be close to campus when they're gone. I wonder, since the cemetery is a **monopoly,** whether it is extracting all the **consumer surplus** from buyers. $2,000 seems like a low price to me. I also wonder whether cemeteries at other schools would be or are charging more, perhaps a good measure of the **price elasticity of demand** by deceased alumni of different schools. A neat project would be to infer the extent of school spirit from the estimate of the price elasticity implied by the prices that different university cemeteries charge.

Q: *Although the schools have a monopoly on their own cemeteries, the market for colleges is quite competitive. Once students have chosen their school, they are subject to monopoly pricing when it comes to alumni services such as on-campus cemetery plots. This is similar to manufacturers of printers charging a monopoly price on ink and manufacturers of razors charging a monopoly price on refill razor blades. Can you think of other examples of this type of monopoly?*

12.7

We saw the musical *Urinetown* last night. This 2001 piece, which contains wonderful take-offs on musical numbers from a wide variety of well-known musical shows, is based on the premise that a worldwide drought has created a severe water **shortage** and that the government has given the Urine Good Company (UGC) a **monopoly** on toilets. No private toilets are allowed, and using trees and public places is punished severely. UGC is free to set whatever price it wants. This would be a great monopoly to have—enforced by the government, and with a **demand curve** that has a **price elasticity of demand** of nearly zero. If I were the owner of UGC, I would set prices just high enough to keep the population at subsistence level and make sure that the government severely punished anyone who tried to cheat by failing to use my toilets. Indeed, that is exactly what happens in the play!

Q: *What would this pricing policy do to the willingness of the public to bribe government officials to ignore the use of trees and bushes? What would happen to the average bribe offered?*

12.8

Whenever I lecture on **monopoly,** I ask the students for examples. Good ones are hard to come by, with the diamond cartel being by far the favorite example among economists. Over the years I've gotten a few others, including Luxfer air tanks for scuba diving, and the Paul Ecke Ranch for the propagation of poinsettias. Today, a student pointed out an example that, if I had thought about my own experience, I would have known: The example is Topps sports cards. This has been a long-standing monopoly: As a kid in the early 1950s, I bought the cards and bubble gum and threw the gum away, and so did my sons in the 1970s. Topps maintains its monopoly by signing leagues and/or individual players. Topps pays players more to sign with the league contract because a complete set of cards of the same type is likely to be worth more per card than individual miscellaneous cards.

Q: *A few years ago, a publisher brought out economists' trading cards, with pictures of an economist on the front and his or her biography on the back. The publisher just gave the cards away. Why were there no monopoly profits to be made on these cards?*

12.9

The old James Bond movie *Live and Let Die* begins with a funeral procession in New Orleans. In the movie, Mr. Big, the chief villain, hatches a scheme to give heroin away for free. The purpose of this plan is to drive out his competitors. Once he has succeeded in monopolizing the market, he plans to raise prices to their **monopoly** level. He implicitly believes that the short-run losses he incurs by giving the drug away will be more than made up for by the monopoly profits he will make once his competitors have been driven out of the market. His predatory pricing—selling below **average variable cost** —makes sense only if he can survive those losses better than his competitors can, and if he believes it will be difficult for new competitors to come into the market. If he's correct, he will reap monopoly profits for a long time.

Q: *Will Mr. Big's plan work better if the demand for heroin is inelastic or if it's elastic?*

12.10

At the opera last night, we pre-ordered a glass of wine for the first intermission. We paid before the opera, and the glass was at the pre-arranged place after Act 1. We've done this many times in Germany and increasingly in the U.S. Why do the opera houses do this? Competitive pressure is absent: they have a **monopoly** on food and drink at intermission. Despite this absence, providing this opportunity raises the house's **profits.** Without the usual long wait at intermission, more customers will buy food and drink—so **revenue** increases. This policy also puts less pressure on workers— they don't have to rush during intermission to serve people. In the long run, this reduces the wages that the opera house has to pay for equal-skilled labor—**costs** are reduced. Everybody wins, and I'm surprised this policy isn't more widespread.

Q: *There must be reasons why this practice is not very widespread. List some.*

12.11

A student writes that she became the Midol **monopolist** in her dorm—hoarding Midol to sell to her dorm-mates at a time of the month when each had a quite **inelastic** demand for this product. She also realized that at that time there is an increasingly inelastic demand for chocolate-chip cookies, so she hoarded and sold those, too. She correctly notes that the two goods are **complementary** over time—more of both consumed on some days than on others. But I bet that over a short interval they are **substitutes**—the satisfaction from one reduces the demand for the other. This illustrates how we need to think about the time dimension of consumer choice. I would also bet that her monopoly doesn't last long. Anybody can bring the two products to the dorm and sell them—there are few barriers to entry. A better description is that she's an innovating entrepreneur in what inherently will be a competitive industry.

Q: *In which of her monopolies, Midol or chocolate-chip cookies, would it be easier for her to maintain control?*

12.12

Two of my economics-major students were commenting on how good the food is at the privately run food stand on campus and how they hoped that the young immigrant who runs it makes lots of money. I hope not, and I bet not. The university leases the rights to set up a stand in that location. The university has a **monopoly** on the space on campus, while the number of potential bidders to operate food stands is large. If the officials who determine which stands can be operated are clever, they should extract from the winning bidder all profits above what he or she would earn in a competitive market. The winner would make just enough to cover capital costs and the **opportunity cost** of labor time. If the university does not receive this much from the lease it writes, then it will be sharing its monopoly profits with the operator of the food stand.

It will be reducing the university's **revenue** and hurting the citizens, who pay taxes to the state that supports the university, and the students who pay tuition.

Q: *Are there any reasons why the university might not want to push the winning bidder down to zero* **economic profits?**

12.13

In the movie *District 9*, the aliens ("prawns") have developed a tremendous **addiction** to cat food. A Nigerian gangster lives in the prawns' preserve and has a **monopoly** on the sale of cat food to the prawns. How can he maintain his monopoly—what **entry barriers** are there to other sellers? Simple—the government does not allow the prawns to leave the preserve, so they can't buy from sellers elsewhere in Johannesburg. Every seller must live near them. Since the Nigerian cat-food sellers are heavily armed, quite literally no competitors can enter the market (the preserve). Some entry barrier, either natural (**economies of scale**) or artificial (as in this case, with restrictions imposed on both buyers and potential sellers), is required to enable a monopolist to keep price above **average cost.** As is so often the case in a monopolized market, here, too, the restrictions that create generate monopoly power result at least partly from government action.

Q: *If you had access to government or military resources which you could use to create a monopoly for a product, which product would you choose? By what means would you choose to enforce the monopoly?*

12.14

For many years, a common *graffito* in men's rooms was, "Wash hands, place under blow dryer, dry hands on pants." The old-fashioned low-powered dryers didn't have enough power to dry hands well in any reasonable amount of time; but no more. About ten years ago, the Dyson Airblade was marketed, and it was revolutionary: In 10 or 15 seconds, one's hands really were dry. I assume that they were expensive, which is why I only saw them in a few places, even in the U.K. Today, they are much more widespread. They aren't cheap (I see a discounted price of £615), but I bet they have come down in price. Why? The answer is **competition:** Other companies are now making equally effective products, both in the U.S. and the U.K. An innovating entrepreneur may enjoy a **monopoly** for a while, but competitors with similar products will enter the market, forcing prices down (and increasing **consumer surplus** for users like me!)

> **Q:** *List three other new devices that improved people's lives and that started out as monopolies but became more competitive as substitutes were created.*

Monopolistic Competition

12.15

I've heard of **product differentiation** by location, and of differentiation arising from slight differences in physical product, but never one obviously based on a combination of these two. Honolua Surf Company is a clothing line selling in its own and other stores. It originated in Maui, as the name implies, and is really big on the island. The stores sell other clothing lines, including Billabong; indeed, for the past five years, Honolua has been a subsidiary of Billabong (unsurprisingly, originally an Australian company). I wouldn't buy a Billabong shirt in the Honolua store in Hawaii, and I wonder why the stores even stock them. The Honolua shirts are slightly different, but most important they carry the cachet of being local. A "made in China" souvenir is generally not as attractive as one made locally, even if they were otherwise physically identical.

> **Q:** *What if I were looking for a shirt like this in Texas. Would it matter as much which one I bought?*

12.16

Traveling through Istanbul, I noticed numerous groups of freestanding kiosks with several, as many as six ATMs, each from a different bank. This struck me as being bizarre; and a Turkish economist said that some of the banks even let you withdraw from your account using a competitor's ATM at no extra charge. Why would these joint locations exist—why advertise for each other this way? One possibility is that it's an issue of **monopolistic competition:** As with multiple gas stations on a corner, people expect to find ATMs at certain locations, so each competitor has to locate there. Another possibility is that there are **economies of scale** in servicing the ATMs. Perhaps several banks use the same armored service to insert cash, in which case each would lower its **total cost** by locating at the same place. Neither story explains why I've never seen this in any other country.

   Q: *If you were to open a new bank in Istanbul, would you locate your ATMs near other banks' ATMs, or would you use another method to choose ATM locations?*

12.17

Your main text is one of around thirty economics principles books. These books appear in new editions every two or three years. Why? Partly because the material becomes obsolete fairly fast. But if that were the sole cause, we wouldn't also see new editions of basic math books every few years: It's hard to believe that college math changes every three years. Frequent new editions also can't stem from the used-book market killing off sales of new copies. If that were true, the book publishers would price high enough to account for the multiple resales of each new copy. Anyway, the three-year cycle of economics texts started before there was much of a used-book market. The best explanation is a combination of the partial obsolescence of the material and the need for the **monopolistic competitors** to **differentiate the product** from its competitors by adding new bells and whistles in new editions. Each book tries to carve out a niche in the market in terms of presentation and approach. When another book in that niche adds a new feature—online updates, interactive CD-ROMs, or whatever—its competitors must update their editions to remain viable. If there were no obsolescence of the material, new editions might not come so frequently. But the books would still be updated regularly as a competitive response to the improvements of the slightly differentiated products with which they compete.

   Q: *The decision to assign the texts is made by your professor. If students could choose the book, would they choose an old edition or a new edition? Why? Would the cycle of new editions be as rapid as it now is?*

12.18

In Episode 3 of the hit Showtime series *Weeds,* Nancy's client (the Kevin Nealon character) has bought a huge supply of medical marijuana and doesn't seem to need her as a purveyor any more. Nancy's business is in big trouble. Partial removal of the **ban** on selling a product, such as the legalization of medical marijuana, reduces the artificially high market prices that the state had fostered and that had benefited illegal suppliers like Nancy. Nancy responds to the competition by upgrading the quality of her product—relying on the demand of her clients for better weed. In addition to her now **differentiated product,** she also uses her locational advantage as a **monopolistic competitor**—the medical marijuana store is in the city, while she sells direct from her house. Who would drive 20 miles to a gas station? Why drive to the city to a grass station?

Q: *How else could Nancy differentiate her product from those of her competitors?*

CHAPTER 13

Price Discrimination

13.1

My teaching assistant went to the House of Torment, a commercial "haunted house" where you walk around in the dark and get scared. She says the proprietors charge $13 for adults, $11 for students. The tour is the same for each person, and the **average total cost** of operating the business is the same whether the customer is an adult or a student. This is a good example of demand-based **price discrimination.** They also offer a special deal: If you want to go through the house a second time, the price is only $5. Why such a low price, when again, the average cost of letting you go through a second time is the same? If you're going a second time, the **marginal utility** is lower than the first time, and you're unwilling to pay as much. The lower price for the second trip through the house is another way the business price discriminates.

    Q: *How much should the price be for a third trip through the House of Torment?*

13.2

Midnight Rodeo, a country-dancing bar near the University of Texas, double price-discriminates. Its entry fee is:

Women < 20: $5   Women 21+: $2
Men < 20: $10   Men 21+: $5

Charging less to women than to men is sensible and standard **demand-based price discrimination:** The women may be less interested in drinking at a bar and have a more **elastic** demand, and without the lower price the bar could have far more male than female customers. Charging more to younger customers may represent **cost-based price-discrimination:** The 21+ customers will buy drinks, on which the bar has a large price mark-up. Thus, the cost of having these "older" customers taking up space in the venue is in some sense lower than that of the under-21s.

Q: *Can you think of any other dimensions along which the bar can price-discriminate that might increase its profits even further?*

13.3

A bottle of eighteen-year-old single malt Scotch whiskey typically is priced at least twice that of the same distillery's twelve-year-old product. Why is the eighteen-year-old malt so much more expensive? After all, the production cost to the distiller is less than 50 percent more than the younger malt. The only extra cost is the additional six years of aging in the cask. The reason must be that the distillers recognize that only real Scotch drinkers are going to buy the more mature whiskey. They assume that such aficionados have a lower **price elasticity of demand** for Scotch than does the average whiskey drinker. They **price discriminate** based on their ability to separate the markets for the different types of Scotch (the consumer who buys the less expensive, younger whiskey can't convert it into the more desirable product) and the different demand elasticities of the two types of buyers.

Q: *How does your answer to the question in the second sentence above change if people get pleasure from snobbishly showing that they are willing to serve the more expensive Scotch to their guests?*

13.4

The Mandalay Bay hotel in Las Vegas boasts the Moorea Club, which it advertises as offering a "European-style beach," with entry limited to ages 21 and over (http://www.mandalaybay. com/thingstodo/mooreabeachclub.aspx). It does not advertise that the price of day use is $50 for male customers, $10 for female customers. While examples of price discrimination are ubiquitous, this is one of the purest examples of **demand-based price discrimination.** The service the Club offers is the same to men and women: A place in the sun, which is equally costly to the Club regardless of the patron's gender. Presumably, women's **price elasticity of demand** for the pleasures of the Club exceeds that of men, justifying the price differential. As a vacation spot, I'm not impressed with the Club, preferring a real beach in Europe. But I suppose the overall cost of going to an artificial European beach in

Vegas is less—no need to buy a transatlantic air ticket. This Club is useful, though—it offers one of the most clear-cut examples of this type of price discrimination.

> **Q:** *Can you think of other situations in which men and women are charged different prices for the same product or service? Why is gender a common characteristic used to price discriminate?*

13.5

Denny's breakfast menu in Provo, Utah, offers something that combines demand-based and cost-based **price discrimination,** but is neither. The "French toast slam" is two pieces of toast and two eggs, two strips of bacon *and* two sausages for $6.99. The "senior French toast slam" is one piece of toast and one egg, and two strips of bacon *or* two sausages for $5.49, and you must be at least age 55 to buy this. Pay 20 percent less and get half as much, but why restrict it to older people? Denny's cost saving on the senior slam is probably less than 20 percent. Perhaps the **demand elasticity** of the 55+ is higher than that of the younger set, so that explains the price difference as demand-based. Some seniors would prefer the smaller meal and happily pay as much or even more for it, rather than the regular slam where they would feel compelled to eat everything.

> **Q:** *Why does Denny's have what seems like an unusual pricing scheme?*

13.6

The care and feeding of my iPhone provides an interesting illustration of the role of **competition** and the ability of suppliers to **price discriminate.** I wanted apps that would translate words (no need for full phrases or sentences—that's done nicely on iTranslate) between German and English, and between Dutch and English. There were expensive ones, but the Dutch app was $24.99, while the German app was "only" $19.99. Far beyond my price range, so I shopped for cheap ones. The German app was $0.99, the Dutch app $1.99. The German apps at each level of complexity were more numerous than the Dutch, so it's not surprising that with more competition they should be less expensive.

> **Q:** *How does increasing the total number of suppliers change the elasticity of demand facing each individual supplier?*

13.7

We spent Labor Day weekend at my aunt's funeral in Los Angeles. She is "buried" in an outdoor, above-ground crypt, essentially a 10-foot-high and 10-foot-thick wall that contains a large number of columns, each with seven niches on top of one another. Each niche contains two caskets. The owners of the crypt charge different prices depending on where in the column the niche is located. The highest prices are for niches 3, 4, and 5—the ones that are roughly eye level, while the lowest prices are for the top and bottom niches. The differences in price can't be based on costs—indeed, the **marginal cost** of building the top niche is probably higher than that of the middle niches. The price differences must be due to demand-based **price discrimination.** People want to be able to see their loved-one's grave at eye level, and do not want to bend over or stand on a ladder to touch it or view it closely.

Q: *The crypts are bought in most cases before the person is dead, with the person himself or herself often deciding which niche to purchase. Why might the person care which one is bought?*

13.8

I just got a very nice haircut at the beauty parlor down the street in Bonn, Germany. The young lady washed my hair first and dried it very carefully afterward—neither of which is done at home. The whole thing cost only €10, much less than I pay at the beauty parlor that my wife patronizes in Austin. On the price list, though, there was no price as low as €10. I asked why, and I was told they give a special price to those like me who are—as we might say in the U.S.—follically challenged. I observed a hirsute fellow in the next chair whose haircut lasted much longer than mine. Clearly, the shop was engaging in **cost-based price discrimination.**

Q: *Do you think that the price difference between my haircut and the hairy guy's fully reflected the difference in the hairdresser's time, more than reflected it, or less than reflected it?*

13.9

I talked about the Dutch and German spas last night to a large undergraduate audience. One student pointed out that the Dutch spa faces competition from a different German spa that is only 20 miles away. Trying to attract German customers, on its Web site the Dutch spa posted a special price of only €21.50 per day. BUT:

This special price was only advertised on the German-language version of the website—the Dutch version advertised the full price of €31.50! This is clearly **demand-based price discrimination;** quite sensibly, the owners believe that German customers have a more elastic demand—for them more than for the Dutch customers the German spa is a close substitute. What is neat is that the method used to **separate markets** is not the usual gender, age, or time of day, but rather language usage.

Q: *What if you believe that most Dutch speakers can read German, but most German speakers can't read Dutch. What would be sensible pricing behavior by the owner of the Dutch spa? The German spa?*

13.10

Price discrimination requires preventing people who pay a high price from being able to buy it at a low price. This is done by separating the markets—linking the price to different times when it is bought, such as day or night, weekday or weekend; or different ages of customers; or others. Another market separation gimmick is underscored by a squib in the latest *Consumer Reports*. Dr. Leonard's catalog sells the Barber Magic hair trimmer for $12.99, but in the same catalog offers the identical product, called the Trim-a-Pet, for $7.99. Other than the names on the packages and a bit of different description, the products are identical; and even the styles of the packages are identical. Putting advertisements for both packages in the same catalog is a poor way of creating **market separation:** If I had hair and needed to cut it, I would simply buy the Trim-a-Pet for my personal use and save the $5. This attempt at market separation might work if done in stores—pet stores could sell the Trim-a-Pet at lower prices than drug or hair-care shops sell the Barber Magic. But without some kind of geographic separation, successful price discrimination would be difficult to maintain.

Q: *This seems like demand-based price discrimination; but can you in any way rationalize it as cost-based price discrimination?*

13.11

Resident undergrads at the University of Texas at Austin pay $10,000; nonresidents pay nearly twice as much. Why does the university **price discriminate** since the **marginal cost** of educating in-state and out-of-state students is about the same? One rationale is

equity: Parents of in-state students pay the taxes that cover about 20 percent of the university's costs. But out-of-state tuition seems too high to be justified on this basis alone. Instead, it's a way that the state raises **revenue**—it represents demand-based price discrimination. The university is not a **monopoly,** but it does have some monopoly power. Out-of-state students who are especially interested in the fun of being in Austin, Texas, or who want to major in a particular subject that the university excels in (petroleum engineering, for example), are willing to pay the high tuition. A very large fraction of out-of-state students say that there is something very special about the university that attracted them (and that made them willing to pay this high tuition).

Q: *What does this discussion suggest will be true about the mix of in-state and out-of-state hotel management majors at Michigan State University, one of the few institutions to offer a major in the hospitality business?*

13.12

One of my students was visiting Chicago last year. She and a friend from Northwestern went to the CVS drugstore, and the friend noticed that the same brand of condoms was much cheaper in the city than in the suburban CVS store adjacent to the Northwestern campus. This illustrates the advantage of a local **monopoly**—the CVS store at Northwestern faces a **less elastic demand** than the others and can therefore **price discriminate** based on differences in the **demand elasticity.** My student noticed her friend "stocked up" at the Chicago store, obtaining substantial extra **consumer surplus** by buying there. My student then checked out the situation around our campus. While the stores are not part of the same chain, stores in the private dormitories charge much more for these items than the Student Services Building charges. Again, a local monopoly allows this higher price.

Q: *Given the huge price differentials, why don't students do all their purchasing where the prices are lower?*

13.13

A student described her summer job at an arcade. In the "crane" game, you win prizes by manipulating a claw to grab stuffed animals or basketballs, but the arcade owner can and does manipulate the odds of winning. If a new crane machine is played rapidly, the crane is automatically adjusted from its normal settings to make it more difficult to win because the player is signaling an **addiction** to the game. If the machine lies idle for a while, the odds are made more favorable than normal. This three-tier **price discrimination** takes advantage of implied differences in players' **demand elasticities.** This is the first example I've come across of price discrimination based on manifestations of individual-specific differences in demand elasticities rather than those based on the demographic or timing characteristics of demand.

Q: *Could this principle of price discrimination apply to other games at the arcade? How would you implement it?*

13.14

In Japan, there is an extra charge of ¥100 (about $1.20) if you withdraw cash from an ATM on evenings or weekends. One wise-guy friend suggested that perhaps this is to give the capital equipment the same overtime pay as received by workers! Seriously, though, the only possible argument for **cost-based price discrimination** in ATM usage is that workers might have to make sure the machines don't run out of cash at those times, and their labor requires overtime pay. But surely the same thing is true in the U.S. and Europe, and I don't see this ATM surcharge there. A more likely explanation is **demand-based price discrimination**—the banks realize that people have fewer alternatives (no bank tellers available) at those times and price accordingly. Maybe—but the biggest cost to banks is tellers' time, so I should think that they would do anything to encourage ATM usage, regardless of time of day or week.

Q: *Although credit cards are becoming more widely accepted in Japan, it is much more common to pay for everything in cash. How does this create a less elastic demand for cash than in the U.S. or Europe?*

CHAPTER 14

Oligopoly
(Including Game Theory)

Games

14.1

A student described a problem he had with his younger brother. His mom always insisted they clean up their room while she was away; and he knew that Mom would blame him, not the younger brother, if the task wasn't done. This is a classic game-theory problem. The two parties are you and your little brother; the strategies are work and loaf; and the **"payoff bimatrix"** is

		Little Bro	
		Work	**Loaf**
You	**Work**	(3,1)	(2,4)
	Loaf	(4,1)	(1,4)

Work and loaf are each of your strategies, the pair (3,1) indicates that your payoff is 3, his is 1, if you both work. The other pairs are read similarly. It's not clear what you should do—you're not uniformly better off independent of what he does. But it is clear for him: No matter what you do, he's better off loafing. Loafing for him is a **dominant strategy.** You know that; therefore, you choose to work because you're better off working if he loafs than loafing if he loafs. (If you both loaf, your mom punishes you and not him.)

> **Q:** *How would the payoff bimatrix change if your Mom were to punish both of you equally if the task were not done?*

14.2

The Homer Simpson approach to purchasing wine at restaurants is to buy the second-least expensive wine on the menu. What if everybody behaved this way? Restaurateurs would have an **incentive** to price the wine that costs them the least higher than before, to enhance profits. But if customers know the owners will do this it becomes a game between customers and owners, with the customers' **strategies** being Buy Second-Least Expensive, Buy Something Else, and the owners' strategies being Price Fairly (to reflect costs), Don't Price Fairly. As always, the outcome of the game depends on the payoffs, and one can construct them in ways that will make Homer's approach look good, or look bad.

> **Q:** *How would the policy change if owners know customers are snobs and like to buy the most expensive wine on the list? What if they know customers are cheapskates and like to buy the least expensive wines?*

14.3

One of the well-known game-theory examples is called the Battle of the Sexes game. This came to life for me one spring weekend in 1994. The movie *Little Women* had opened, and my wife desperately wanted to see it. The thought turned my stomach, especially because another, locally made movie about young women, *Teenage Catgirls in Heat,* was playing in town. My wife had no interest in seeing that. The alternative to going out was staying home and watching a *Star Trek* rerun. If we stayed in, we would have been together watching the rerun, which was better than being separated and watching separate movies, but neither of us would have been very happy. There is no single solution to this game, so I proposed that we alternate by seeing *Little Women* that weekend and *Catgirls* the next. This "mixed-strategy" idea is an equilibrium solution for this game. We saw *Little Women,* and my wife was happy. Regrettably, *Catgirls* never showed after that weekend. Years later, I bought a DVD of it and sadly wasted 90 minutes watching a truly awful movie.

> **Q:** *What would the outcome have been if either my wife or I would have preferred to see the other person's movie than watch the* Star Trek *rerun?*

14.4

I'm a thief—I just swiped my eighty-nine-year-old mother's car keys! The retinologist told her that she absolutely should not be driving. Mom asked if we should sell her car, and I said let's wait, see how her vision goes. My wife and my sister, both of whom are convinced that Mom is a menace on the road, told me that I missed my chance. They suggested that I steal her keys to remove temptation. Thinking about this, I realized stealing her keys would be a good **strategy:** If Mom asks where the keys are, I can respond, "Mom, why does it matter, since you are not supposed to drive?" If Mom remembers the prohibition, her optimal strategy will not be to ask since asking indicates that she intends to defy the prohibition on her driving. Assuming Mom is rational, my "steal the keys" strategy leads us to a **Nash equilibrium** in the car game.

> **Q:** *Ignoring the morality of what I did, are there any other strategies you can think of that would have kept Mom off the road?*

14.5

Another professor has caught a cheater. It's an open-and-shut case. If the professor files a formal charge with the university, however, she may be required to participate in a long judicial hearing. Her strategies are file the charge and don't file the charge. If she files, the student faces university-wide disciplinary charges. The professor has given the student the choice of taking a course grade one level below what he otherwise would receive or facing a university hearing that could lead to his expulsion. Which choice—which strategy—will the student pick? Unless the student is a tremendous risk lover, he will choose to take the lower course grade and not risk expulsion. Taking the lower grade is his **dominant strategy.** The professor knew this when structuring the choices for the cheater, and she designed the choices to minimize the time she would have to spend on this case.

> **Q:** *Is this equilibrium **Pareto optimal**; that is, are both parties at least as well off as they would be in any other outcome of these strategies?*

14.6

In the original *Star Wars* movie (Episode IV), Luke Skywalker pleads with Han Solo to help the Rebel Alliance battle the Empire, but Han refuses and a disgusted Luke storms off. Chewbacca, being a student of game theory, lays out the payoff **bimatrix** to Han in their "conversation":

		Han Solo	
		Fight	Don't Fight
Rebel Alliance	**Fight**	(10,8)	(7,5)
	Don't Fight	(−5,−7)	(−5,6)

Han understands that the Rebels have a **dominant strategy** of Fighting. Knowing that, although he has no dominant strategy, being the self-centered person he has already shown himself to be, Han realizes he is better off choosing to aid the Rebels and fight. (Fight, Fight) is a **Nash equilibrium** and also a **Pareto optimum**.

Q: *Can you make up any other Star Wars games?*

14.7

A student was interested in seeing the *Twilight* movie, *Breaking Dawn Part 1*. And her roommate, a "Twi-Hard," even had an extra ticket for the opening, midnight showing. The student likes seeing the vampires and werewolves occasionally, but cannot stand the continuing screams of the pre-pubescent audience. She views her situation as a game with the payoff bi-matrix:

		Twi-Hards	
		Go to Movie	Don't Go
Student	**Go to Movie**	(−3, 5)	(3, 0)
	Don't Go	(0, 5)	(0, 0)

She has no dominant strategy; but understanding that the Twi-Hards do—that they will go to see Edward and Jacob on opening night no matter what—her best choice is to stay in her dorm room. (Don't Go, Go) is a **Nash equilibrium** and a **Pareto optimum**.

Q: *Change the payoffs to reflect the possibility that the Student hates vampire and related movies. How does that change the equilibrium?*

14.8

One of the most widely read books in American high schools is *The Catcher in the Rye*, by J. D. Salinger. At one point the hero, Holden Caulfield, is thinking of running away from New York City. He thinks his little sister Phoebe will follow him if he does, and he hates the idea of her missing out on her school play. He also likes the idea of being with her. One might view this as a game, with the **payoff bimatrix:**

		Phoebe	
		Run Away	**Stay**
Holden	**Run Away**	(4,4)	(5,4)
	Stay	(−2,− 2)	(6,6)

Holden has no **dominant strategy,** but Phoebe does: She will stay in New York no matter what. Knowing that, Holden is best off staying; and both of them staying is a **Nash equilibrium** and a **Pareto optimum.** Indeed, Salinger writes, "Life is a game, boy. Life is a game that one plays according to the rules."

Q: *How would the payoff bimatrix change if Holden didn't care about his sister's missing her school play?*

14.9

In *American Pie 2,* a guy tells his buddy that with women you need to use the Rule of Three: To find the truth, multiply by three the number of guys a woman says she's slept with. In the next scene, a woman tells her friend that with guys you need to use the Rule of Three: To find the truth, divide by three the number of women a guy says he's slept with. Assume that each sex believes its own Rule of Three about the other sex: that guys seek to impress women with their prowess, and that women seek to impress guys with their demureness. What will each sex's strategy be, and what will the **equilibrium** be? Guys will claim as many women as is remotely credible; if they know women will divide by three, they should multiply the actual number by four. Women will claim as much demureness as is remotely credible; if they know guys will multiply by three, they should divide the actual number by four. The equilibrium will not be the truth or even three times (for men) and one third (for women) of the truth. Instead, the sexes will go to opposite extremes, restrained only by the credibility of their claims. Rules of Three may be only a temporary equilibrium: If both sexes realize what's going on, each may develop a Rule of Four, a Rule of Five, or more.

Q: *What if a woman announces that she is telling the truth? How will guys' strategies change?*

14.10

Every time an opposing player is penalized at a University of Michigan hockey game, the student fans begin chanting long strings of obscene epithets. After the first few times this happened the band began playing loud music (lots of drums) to drown this out. This is a **repeated game,** with the students as the first-mover, **strategy** chant/no chant, and the band a follower, play/don't play. By now, with many rounds (penalties) having occurred, other fans can't hear the students at all—the second they begin to chant, the band begins playing. This is not a desirable equilibrium for the students. What should they do to have some impact (assuming they aren't just chanting to hear themselves)? They will always be first-movers, which is a disadvantage in this case; but perhaps if they randomize chanting—chant only at random penalties—they can surprise the band and have a few seconds of audible chanting. Of course, after a while the band will simply start playing at every penalty, so that randomized chanting won't work either. I think the equilibrium is that the students will never be heard.

    Q: Can you think of a strategy for the students that might allow their obscene chants to be heard at least sometimes?

14.11

During our family's beach week, the grandkids decided that my name is "Tammy," and they called me that the entire week. On the last day, the four-year-old asked, "Grandpa Dan, if you give me a dollar I won't call you Tammy anymore." I thought this was a good deal, and gave a dollar to her, her brother, and her cousins, all of whom made the same promise. Was this a good strategy on my part—was my behavior **subgame perfect** in the context of the **repeated game** that is our beach week each summer? No—my behavior was not subgame perfect. They will probably not call me Tammy again. (I told them that, if they did, they would have to pay me one dollar *plus interest*.) But next summer they could, for example, start calling me Georgina or something equally silly for a fifty-nine-year-old man. If I played the same strategy next summer, the grandkids could wind up taking me for a dollar per grandkid each summer. If they pick another name next summer, you can be sure that I will not choose the subgame imperfect strategy of paying them not to call me that *particular* name! In fact, my surmise about their behavior was correct: I saw all four kids just three months later at a family occasion—and they all immediately decided that my name was "Cheesie," and called me that the entire time! This time, though, I didn't try to buy them off.

Q: *What should I have told them about names for me when I paid the four grandkids a dollar each?*

14.12

In John Grisham's *A Painted House*, the seven-year-old hero Luke Chandler has the following thoughts: "If I told him about Hank, I knew exactly what would happen. He'd march me down the front yard to Spruillville and we'd have a confrontation. . . . Hank would misjudge his opponent, and before long the stick would come into play. . . . The Spruills would lick their wounds . . . and we'd be left short-handed. I'd be expected to pick even more cotton. So I didn't say a word." Even a (fictional) seven-year-old understands the need to choose **subgame-perfect** strategies since, without them, he is liable to wind up doing more arduous labor than would otherwise be required of him.

Q: *As a young child, you probably went through a similar train of thought that led you not to do something that would have been the morally correct thing to do. Give an example.*

14.13

My granddaughter won $72 in a music composition contest and wants to spend $4 of it on some artificial fingernails. I accompany her to the store; being a proud grandfather, I'd like to reward her for winning the contest. So after she picks out the nails and we walk to the cashier, I offer to pay half. I figure this way I am transferring income, showing pride, but not lowering the price of fake nails and not giving her an **incentive** to spend more on fancier fake nails. This little **strategy** seems sensible for a one-shot game; but in a **repeated game,** she will catch on and walk back from the cashier with whatever she purchases and spend more money. I like to transfer income, but I don't want to subsidize specific purchases.

Q: *Think of a time when you were out at a restaurant and knew that someone else was going to pick up the bill. Did you order differently from what you normally would have done?*

Oligopoly Behavior and Antitrust Policy

14.14

I earned two free one-way coupons on Southwest Airlines. I tried to redeem them for a round-trip flight, but there were no coupon seats on the return flight. So I redeemed one coupon and now have one left over. That's the result of a clever **strategy** by Southwest, as I will now use the other coupon as part of a second round-trip. Unlike the older trunk carriers, Southwest prices solely on one-way tickets—there is no gain to buying a round trip. That means that I have an incentive to pay (either with cash or coupon) for two Southwest trips. When I use my mileage to obtain a "free" ticket on the other main carrier out of Austin (American Airlines), it always pays me to use it for a round trip. Southwest's pricing and coupon policy tie me more strongly to them. American's does allow use of mileage for a one-way ticket; but given their pricing policy, that only pays if I am planning one-way travel.

> **Q:** *Knowing that the airlines have these strategies for redeeming frequent flier miles, how should I change my purchasing behavior in the future? Can the airlines easily change their strategies in response to my behavior?*

14.15

Digital TV is much better than analog—a crisper picture, better sound, and less space required on the radio spectrum to send the signal. For many years, TV manufacturers had been able to make and install digital tuners, and broadcasters had been able to send digital signals. Yet only a tiny fraction of TVs and TV broadcasting were digital. This was a **prisoner's dilemma:** Manufacturers chose between make digital and don't make digital. Making digital was profitable only if there were lots of digital broadcasts. Broadcasters chose between broadcast digital and don't broadcast digital. Broadcasting digital was profitable only if there were lots of digital TVs. The **equilibrium** was don't make, don't broadcast. Everyone was worse off—this was an inferior equilibrium, but neither side wanted to risk the chance that the other side wouldn't go digital. So, the government imposed a solution: Now all stations must broadcast in digital. The new equilibrium is make digital, broadcast digital. Both manufacturers and broadcasters are better off since the more attractive viewing brings in more customers. But without intervention from outside this game, the desirable equilibrium would not have been reached.

Q: *Write down a* **payoff bimatrix** *for this game, and show that the initial equilibrium was don't/don't.*

14.16

Textbook publishers customarily send professors free "examination copies" of books they would like the professors to require their students to buy. A game theorist colleague has received an advertisement for a textbook on game theory. The publisher will send an examination copy if the professor returns a reply postcard and $3. Why the $3 charge? It's a trivial amount, not even enough to cover the **marginal cost** of printing and sending the book. The strategy is presumably designed to avoid sending books to professors who have no intention of assigning them in class. The publisher has defected from the **Nash equilibrium** of free copies for interested professors. My colleague has three strategies: forget it; send in the $3 with the postcard; or a third, clever strategy—send in the postcard with no money and punish the defector. He chose the third strategy. My guess is that other good game theorists will, too. They will call the publisher's bluff. I expect the publisher will find that adding this charge doesn't work, and the game will revert to the Nash equilibrium of free copies to any interested professor.

Q: *How would my colleague's strategy change if the charge had been $10? Would a different charge alter the Nash equilibrium?*

14.17

The Antitrust Division of the U.S. Department of Justice must approve mergers between American companies. It charges companies a fee of $75,000 to review a medium-sized merger, and $150,000 to review a larger merger. The Division can be viewed as the **monopoly** seller of "merger approvals," and the companies that are merging can be viewed as the **monopsony** buyers of approvals from the Division. A buyer will presumably gain additional profits when the merger is approved. Otherwise, why would they be seeking the merger? This situation is a **bilateral monopoly**—one buyer, one seller—in which there is some pot of extra profit that will be generated after the merger. The question is: Why does the Division charge so little? Surely the merger is worth far more to the parties than the measly $75,000, or even $150,000, that the Division

charges. The $75,000 far exceeds the cost of the Division's work-
ers' time, and in fact in a good year the Division returns more than
$200 million to the U.S. Treasury. If it were a profit-maximizer it
would charge a lot more—it would bargain for a large chunk of the
profits to be generated by the merger. It doesn't maximize profits,
though—political pressures limit its ability to extract much of the
merger's profits and return them to the taxpayer.

> Q: *If this were a competitive industry and the merger generated
> gains in efficiency in production, who would benefit from the
> merger, and why? Since it is a monopoly, who benefits, and why?*

14.18

Each year in my five-hundred-student principles class, I gather a
group of eight students together and tell them that I will auction
a $20 bill to the highest bidder. If two or more students bid the
same thing, the difference between $20 and their joint bid will be
divided among the winning bidders. They can collude to fix the
price just like **oligopolists** who violate antitrust laws; but they must
mark down their bids in secret. Today, seven of the students stuck
to the collusive agreement, and each bid $.01. They figured they
would split the $20 eight ways, netting $2.49 each. Ashley, bless
her heart, broke the agreement, bid $0.05 and collected $19.95. The
other seven students booed her, but I got the class to join me in ap-
plauding her, as she was the only one who understood the game.
It showed that, even in a market like this one, with very few players, collusion is difficult to maintain. There are tremendous **incentives** for one or more parties to cheat and move the market toward
a competitive outcome. Unfortunately, nobody has ever gone as
high as the predicted equilibrium bid of $17.50, an amount that one
student was clever enough to suggest to me after class.

> Q: *Suppose there were only four students participating. What
> would they collude to bid, and how much profit would each make?
> Do you think this collusion would be sustainable? What does this
> say about the number of oligopolists in a market and the potential
> for earning economic profits?*

14.19

One of my students is active on eBay, where he sells autographed
items that he has bought elsewhere. His current gimmick is a new
CD recorded and autographed by Janet Jackson. Only fifty were

sold initially, all at stores in New York City. My student is selling twelve on eBay, and his friend is selling nineteen. Together, my student and his friend are almost **duopolists;** their problem is how to maintain collusion. Their problem is enhanced by the fact that in a few days Janet Jackson will be signing five hundred copies of this CD in stores. As that date approaches, and as potential customers discover that the supply of autographed CDs will be expanding greatly, the value of his twelve, and his friend's nineteen, will drop drastically. Each will have a tremendous incentive to cut prices in order to unload the inventory before its value plummets. It is difficult to reap **monopoly,** or even duopoly profits, when customers realize that your monopoly or duopoly is about to end.

   Q: *The student only has five days left to unload the CDs. If you were in his position, how would you price them during this five-day period?*

14.20
The Fox TV network will try a new strategy this year—it will premiere its new fall program lineup in the summer, when the three main networks are generally showing reruns. The idea is to get viewers hooked on the new shows, so that by the time the other networks introduce their new series in the autumn many viewers will remain with Fox. Think of this as a game—with the **strategies** being: Premiere in summer, premiere in fall. What Fox is doing is **jumping the gun**—pushing backward in time the point when the **equilibrium** in the game occurs. What if Fox is successful, and gets a lot of new viewers? The other networks would respond by scheduling some of their premieres in the summer, too. Fox's **strategy** may be a short-run success; but if it is, the end result will be a new equilibrium with many network premieres occurring in the summer.

   Q: *Look at when the 2015 model cars are introduced. Is it in 2015? What has happened to the dates of introduction of new car models over the last two decades?*

14.21
Zocor®, a cholesterol reducing drug designed for heart patients, is one of the most widely sold prescription drugs in the world. Unfortunately for its manufacturers, the **patent** on it ran out in 2006, meaning that their **monopoly** power over the drug's sales ended.

Even before the expiration date, however, an upstart company was marketing a generic version of the drug at a much lower price. Rather than wasting money on protecting its patent for the few remaining months, the manufacturer of Zocor chose instead to undercut the price of the generic competitor. That generated a rebuke from a U.S. senator who accused the manufacturer of **predatory pricing**—taken literally, pricing at below **average variable cost.** While possible, the accusation is not very credible—the average variable cost of an existing drug is tiny, far below even the lower price that the manufacturer began charging.

Q: *The upstart company chose to infringe on this patent, knowing that the drug was protected. What are they assuming about the payoffs of protecting the Zocor patent versus not protecting it? Do you think they considered the possibility of predatory pricing on the part of the Zocor manufacturer?*

14.22

The Federal Communications Commission has changed its views and is now proposing to require cable television providers to allow consumers to select which specific channels they want rather than select from among a small set of packages. The cable companies vehemently oppose this. The current set of packages is a classic example of a **tie-in** sale: If I want to get CNN, I also must purchase the Fox News Channel, which I do not want. My well-being would increase if I could pay less and get the very few (no more than 10) channels that I ever watch. I imagine that's typical of cable consumers. The **average cost** per channel offered would probably rise: Cable companies would have to spend resources offering tailor-made combinations of channels to each customer; but I would expect that the overall price to the consumer for his/her desired set of channels would fall. Consumer well-being would increase.

Q: *If the cable business were not monopolized, would this be an issue?*

14.23

Today's *Wall Street Journal* reports a class-action lawsuit and an inquiry by the U.S. Department of Justice into charges of **price-fixing** by modeling agencies. Price-fixing is illegal in the U.S., but it's hard to believe that modeling agencies, of which there are many competitors, would be a likely suspect for charges of price-fixing.

Unfortunately for them, the agencies' executives made the mistake of taking detailed minutes of their discussions in meetings. In the past, including in the most well-known case, the Electrical Conspiracy in the 1960s, it was the detailed notes that got the executives convicted and even sent to jail. This written evidence may be enough to convict members of an industry that very possibly would otherwise have not been a target, or at least would have escaped investigation fairly easily. Moral of the story: If you're going to engage in illegal economic behavior, do not keep records of your activities!

Q: *If there hadn't been minutes of the meetings, what evidence could the government use to demonstrate the existence of price-fixing?*

14.24

You don't see too many **cartels** in the news these days, but a story today reports on a lawsuit by wholesale grocers that charged the United Potato Growers of America with **price-fixing**. My initial reaction was disbelief: As in most agricultural industries, there are lots of producers, so how can quantity restrictions be enforced in this **competitive** industry? Not easily, but modern technology helps—the cartel is accused of using spy satellites to make sure each cartel member abides by limits on production. Like most cartels, this one grew out of a period of low prices. One member said farmers "... hauled their potatoes out in the field with the manure spreader, dumped them and plowed them under," implying that the price didn't even cover **average variable cost.**

Q: *What if we discover that a diet of potatoes reduces the risk of cancer? How would this affect the cartel's power and stability?*

Tips on Hunting for Economics Everywhere in Part II

1. Look at how companies produce things—the techniques that they use as they produce more—and how you and your friends choose to do different activities. When the cost of producing changes, look at how the method of production changes.
2. Consider whether fixed costs are ignored in deciding on a course of action for the present and the future. Is a company—or are you—behaving in a maximizing way?
3. Consider how the price of a good is determined by costs and by ease of entry into the market. Think about why the price of a competitively produced good might differ across geographical areas.
4. Look for shocks to markets. They are always occurring, both naturally and because of government actions. How do they affect price and quantity? How do changes in cost and technology affect price, quantity, and the size and number of suppliers? How do changes in product demand alter the number of firms, and the size of the typical firm?
5. Search for cases where people are dividing some fixed amount of anything. Can the group be made better off with a different division? If the amount changes, does the new distribution make everyone better off? For any change, think whether the group should be defined narrowly enough so that every member might be benefiting.
6. If there is only one supplier of a good or service, why? How is its monopoly protected? Does the monopolist take into account the impact of raising price on the quantity he or she sells?
7. Look for monopolists charging different prices for the same good or service. Why are they doing it—is it cost differences or differences in demand? How do they succeed in separating markets?

8. Look for suppliers colluding. Do they succeed? How do their strategies follow the ideas of game theory? Consider people's or companies' interactions in light of game theory. Are they behaving optimally in light of the repeated interactions they have with other firms? What are the implied payoffs to the strategies that you choose—and that others whom you deal with are choosing? Are your strategies in your own career consistent with long-term rational interactions with others?

PART III

*I*nput Markets, the Public Sector, and International Markets

CHAPTER 15

Discounting and Present Value

15.1

I am installing over thirty solar panels on our roof in Austin. It costs $25,000. The City of Austin currently offers a rebate up to $15,000, or 60 percent of the cost, and the federal government gives a 30-percent credit on the remainder. With those subsidies the **rate of return** on our own investment is 17 percent, making this is a superb deal. I noticed that a neighbor here in the Netherlands has four solar panels on his roof, which seems like a strangely small number. I asked him why. The answer is very simple: The Dutch government will pay up to €1,500 if you install a solar installation. Each solar panel costs him €450, with a **fixed cost** of about €200 to do the installation. Thus, the average rate of return on his four panels is about 25 percent, a great investment. The rate of return on a fifth panel, which would not receive the subsidy, would only be 4 percent, a much less attractive deal. Small wonder that my neighbor has his unusual solar installation.

> **Q:** *What would be the rate of return on my investment if there were no subsidy from the City of Austin?*

15.2

The U.S. Postal Service is planning another rise in the price of a first-class stamp. Until 2007, at each price increase they issued a special letter stamp usable at the new price (since they didn't know how much the new price would be until shortly before it went into effect). Since then, the USPS has been selling something new: A "forever stamp"—a generic first-class stamp that will always be good and will be sold at the current price of a first-class stamp. If I buy the "forever stamp" when the price is 45 cents, say in 2013, I'll be able to use it in 2023 when first-class postage costs, for example, 68 cents. So why not stock up on first-class stamps now—buy a lifetime supply—and save money later on? If I spend $450 to buy 1,000 45-cent forever stamps in 2013, I will save spending $680 on postage in 2023; but I could put the $450 in a bank in 2013 and let it grow for ten years. The **present discounted value** of $680 to be spent in 2023 is less than $450 if the interest rate is above 4 percent. Only if I expect interest rates to be below 4 percent for the next ten years should I stock up on forever stamps.

> **Q:** *If I expect the 2023 price of stamps to be 88 cents, then what would be the highest interest rate for which it is profitable to stock up on stamps now?*

15.3

I have been running for exercise since 1967, in the early days averaging 25 miles a week, and these days 12 miles a week. Now my knees and hips hurt often. I always ran because I enjoyed it and thought it would be good for my long-term health. If I had known forty-seven years ago how much my lower body would hurt (and how likely it is that someday I will need knee and/or hip replacements), would I have run so much? Is our **forward-looking maximizing behavior** the same as the behavior we would have undertaken if we knew the long-term consequences of our activities? Do we **discount** the future at too high a rate when we are young?

> **Q:** *How does this vignette apply to your behavior in timing your studying for economics over the semester? Give examples of cases in which your behavior implies that you discount the future at a very high rate.*

15.4

California is considering banning teenagers from using tanning salons. The argument is that their using the salons will increase the incidence of skin cancer, especially its deadly form, melanomas, many years in the future when the teens are in late middle age. For economists, the question is whether the teens have a sufficiently low **discount rate** that they will properly account for their future risk of getting skin cancer when they decide whether to go tanning now. If they do, then they will make a correct choice in comparing today's pleasures from being tan with the future risk of skin cancer and its costs. If not, and if the government is better at accounting for these future risks, banning teens from tanning salons makes economic sense. Judging by the teens whose behavior I have observed closely (my sons), I doubt that teenagers' discount rates are low enough to account for these future risks. So banning tanning by teens seems like a good idea.

Q: *Short of banning tanning, what could you do so that teens account more fully for the future risks that their current actions will cause?*

15.5

A student reports that she decided to examine her brothers' **discount rates** with an experiment. She told both of them that she would put a freshly baked cookie in each of their rooms. If the cookie was still uneaten after 10 minutes, she would give the brother a second cookie. When she went back to the three-year-old brother's room, the cookie was gone. The fifteen-year-old brother, though, had a sufficiently low discount rate that he left the cookie uneaten, got the second one, and devoured both. Very young children are extremely impatient—have very high discount rates. As we get older, our discount rates drop, but: At some point they must rise again. If I expect to live only one more week, I would have a very high discount rate indeed—there would be almost no future left for me to discount!

Q: *How has your willingness to wait for rewards changed over time? Do you have a higher or lower discount rate than you did five years ago? Do you predict that it will be higher or lower five years in the future?*

15.6

Yesterday's local paper gave some remarkably bad advice about lottery winnings. The columnist was asked about Lotto winnings when one chooses the cash option (all the money at once) or the option of twenty-five equal annual payments. She responded, "If you selected the cash option for a $100 million jackpot, you would receive about one half the money. . . . Then 25 percent for taxes is taken out. Your check would be $37.5 million. If you selected the annual payment option, you would receive considerably more—twenty-five annual payments, less the 25-percent income tax. Each payment would be about $3 million [totaling about $75 million]." Now each sentence here is correct. But the columnist makes it sound like the annual payment option gives you much more. It gives you more dollars, but it gives you dollars in the future, up through twenty-five years from now. When you take the **present**

discounted value of those dollars, you find that the annual payment option yields a present value exactly equal to the cash option. So which one should you take? That depends on how badly you want the dollars now. If you are impatient—if $.95 today is worth more to you than $1 next year—you should take the cash option; if not, go for the annual payment option. Most lottery winners take the cash now—they are pretty impatient.

Q: *How should your choice between the two options be affected if the Lotto suddenly figures the interest rate is 20 percent per year and discounts the cash value amount accordingly?*

15.7

One of my favorite stories about compound interest is from a science-fiction vignette I read as a teenager, entitled "John Jones's Dollar." Set around the year 3000, the idea was that a kid had put $1 in the bank in the 1950s, and it had grown at compound interest for 1,000 years because neither Jones nor his descendants ever touched the interest, instead re-investing it so that their account owned most of the assets in the solar system. If the interest rate after inflation is 3 percent per year—about what it has averaged over the past fifty years—and someone invested $1 today, it would grow to $6.7 trillion by 3009, which matches the total of nearly half of the value of all goods and services produced in the U.S. today. So, one family could become phenomenally rich this way. But if the whole economy also grew at 3 percent after inflation, as it often has, while the family would be extremely rich it would still only control a tiny fraction of the output produced because the whole economy would be growing at the same rate as John Jones's dollar.

Q: *How much would John Jones's dollar be worth in 1,000 years if the interest rate after inflation was 5 percent?*

15.8

I often see one of the associate deans of our college at my health club. He does nothing but run on the treadmill. Today, he informed me that he was quitting the club. He pointed out that the dues are $1,000 per year, and he can buy even the fanciest treadmill for use at home for $3,000. So I thought: How high would the interest rate have to be to make saving $1,000 of dues per year a bad deal? Assume that the treadmill will last forever. Then the question is what interest rate would make the **present value** of $1,000 per year less than $3,000? The present value of $1,000 each year forever is $1,000/[r] where r is the interest rate; so any interest rate below 33.33 percent would make his investment in the fancy treadmill worthwhile. In fact, it's a better investment even than that since by having the treadmill at home he saves the costs of gasoline used while driving to the health club, and he avoids losing the **opportunity cost** of the time he would spend traveling to the health club.

Q: *Calculate what the maximum interest would be to make the purchase of the treadmill worthwhile if it cost $4,000 instead of $3,000.*

15.9

The price offered to coffee growers who turn in their "cherries"— ripe coffee beans—at Greenwell Farms in Kona, Hawaii, is 90 cents per pound if they are paid weekly, $1.05 if paid monthly. The weekly price offered is lower because it takes the company's accountants more time to work out and record pay if they do it weekly rather than monthly. But what does this price differential imply about the grower's **discount rate**? If he takes the weekly rate, on average he is getting 90 cents one-half month earlier than he would get $1.05. That implies an annual discount rate of nearly 4,000 percent—$(1.05/.90)^{24} - 1$—a truly remarkable rate of impatience. Despite this, the tour guide tells me that a lot of growers do take the lower rate of pay.

Q: *Think about your friends who get paid weekly or bi-weekly versus those who get paid monthly. Is one group more likely to run out of money before their next paycheck? Given a choice, how often would you prefer to be paid?*

15.10

The Hebrew calendar is lunar, so a leap-month has to be inserted every once in a while to keep the seasons and holidays at appropriate times. But when to insert the month, and what group should decide? According to the *Talmud Sanhedrin 18b*, the king was excluded from the group. Because he paid his soldiers on an annual basis, it was felt that he would have an **incentive** to insert extra months since that lengthened the year and saved him money. If the king only expected to be in power for a few years, or if he had a very high **discount rate** and didn't care about the future, this explanation might make sense. But the calendar couldn't get too far off—the king couldn't keep inserting months year after year. Otherwise, for example, harvest holidays would come during planting times. One might even argue that the king had the opposite incentive: By avoiding excessive intercalations, he would demonstrate to the soldiers and the people his confidence in a long reign.

Q: *How would incentives differ for a new, young king and a king who was age 70?*

15.11

The behavior described in the previous vignette is made even clearer in Clay Walker's song "Then What," where he addresses a man about to engage on an extramarital affair: "Then what, what you gonna do, when the new wears off and the old shines through, and it ain't really love and it ain't really lust, and you ain't anybody anyone's gonna trust, when you can't turn back for the bridges you burn." The guy in the song is willing to throw over his marriage, even though he may know that in the future the affair will come to nothing and he will lose his family. He values the present pleasure much, much more than he worries about the future pain. It's not just that he has a high **discount rate;** he values pleasure now much more than he is bothered by pain next year, even though, if he were asked about the affair in three years, he would choose not to have had the affair. Economists call this strange valuation of present and future **hyperbolic discounting**—people overemphasize current pleasure and pain in comparing actions at different points in time. It provides one explanation for why people have trouble giving up **addictions.**

Q: *Would you be more likely to exhibit hyperbolic discounting in investing your money or in dealing with beers offered to you at a party?*

CHAPTER 16

*L*abor Markets

Labor Demand and Supply

16.1

A story in the *Washington Post* illustrates how valuable good Santa Clauses are. It points out that mall owners, "consider having a premium Santa an important business lure." A good Santa is one who is drug free, not likely to harass the children, and who is "child-friendly." Such a Santa has a high **marginal revenue product**—some Santas develop reputations and generate repeat business year after year. The people lured into the mall by the Santa add to the storeowner's revenues, and thus to the rental fees the mall owners can charge the storeowners.

> **Q:** *Suppose you were a popular Santa with a reputation for bringing many customers to a local mall. How would you use the concept of marginal revenue product to negotiate a higher wage?*

16.2

The Jewish New Year is announced by blasts on a ram's horn (*shofar*). Many people use much larger horns (from a kudu, for example) instead. This year, as part of the religious service, a woman picked up the ram's horn to blow a few sounds, and not much came out—a few feeble toots. After squeaking out half the required notes, she switched to the kudu horn—she switched to using additional **capital.** With the larger horn, she blasted the entire congregation out of their seats with truly wonderful sounds. Even in a religious service, we can observe that the **marginal product** of labor is enhanced by additional capital; even in this context, labor and capital are **complements** in production.

> **Q:** *My older son is an accomplished shofar blower. How much improvement would he get if he switched from a ram's horn to a kudu horn as compared to the woman in the story?*

16.3

A student came to my office hours yesterday with a question about the course. He then said he had an unrelated question—but in fact it wasn't unrelated at all: "Why do we tip the same percentage at cheap restaurants and expensive ones so that, for the same amount of time serving you, the waitperson at the cheap restaurant earns much less than the waitperson at the expensive one?" Very good question indeed! My answer is that it is probably partly custom; but it's partly, too, that if the workers seeking waiting jobs and their potential employers know about this behavior (and I'm sure that they do), the best, most productive waiters will look for and obtain jobs at the fanciest restaurants. The least productive waiters will get jobs at the cheap restaurants. So because workers sort themselves among employers, in a real sense the higher dollar-amount tip at the fancy restaurant means you are paying for the waiter's higher **marginal product of labor** there. You are paying for the same amount of time as at a cheaper restaurant, but you are paying for quality service.

> **Q:** *What would happen in this situation if the government passed a law requiring all tips to be at least $2 per customer?*

16.4

A story on the Web discussed a new personnel policy: "rank and tank." The idea is to have managers rank their employees each year, with the bottom 10 percent being dismissed. The purpose is to avoid the "Lake Wobegon effect," in which all the employees are rated as better than average. This may be a reasonable one-time policy, as it forces managers to disclose which workers they believe are sub-par. But it is a very stupid policy if continued beyond a year. In each successive year the bottom 10 percent become better and better relative to workers elsewhere and to their potential replacements. Moreover, workers who expect this policy to continue become increasingly uncertain about their own futures. If no other jobs were available, fine; but in a modern economy, workers have alternatives—**monopsony** is very rare—and this policy will increase the workers' quit rate. Beyond the one-time beneficial effect of a surprise ranking, this idea is a good way for a firm to lose some of its best workers and to decrease its labor productivity as its workers' morale drops.

> **Q:** *Can you think of more sensible ways for employers to avoid the Lake Wobegon effect?*

16.5

Newsweek quoted Keith Richards explaining why tickets to shows on the "final" Rolling Stones world tour cost much more than tickets to see Sir Paul McCartney: "There's more of us." Richards implicitly believes in the Marxian **"labor theory of value"**— that the price of a product is determined by the cost of the labor input in production. Labor costs matter, but they aren't the only thing that matters. Indeed, in this case the tickets probably cost more simply because there is more demand to see the entire Rolling Stones group than to see a single Beatle. It's the greater demand that allows the Stones to charge a higher price than Sir Paul charges.

> **Q:** *A ticket to see Simon and Garfunkel recently cost only half of what it cost me to see the Stones. Is this because the Stones consist of four main players, while Simon and Garfunkel are only two people?*

16.6

Classes start in three weeks, and the bosses have mandated a revolution at UT-Austin: We can no longer give only A, B, C. . . grades, but must give $+$/$-$ grades too—A, A$-$, B$+$, etc. With six hundred students this Fall, I can imagine a big change in griping. One colleague says I'll get fewer complaints—with less to argue over, each argument will be less heated. I say more complaints, though—there are more dividing points, so more students will think that they're on the edge of a better grade. The first effect is a beneficial change at the **extensive margin,** the second a detrimental change at the **intensive margin.** The issue is analogous to the effect of some **incentives** on hours per worker (the intensive margin) or **labor-force participation** (the extensive margin). It's similar too to the breakdown of the unemployment rate into the duration of unemployment spells and their incidence (number of people unemployed this year). The burden of workplace injuries also depends on their severity and number.

In these other examples, the costs to society are greater if duration or severity increases than if the number affected rises. With grading complaints, though, it takes me less time to deal with a few very unhappy people than lots of somewhat unhappy people. In the end, two years of experience showed that my expectations were correct: I've gotten many more students complaining about their grades than before, and my colleagues report the same annoying phenomenon.

> **Q:** *What kind of incentives does this new grading policy give to students? Do you think it encourages them to work harder and supply more effort to studying?*

16.7

One of my introductory economics students came into my office to ask a question, and we started talking about running. I asked him if he was on the track team; he said yes. I asked what event, and I was wowed when he said decathlon. I ventured a guess as to how many points he achieved in a meet, and he said I was way low. In fact, he is the American junior champion, ranked, he said, twentieth among decathletes of all ages in the world. Clearly, since decathletes peak in their late twenties, he has a decent shot at being in the Olympics and even winning a gold medal. He is a superstar among track and field athletes; sadly, however, he will not be what economists call a **superstar**—he is unlikely, even if he wins a gold medal in 2016 or 2020, to make huge earnings from his decathletic prowess. The reason is that very few specialists in that sport get many endorsement contracts—I can only think of Bruce Jenner and Bob Richards in the last fifty years; and there is no repeated broadcasting of their performance over long periods, as there would be for pro baseball, football, basketball, or golf. My guess is that even the 500th-best major league baseball player will wind up earning more from his athletic skills than will this incredibly talented athlete.

> **Q:** *How do you think his earnings would compare with those of the best rodeo rider in the U.S.? The best bowler?*

16.8

A graduating senior comes to talk about the course and about what he's going to do after graduation. He's thinking of getting a master's degree next year. He reasons that the job market is currently very tight, so the **opportunity cost** of being in grad school will be low because it would be hard for him to find a job. He figures that in a year the job market will be better, and he will be well positioned to get a good job with his new advanced degree. Maybe he's right. But a lot of studies suggest that, if everybody thinks this way, the market becomes glutted with newly degreed people. They all entered grad school thinking they would earn a lot on graduation. When they come out on the job market, the large supply of new graduates drives down their earnings. My student may be in for a rude surprise.

Q: *So, how should you time grad school—if you go during good times, you give up job opportunities now, but you have fewer competing graduates when you finish your program? Is that a better or a worse choice for you than the choice outlined in the vignette?*

16.9

Today's *Wall Street Journal* has a story about an interesting interaction between technical change and the **marginal product** of labor (and thus in the payment generated by a personal characteristic). We have always thought that television stardom required the most beautiful face—no blemishes, perfect features. With the advent of HD television, which shows every detail of one's features, you might think the new technology would require even more perfection from TV actors; but it also shows every movement of one's facial features—and their immobility. The rigid skin of the Botoxed, face-lifted actor or actress is unexpressive, and HDTV puts an increased reliance on expression. One might soon expect to see more television stars who do not look like their skin is ironed out and pasted onto their skulls.

Q: *How will HDTV affect the earnings of television actors in relation to their ages?*

16.10

One of my students informed me that he and his team of six students won $3,000 at a recent cybergaming tournament by taking eighth place in the tournament. The first prize was $25,000 and the second prize was $10,000. The extra prize for each additional step up the ladder increases rapidly in this as in most other tournaments. Why? The answer, which comes from economists who have developed a theory of **tournaments,** is that rising prize money is needed to get contestants to work hard to demonstrate they are better. Early in a tournament, the top seed doesn't need to put forth much effort to beat the bottom seed—and he doesn't need a large monetary incentive to be induced to do so. In the championship round, however, the contestants are nearly evenly matched. The only way to get them to give their best so that the one who is slightly better can win, is to give them a big monetary incentive to put forth the effort necessary to win.

Q: *How might this theory apply to the pay of executives as you move up the corporate ladder?*

Equilibrium in the Labor Market

16.11

The Texas legislature has been debating a law allowing people to carry concealed weapons on campus. Having observed enough shootings of professors by students in the U.S. over the past forty-five years, I think this is a dreadful idea. But it has interesting implications for wages. Some people who might be willing to take jobs at Texas campuses will be hesitant to do so. Unless there are enough other people who welcome guns on campus (which I doubt), Texas universities will have to pay professors more— the **equilibrium** pay for profs will have to rise—there will have to be a **compensating differential** for the risk of being shot. Interestingly, although there are many more undergrad than grad students, it seems like the large majority of shootings of professors are by grad students. Assuming that's true, the new law will cause a change in wage differences between those who teach mostly undergrads and those who teach most grads since teaching grads will become relatively riskier. I doubt that our legislators thought about the extra labor costs that their ideas are likely to create.

Q: *Under what conditions might the passage of this law actually decrease the wages that Texas universities would have to pay professors?*

16.12

Because my undergraduate econometrics class has sixty students, I do not have the time to work with each student to develop the short term paper that I require. Instead, I am asking students to work in pairs. The **matching** of students to form these pairs is an interesting example of two-sided matching, something that economists have studied in a variety of entry-level job markets. If all that matters is getting the best grade on the term paper with the minimum of effort, each student will want to match with the best student (in terms of both ability and willingness to work) in the class. If the best student is already matched, the remaining students presumably will want to match with the next-best student, and so on. If there is perfect information about each student's ability, the equilibrium will be the optimal one for eliciting performance: The top student will match with the next-best, students 3 and 4 will match, and so on. Unfortunately, information is far from perfect, and factors other than expected performance may enter into matching decisions. Regrettably, I expect to have a number of pairs where one student winds up doing almost all the work.

> **Q:** *How is the matching process described here affected if I allow some students to write a paper alone (without any co-worker)? Now consider matching in the market for spouses. How does the two-sided matching in that market resemble that in the "market" for paper coauthors? What is the equivalent in the marriage market of a student writing a paper alone? How does it affect the equilibrium matching in that market?*

16.13

A story on Yahoo.com today reports the settlement of a class-action suit objecting to eHarmony's maintaining separate services for straights and gays. The company has agreed to link its two services and allow participants to use both Web sites for one registration fee. The economic issue here is that of **matching** in the dating market, which is the purpose of the service, and of price in relation to **average cost.** Presumably, the linkage raises eHarmony's average cost, although I doubt by very much. As such, I would expect the price of the service to rise slightly for all participants, unless eHarmony had been discriminating in pricing against gays, or straights, before. Bi-sexual people benefit a lot, though: They no longer have to pay double to register on both matching services. So this seems like a standard example in economics of most people facing a small loss, with a few—bisexuals in this case—reaping a substantial gain.

> **Q:** *Imagine that there are two separate employment Web sites listing postings and resumés for, say, the accounting industry and the information technology industry. Would we see similar changes in well-being from linking those two sites? Who would gain the most?*

16.14

In the delightfully sophomoric movie *Clerks 2*, Randal tells Dante, "Odds are there's someone out there who's a better match for you than the girl you are about to marry." Even if Dante engaged in the most thorough possible search for a wife (which he certainly didn't do in the movie), Randal's statement is correct. Despite that, rational marital **search,** job search, or search for a high-quality/low-price product should stop when the gains from additional searches begin to fall short of the cost of spending the time and money searching and of giving up the pleasure of what you already can get. There is always some job out there that will suit you better, some better match as a mate, or a better deal on a purchase. Randal's implied advice is bad economics. If followed, it would guarantee permanent bachelorhood for Dante.

> **Q:** *Are you more likely to spend more time looking for a good price when buying a new camera or when buying a new car? Why?*

16.15

A story on Yahoo.com talks of raids by the Department of Homeland Security in a small town in Georgia where numerous illegal immigrants were employed by a large plant. The illegal immigrants either fled or were arrested. With these workers gone, the **supply curve** of labor to the plant had shifted to the left. Not surprisingly, the plant is now paying a dollar an hour more than before the raid, to draw new workers from neighboring counties. "With the illegal immigrants gone, Americans have a chance to make more money," says the former plant manager. He also noted there are more jobs for workers who live in the area. He did not note that, with the higher labor costs, the products produced by the plant will be more expensive and American buyers of the products will be paying more.

> **Q:** *How does this change affect the company's chances of survival? How does it affect foreign companies selling to the U.S.?*

16.16

A friend has signed up for It's Just Lunch, a matchmaking service that has a franchise in Austin. The service promises to arrange fifteen dates for her over a one-year period. This is not an ordinary dating service, however: Each participant is interviewed at length in order to **match** him/her better with another of the roughly 1,000 participants. This is a costly, but very high-quality **search** procedure. The price is the same no matter what the member's sex or age. The price is $1,500, even if you wind up marrying the first person you date. The question is why the company charges the same price for everybody. Why not **price discriminate**—charge less to participants who are easy to match, more to those who will take more than the usual work in finding matches? Perhaps charge more to men if women are scarce. One reason for a uniform price might be that different prices might convey different quality—if someone is charged little, he or she might infer that the matches may not be so good. That might cause fewer people to sign up.

> **Q:** *Would someone be more or less likely to sign up if there are more or fewer people already signed up? Is there an optimal number of participants?*

16.17

We took a walk along the Great Barrier Reef in Australia with a naturalist who explained the life cycle of coral. These polyps clone themselves, but they also reproduce sexually, spewing forth sperm or eggs. In some years, all the coral in an area spew forth gametes within several days of each other; in other years, some do it in November, others in December. The first kind of year, he said is better, resulting in more fertilizations. This is exactly what an economist would expect: With more jobs in an area, for example, more workers will get **matched** to a job that fits them. Just as simultaneous emission of gametes results in more baby coral, this results in lower unemployment rates and a lower rate of job vacancies. Similarly for men/women seeking spouses.

> **Q:** *How does the recruitment cycle of new college graduates fit into this pattern? Would you expect a higher or lower likelihood of getting a job if your school year ended at a different time from that of most other schools?*

16.18

Garth Brooks sings in his song "Big Money," "My older brother Tommy was a [telephone] lineman, rest his soul/He said it pays big money and man I'm into that/It pays big money but he sure can't spend it now." Garth's "late uncle Charlie was this demolition hound," for the same reason (money), and with the same result: both Tommy and Charlie were killed on the job! **Compensating wage differentials** are alive and well in country music. And they're alive and well in my freshman students' high-school jobs. The best example I got this year was a student who made $20 per hour as a sixteen-year-old, removing asbestos from houses one summer (and who lived to tell me his story!)

Q: *What is the most dangerous job you have ever held? Did it pay more than other jobs you or your friends had?*

16.19

A report on BBC World discussed the problems of gatherers of wild honey in the mangrove forests of Bangladesh. This is an extremely risky job—not because of problems with the bees that produce the honey—they're mainly harmless. The problem is with tigers that live in the swamps and like to eat the honey (and also unfortunately the honey-gatherers whom they confront). Indeed, in the past summer alone tigers ate two of the roughly four hundred honey-gatherers. Why would anyone take this kind of risk, a one-half percent chance each year of being killed on the job? The reason is that a honey gatherer can earn in three months what an agricultural laborer earns in a year. This 400-percent wage premium (a monthly wage four times that in agriculture) is a sufficient **compensating wage differential** to induce workers to face an annual risk of on-the-job death of 0.5 percent, far higher than the risk in any occupation in the U.S.

Q: *Look up in official government statistics which kinds of jobs in the U.S. have the highest risk of death on the job. What do you expect to observe about wages paid for such work?*

16.20

When I discuss **compensating wage differentials** in class, I ask students if they ever had a really lousy job in high school. One young woman reports that she had a job during the school year that paid $20 per hour, a very high wage for a sixteen-year-old student. She was hired by a nursing home to work the early morning shift. Aside from having to awaken at 4 AM, and falling asleep regularly in her classes, her tasks including showering residents, cleaning and feeding them, changing diapers, and cleaning the rooms. The job was dangerous: One resident, suffering from Alzheimer's disease, was constantly belligerent and threw things at her, resulting in several bruises. Once the student had made enough money to finance her spring-break trip, she quit the job.

Q: *What is the best-paying summer job you have held? Why did it pay more than the other ones you have had?*

16.21

The song "Proud Mary" by Creedence Clearwater Revival begins, "Left a good job in the city, workin' for the Man every night and day." This is a really silly sentence. If the person was working "every night and day," it couldn't have been "a good job." That implies many hours of work each week. In the U.S., only a small fraction of workers put in more than 50 hours per week, many of them self-employed professionals and highly paid managers, not the kind of person who might be singing this song. Also, if the person worked at night, it is unlikely that the job was good: Nighttime work is most common among workers with few skills and low wages. It is also more prevalent among workers in minority groups that are discriminated against. Night work pays better than comparable day work—there is a **compensating wage differential** for night work—but not much better. Work at night is typically undesirable work.

Q: *Find a want ad for a nighttime job. Look at the wage being offered and compare it with a want ad for a similar job with a daytime schedule.*

16.22

The big story on campus is the appearance of several University of Texas students in *Playboy's* feature, Girls of the Big 12. One of the students featured is quoted in the local newspaper as noting that some of the women in the article kept their clothes on: "That's so not fair. I hope they didn't get paid for wearing those skirts." In fact, *Playboy* paid the unclothed women $500, but paid less to those who were semi-nude, and paid even less for fully clothed pictures. There is a market for supplying such pictures, with the offer price rising as the amount revealed increases (since revealing more requires a **compensating wage differential**). Five hundred dollars seems like a pretty low price, but it reflects sorting: Most women would not do this for $500, but there are enough who are willing that the market demand can be satisfied with an offering price of only $500.

Q: What would happen to the price that Playboy *would be willing to offer if the fraction of homosexuals among the male population increased?*

Economic Rent

16.23

Listening to Mick Jagger sing "Satisfaction" today reminded me of my favorite example of **economic rent**: two guys, each seventy years old, each having majored in economics in college, each running long-distance for exercise, and each having a child who graduated from Yale. The two guys are Mick Jagger and I. We probably have the same **opportunity cost**: For both of us the alternative uses of our time aren't great. Both of us earn more than our opportunity cost, but Mick earns much more than I do, so he is receiving much more economic rent than I am. The British or American government could tax Mick's music earnings a lot, and he would still be willing to continue singing. If they imposed a huge tax on my earnings from economics, they'd be taxing away more than my economic rent, and I'd quit teaching economics.

Q: Let's say I earn $100,000 as an economist and my next-best alternative is as a singer earning $20,000. How much could the government tax away without me leaving economics to become a singer?

16.24

Until 1975, the federal National Institutes of Health (NIH) identified young scientists and offered them career-long financial support (salary only) to do research at their own university laboratories. Only ten such grants were in force at any time. The NIH discovered that about half the scientists continued to do good research over most of their lifetimes, while the other half soon stopped doing serious research and happily enjoyed their sinecures. To someone who thinks economic considerations dominate everything, the surprising fact is that half the scientists continued to work productively. Financial incentives do matter, and no doubt that is why the NIH abolished the program and replaced it with five-year renewable grants. But nonfinancial incentives—the desire to excel, the desire to avoid embarrassment, and the love of one's work—provide an important spur, too. For people who are motivated by these incentives, the financial rewards are at least partly **economic rent** to an activity they would pursue even at lower pay.

> **Q:** *Michael Jordan made $40 million per year playing basketball and endorsing products. If the government taxed away $35 million, would Michael still have played basketball and done product endorsements? How much of his $40 million earnings is economic rent?*

16.25

At the annual meeting of the American Economic Association, its President announced that the medal previously presented biennially to the top economist under age 40 will henceforth be given annually. Sounds like a lot, but in this profession the **supply** of honors is very small relative to the **demand** (the number of economists). Sociologists present many more awards per capita, and I believe that is also true in other disciplines. But the more awards you give out, the less worthwhile to current and past winners. (One Nobel Prize winner whom I know has often complained about the quality of his successors, implying that their awards devalue his.) From an **efficiency** viewpoint the purpose of these awards should be to maximize the incentives to produce great work. I wonder, however, whether the **elasticity of supply** of effort in response to awards exceeds zero—and I frankly doubt it. I believe that such awards only represent **economic rent** to the recipient and have no **incentive** effects so that the only question about them involves the distribution of rents among potential recipients.

> **Q:** *Think about awards you or your friends have received throughout your schooling career. Did these awards create extra incentives to produce good work, or were they merely economic rents going to the students who were already motivated to work hard?*

16.26

A recent article mentions that the annual price of a hot-dog stand license near the Metropolitan Museum of Art in New York City is $362,201. Licenses are very limited and are bought at auction. The price presumably reflects the **economic rent** associated with the particular site (the price would be a lot lower in the middle of Central Park). Yet at a **fixed cost** of the license of $1,000 per day, how can a vendor make enough money to cover his **variable cost,** including the value of his own time? If on average he sells only one hot dog and drink every minute the Met is open, with average daily opening minutes of about five hundred, that's five hundred servings per day. If he charges $3 for the dog and drink, his **revenue** of $1,500 leaves him $500 per day to cover variable costs. Seems possible, but I would expect that he's not making **economic profits.** If the city were to issue many more licenses, we would see more vendors, cheaper hot dogs, but, in the end, no higher net returns to the vendors.

    Q: *Suppose the city decides to stop charging for the licenses and instead issue them by means of a lottery system. Who would receive economic rents? Would the most efficient firms end up selling hot dogs?*

CHAPTER 17

Human Capital, Discrimination, and Labor-Market Policy

Education and Training

17.1

I was chatting with a seventy-year-old man I met who is an independent "software engineer"—a programmer. I asked him how he keeps up with all the young hot-shots who know the latest fancy programming languages. Simple, he said: There are many companies that are just now converting very old systems, and the young programmers don't know the older languages. Being technically obsolete gives him an advantage. We believe that **human capital** and technology are **complements** (something I show by negative example when I can't get my PowerPoint presentations to work on a projector!). But as long as companies don't introduce new technologies, those workers with "obsolete" human capital will do OK. Indeed, this man charges higher than average fees because there are so few other programmers left who can deal with the old technology!

Q: *Can you think of other skills that technical changes have made obsolete but have found uses with new technologies?*

17.2

Benjamin Franklin apparently understood the notion that input prices affect product prices, which is a problem because product demand curves are not completely **inelastic**. Discussing a **minimum wage,** he noted, "A law might be made to raise their [workers'] wages; but if our manufactures are too dear, they might not vend abroad." This is one of the best arguments against a minimum wage: In an open economy—one that faces a lot of foreign competition, which the U.S. increasingly is—the costs of the minimum wage will be at least partly passed on in the form of higher product prices, which will in turn reduce product demand and, eventually, employment. ["On the Labouring Poor," *The Gentleman's Magazine*, April 1768]

> **Q:** *Check out the minimum wage in your state. See if there are some jobs to which it does not apply, and whether it currently differs from the federal minimum wage.*

17.3

Every time I visit Australia, one of the first things I see in the news is a discussion of **minimum wages** since pay rates are to some extent set by government (these days by the Fair Work Commission). Today, there's a story that trade unions will be seeking to have teenagers paid the same wage as adults on the same job. This increase in youth wages will **decrease the demand** for young workers, which is typically quite **elastic**. Worse still, this will prevent some kids from obtaining job experience, reducing their **human capital** and making them less employable in the future.

> **Q:** *If you are 18, 19, or 20, how would you feel about receiving a wage that is less than that of a 22-year-old on the same job?*

17.4

State legislators in a number of states are proposing that college athletes be paid several hundred dollars a month by their universities. Major football programs can certainly afford this small payment; but should payments be made? A college athlete may be spending his or her time just for the enjoyment of the sport, but many are making an investment in developing their **human capital** in the form of athletic skills. This is a very risky investment. Most athletes won't recoup anything—they'll never make the pro leagues; but a very few will strike it phenomenally rich. Since nobody forces college athletes to go to college, or to engage in athletics, one must assume that the college athletes make the choice freely. The only argument in favor of paying them might be that they don't understand how few athletes find that the investment pays off—how risky the investment is. If that's true—if the market is noncompetitive because information about the risks is lacking, the prescription should be better information, not a required payment for the athletes.

Q: *You are asked to develop information for college athletes on the risks of spending much of their college life engaged in sports training. What specific information would you list to illustrate the risks, and benefits, of a college sporting career?*

17.5

The general rule that we tell students is that people should work until the pleasure of earnings from the last hour of work falls below the hardship imposed by that **marginal** hour. In many cases, though, we unfortunately can't make choices about that marginal hour. Our sixty-three-year-old friend, a specialist in pediatric oncology, was, so I thought, a workaholic. Nonetheless, he wanted to cut back a little, perhaps from 100-percent to 75-percent time (which meant from 60+ to 45 hours per week) because the money was less important than before, and he wanted more leisure. The head of his hospital-based practice said the work was either 100 percent or 0 percent—so our friend quit entirely and is now fully retired. He is better off not working at all (and not earning) than working long hours—but he would have been best off earning something and working a moderate amount. Because of his boss's rigidity, he's worse off, the hospital has lost one of its most skilled and devoted specialists, and society has lost the benefits from his large investment in **human capital.**

Q: *Why might it have been in the hospital's interest NOT to let him work part-time?*

17.6

When our younger son was 15, my wife finished law school and began practicing as an attorney. I had already been working as a professor for eighteen years. I told my son that I was tired of arguing with him about increasing his allowance, and that henceforth we would index it—it would increase each year by the same percentage amount as my pay would rise. He immediately said, "Dad, I want my allowance indexed to Mom's wage increases." I thought about this and realized that this fifteen-year-old understood **human capital theory** and the nature of investment in **on-the-job training.** He knew that early in their careers people's wages increase rapidly because they are learning a lot in their job, but that people who have been working in the same job for a long time do not see such rapid increases. Unfortunately for him, I understood the theory, too, and told him, "Sorry, Buster—your allowance will be indexed to increases in my salary, not Mom's!"

Q: *Given this indexing rule, how did my son feel about how I should spend my work time?*

17.7
I've been taking taxis around Seoul, Korea, all week. This may be a mistaken generalization, but the younger drivers have all been efficient—seem to know where they are going, get there quickly and let me out. This is advantageous for them, as (so my former-taxi-driver brother tells me) a cabbie makes the best money on the "drop"—the initial fixed amount, which is almost $2 here. The older cabbies wander around, don't seem to know the city, and have an amazing ability to get stuck in traffic jams. I wonder if this difference is because of the rapid growth of education here—younger people are much better educated than their elders. Perhaps the general education—the **human capital** embodied in younger people—raises their productivity, even in something like taxi-driving that seems so remote from what one learns in school.

Q: *Do you feel that your schooling has increased your human capital in fields beyond the subjects studied in school? How well do you think your training would transfer to various occupations?*

Discrimination

17.8
One of the better-known biblical passages, *Leviticus* 27:1-7, lists the value of pledges of silver to the temple based on the value of a person: 50 shekels for a man age 20–60, 30 for a woman 20–60, 15 for a man over 60, 10 shekels for a woman over 60. Hourly wage rates of workers in the U.S. in 2008 differed greatly from the ratios implied by *Leviticus*. The average female worker age 20–60 earned each hour nearly 80 percent, not 60 percent, of a male worker that age; and the average older male worker earned nearly as much per hour as the average male worker 20–60.

Most older men and women don't participate in the **labor force,** however, and fewer 20–60-year-old women work than men that age. Take *all* U.S. citizens in each age-sex group, whether or not they work, and assume that men 20–60 earned 50 shekels per time period in 2008. Then women 20–60 earned 34 shekels, men 61-plus earned 14 shekels, and women 61-plus earned 7 shekels. The earnings ratios are not that far from what was expected 3,000 years ago.

Q: *Go on the Web and try to find out what the average wage is for men and women nationwide. Then get information on this wage difference for college-age youths, for people in their thirties and forties, and for those in their sixties.*

17.9

A woman weighing 240 pounds had been denied a job as an aerobics instructor by a for-profit fitness center. She sued under San Francisco law, which prohibits **discrimination** based on appearance, arguing that she had been leading aerobics classes for fifteen years. Was she being discriminated against because of her weight? In other words, was this pure discrimination? Or was she not hired because her potential employer felt that her weight would ensure that few or no clients would take her classes? Was this a sound commercial decision based on her likely productivity? It is impossible to decide between these two possibilities, and this is true generally in cases where the source of potential bias is consumer preferences. The same arguments can be made about discrimination against minorities or women: Businesspeople could always rationalize a refusal to hire on grounds that hiring would be bad for business. If determining the underlying cause is so difficult, in the end we have to decide which groups to protect on political, not economic, grounds.

Q: *Give arguments in favor of protecting the overweight against discrimination of this kind. Then give arguments against protecting them.*

17.10

My study on **discrimination** in baseball included the general idea that those who are discriminated against will alter their behavior to mitigate the impacts of discrimination on themselves. But while reducing the impacts, these changes are not costless. For example, if you're a Hispanic pitcher and think that the white umpire is against you, you'll change your pitches. Where will you throw? How will you throw? The paper shows that the pitcher will avoid giving the umpire a chance to use his discretion in judging a pitch. More pitches go into the strike zone, more are clearly balls. More are fastballs, fewer are curves and change-ups. These are rational responses, but by avoiding the umpire's discrimination the pitcher makes it easier for the batter to hit the ball or to walk.

> Q: *Think about racial discrimination in jobs. How might the behavior of minorities be altered by their knowledge that they will be discriminated against?*

17.11

Fox News reports that during the early rounds at Wimbledon a lot of second-level, but good-looking, female tennis players have been featured on *Centre Court*, while some of the stars have been relegated to side courts. An event organizer noted, "It's not a coincidence that those (on *Centre Court*) are attractive." Not at all. The price of TV rights is based on viewership, so the sponsors want to maximize it: "Our preference would always be a Brit or a babe, as this always delivers high viewing figures." The product sold is a combination of good tennis and beauty—and consumer satisfaction is increased by more of both. Event planners would like the top-seeded players to be the most beautiful; absent that correlation, they believe customers are willing to trade off some tennis quality to watch more attractive players. Are they catering to customer **discrimination,** or are they merely indulging consumer **preferences**?

> Q: *Think about the top performers on shows like* American Idol. *Do you think the same principle applies? To what extent are consumers willing to substitute physical attractiveness for musical talent?*

Policy and Poverty

17.12

Deuteronomy 24:15 provides rules for the payment of workers. It says, "In the same day thou shalt give him his hire; neither shall the sun go down on it, for he is poor. . . ." The legal requirement, that a worker should be paid each day for the fruits of his labor, is almost completely ignored in the U.S. and in most developed countries today. Most workers are paid weekly, semimonthly, or monthly, even when their pay is computed on an hourly basis. Why the change? Partly, the reason is that most workers have **long-term employment contracts** with their employers, so they know that they will be attached to the employer for a long time. Moreover, few workers in developed economies live hand-to-mouth. Most of them have enough savings in most cases from their earlier paychecks to tide them over to the next one. In a poor agricultural society neither of these conditions holds. The workers are usually casual laborers, working for one landholder one day, another landholder the next. Workers also often had little or no savings, so that without the daily pay they, and their families, faced hunger.

Q: *This is all true, but what would be the harm if people were still given their pay at the end of each day?*

17.13

In nearly every recession, the U.S. Congress passes a law that extends unemployment benefits from twenty-six to thirty-nine weeks in many states as long as the country stays in a recession. There is a real **trade-off** here. Making the benefits last longer helps maintain the spending of the unemployed, but the longer benefits give unemployed workers an **incentive** to stay unemployed. This is true whether we're in a recession or not. The argument for extension is that, in a recession, the balance tilts more toward helping the unemployed because the incentive to remain unemployed matters little if few jobs are available. There's good statistical evidence that the disincentive to work generated by unemployment benefits is much smaller in recessions. Well and good, but the problem has always been how to turn off the spigot of unemployment benefits soon enough when the economy recovers to prevent them from making unemployment too attractive an option for people who would otherwise easily find jobs.

Q: *If there are few jobs available in the recession, why not allow people to draw unemployment benefits for fifty-two weeks? Or sixty-five weeks? Or until they find a job?*

17.14

At a seminar in Germany last week a crucial EU-U.S. difference became apparent. In the U.S., we define the **poverty line** as absolute—three times the income needed for a minimally nutritious food budget. In Europe, the poverty line is based on relative income, typically 50 percent of the median. This difference says something about cultural differences. With our definition, in a growing economy, so long as inequality doesn't increase too much and food prices don't increase more than average prices, poverty will eventually disappear. We will not always have the poor with us in America. What an optimistic view—and what lack of concern about inequality! In Europe, even with income growth, unless inequality decreases, the fraction of households in poverty won't decline. How pessimistic, yet how concerned about inequality! With sufficient economic growth, but no change in inequality, someday the European poor will be driving BMWs!

Q: *What are some policies that would be affected by these differing ways of measuring poverty? Which view do you agree with more closely?*

CHAPTER 18

Public Goods, Externalities, and Property Rights

Public Goods

18.1

Universities are at least as plagued by **public-goods** and **free-rider** problems as other organizations. The University Coop offers each major College at UT $50,000 if the profs meet the Coop's deadline for book orders. My college (Liberal Arts) is the only one that can't do this—that doesn't take this money off the table. I'm actually surprised that any College does this—there's almost no incentive for individual faculty members since they don't directly receive any part of this large sum. Whether our failure is because management doesn't worry about this or because we are more disorganized as individuals is a tough question. I doubt that it's because the **opportunity cost** of faculty time is higher in my College: Most of us are humanities profs, sadly among the lowest-paid denizens of academe. I wonder whether in other organizations managements fail to overcome this public-goods problem.

> **Q:** *If the Coop is really concerned with getting book orders in on time, how should it change the reward structure? Can you think of a system that would eliminate the public good problem here?*

18.2

As little boys in the Chicago suburbs, one of our biggest thrills was throwing snowballs at passing cars. It took only one person to throw the snowball, but we all wound up giggling if it smashed into somebody's car window. We all benefited from the snowball throwing; and if more of us were in the group, each person would still benefit just as much—no one could be excluded. The snowball throwing was a **public good.** We all knew, however, that there was a risk that the offended driver would stop his car, run after us, and beat up the boy who threw the snowball. Only one person would bear the cost of throwing, and that cost seemed so great that most times nobody wanted to throw the snowball. This public good was underprovided. A student reported on a similar "problem" that he confronted with his high-school buddies: They drove around their Dallas suburb trying to antagonize the locals who hung out at the Taco Bueno stand. The students would drive by the locals, and one of the students would moon them, while the driver honked the car's horn and the other students, sitting in the back of the car, laughed uproariously. The difficulty was that few of the students wanted to do the mooning because the mooner would get beaten up by the locals if he was caught.

Q: *As you were growing up, what similar activities posed similar problems for you and your friends?*

18.3

As I do before each midterm and final exam in an undergraduate class, I held what was supposed to be a 90-minute question and answer (Q&A) session for my students this evening. This is not a review session: Unless the students have questions, I don't say anything. The problem is that most of the students came without questions, hoping that their fellow students would have questions prepared and that my answers would enlighten everyone. Each student relied on the others, hoping to reap the benefits of the **public good** created by my answers. But each student, not wishing to spend time making up questions, became a **free rider** on the other students because very few students brought questions. After 50 minutes and a lot of long pauses, I ended the Q&A session. I hope the students remember what happened in this session when the Q&A for the final exam takes place. The public good problem in this case lasts over two periods. If the students realize the longer-term nature of the public good problem here, maybe they will be less interested in free riding off their fellow students next time.

Q: *What, if any, are the incentives for the students to bring in more questions in the Q&A session before the final exam? Are* *they greater or less than the incentives were in the midterm Q&A session?*

18.4

The most common nationality of the students in my undergraduate class in the Netherlands is German. They pay the same fees as Dutch students. The same would be true for Dutch students in Germany or in most other EU countries, under the agreements referred to as the Bologna Process. Totally different from in-state/out-of-state tuition charges in public universities in the U.S. This is not a bad idea—it encourages university students to flock to schools that they believe (rightly or wrongly) offer a better education. It means that European students in general obtain a better education. The problem is that fees never cover **average cost**. Taxpayers in the net receiving countries subsidize the education of net sending countries' students. I don't see how this can be a stable **equilibrium** politically: If I were a taxpayer in a net receiving country, I would not like having my taxes support the education of foreigners; nor would I be pleased to give foreign taxpayers the incentive to be **free-riders** on the educational policy of the EU. The only hope is that some foreign students remain in the receiving country after completing education—so that the receiving country reaps a return on its subsidies to the accumulation of foreign students' **human capital**.

> **Q:** *Freedom of choice among European universities gives each school a greater incentive to be competitive. However, each country has an incentive to avoid free-riders, which may lead them to under-fund education. Which effect do you think is stronger? Are there any factors that might outweigh the fear of free-riders?*

18.5

One of my young colleagues loves holiday parties; for years, another colleague has gone to the trouble of organizing a party, and the young colleague has happily been a **free-rider** on this **public good** provided by someone else. Having paid nothing, he has enjoyed a substantial **consumer surplus.** This year, the other colleague is not organizing a party, so my young colleague has decided to sponsor one himself. Since he is doing this, one can conclude that the consumer surplus he enjoyed in the past is less than the cost to him of organizing the party. He has, however, persuaded a third colleague to organize the party together with him, so he is keeping more of the surplus than if he sponsored the party himself.

Q: *What about the idea of our Economics Department financing the party by collecting contributions from all the faculty members? Would that work?*

18.6

What is a **public good**? A story today describes a house fire in Tennessee, where the firefighters refused to extinguish the blaze because the owners hadn't paid the annual voluntary fee for fire protection. They firefighters only intervened when the conflagration spread to a neighbor's field and threatened the (fee-paying) neighbor's house. Is fire protection **excludable**? In a small town, with widely separated houses, it may be—after all, what is the harm to me if the house of the family who hadn't paid its tax burns down? In such a case, the best argument for requiring payment of the fire-protection fee is that there are **economies of scale** in providing protection. But then the fee should be compulsory—a tax. In a suburb or city, the density of dwellings means that there are such large spillovers that fire protection is **non-excludable.**

Q: *A similar argument can be made for requiring motorists to buy car insurance. If there were no such law, how would free-riders be a problem?*

18.7

Central Texas is having its worst drought in fifty years, and since May we have been limited to twice-a-week lawn watering. With things getting worse, on August 24 the limit goes to once-a-week. I'll abide by the limit, but I'll set my sprinklers to run longer each session than during the twice-a-week watering. I'm sure I'm not alone; and thus these private actions will partly undo the restrictions. We all water out of a common pool, but the water is NOT a **public good**—each of us uses it. The problem could readily be solved by pricing the water sufficiently high to ensure that we get through the drought with water to spare. Indeed, that's what a free market would do. Unfortunately, the City of Austin hasn't seen fit to mimic free-market pricing of this increasingly scarce resource.

Q: *Think of other goods and services provided by your city. Are any of them public goods? Do you think the pricing of these goods is efficient?*

18.8

The Tigers and Giants are in the World Series, with possibly four of seven games to be played in San Francisco. The majority of games will be played there because the seventh game (if it is necessary) is played at the field of the team representing the league that won the All-Star game. The purpose of the rule, adopted in 2003, is to offer players and managers an **incentive** to provide more effort in the All-Star game. I'm doubtful that this incentive matters much. With large teams each player is to some extent a **free-rider**—why risk injury, why strain yourself if your efforts have little effect? That is especially true if, by July, you realize that your team has no chance of making it into the Series.

> **Q:** *What incentives could Major League Baseball provide for players to perform better in the All-Star game?*

Externalities

18.9

What's an **externality**? My friends tell me that, in the Vondelpark, a delightful reserve in central Amsterdam, it is illegal to let your dog off a leash. But it's perfectly legal to have sex in the park, so long as it is not in view of the children's playground. The argument is that the dog may make a mess that imposes costs on the unwary walker, while the couple imposes no costs on other park users. I wonder which of these two actions would be more likely to be outlawed in the U.S.—implicitly, how do attitudes toward **negative externalities,** as expressed in city ordinances, differ between the U.S. and the Netherlands—or between other Western countries?

> **Q:** *What kind of costs (or benefits) do the two situations described impose on other park users? How do these ordinances demonstrate different preferences between the two cultures?*

18.10

One way to reduce the **negative externality** of the air pollution produced when electricity is generated is to replace fossil fuels with windmills. In a number of areas, a large cluster of windmills can be an efficient alternative source of electric power. But do windmills eliminate pollution? Probably not; while they eliminate air pollution, they create visual pollution in areas where people value the unobstructed view of some particularly attractive natural or even man-made area. People on Nantucket Island off Cape Cod, Massachusetts, realize this and have been arguing against the creation of a forest of windmills just offshore. Similarly, in Ireland at the Giant's Causeway—a series of offshore rock formations that is one of the most frequently visited tourist sights in the country— a large protest movement has been launched against proposals to build windmills that would be visible when viewing the Causeway. The negative externalities produced by electricity generation are not limited to air pollution.

Q: *What about locating windmills in uninhabited areas of no scenic value? Does that solve the problem while keeping other costs down?*

18.11

I gave my final exam yesterday to five hundred students in an auditorium that holds eight hundred fifty people. Most of the students arrived on time and were seated when I handed out the tests. But about twenty-five trooped in late, anywhere from 1 to 5 minutes late. These latecomers imposed large **negative externalities** on their fellow students. They disturbed them as they walked down the aisles and, even worse, climbed over other students to find a seat. How can I reduce the externalities? I could simply ban the latecomers, but that seems harsh. I can't impose a monetary penalty since the university doesn't allow that. Perhaps the best alternative is to make it clear ahead of time that two points will be deducted from the test scores of all latecomers. If they know that ahead of time, perhaps they will adjust their behavior in response to this "tax" and reduce (hopefully to zero) the externalities they are imposing on the rest of the "society," which in this case is the other students

Q: *What if I just say at the end of the exam that I will be deducting two points from the scores of all students who arrived late? Would that solve the problem? Would it solve the problem if it is well known that I teach the same giant class every term?*

18.12

The house across the street and up the hill from our friend's house has been vacant since its owner died two years ago. No maintenance has been done, and the house is an eyesore, with brush overgrown in front. One might argue that its poor appearance imposes a **negative externality** on our friend, perhaps decreasing her property's value. Maybe; but her complaint is about a different negative externality: the risk in this record drought in Central Texas that fire will engulf the parched brush and spread to her house.

> **Q:** *Should the City of Austin have a right to regulate the poor appearance of a vacant house? If not, is such regulation justified when the house might generate a fire hazard to its neighbors?*

18.13

One of the students came up with what is perhaps the most amusing **negative externality** example that I have heard in my teaching career. Her roommate is beautiful, but her roommate's boyfriend, so she says, is very, very ugly. No problem, except that the roommate has a poster-sized photograph of the boyfriend on the wall on her side of the room, a poster that my student has to view whenever she is on her own side of the room. I ask my student why, if the guy is so ugly, her roommate goes out with him, and she answers, "He goes to Harvard; and he's also a very nice guy." This illustrates the importance of **human capital** in the **matching** market that is dating, and also that looks aren't everything, either. We also supply personality and the ability to get ahead, both of which are valued by the labor market and thus by potential spouses. Indeed, careful research shows that, compared with average-looking women, good-looking women marry guys with an extra year of education. Today, an extra year of education is associated with about an extra 12 percent annual earnings.

> **Q:** *Is there any way for my student to reduce the burden of the negative externality that her roommate is imposing on her?*

18.14

My student writes that she is sitting in the lobby of her dormitory at 3 AM on a Saturday because she has, as Tom Wolfe, *I Am Charlotte Simmons* (2004) calls it, been "sexiled." Her roommate is using the room to maximize her own **utility**, but is imposing a **negative externality** on my student. It's worse than that—the paper-thin walls mean that noises resound down the hall, so many other students are kept awake. The question is who has the **property rights** to the room. There's no easy answer, and certainly no **Pareto improvement** is possible. But my student figures that there are enough people who are losing sleep that the sum of the value of their time and utility should be weighted more heavily than that of the roommate. As a neutral observer, I would agree and view the roommate's behavior as piggish.

Q: *How can my student and the other students in the hall combat this externality?*

18.15

A student writes that she had a problem: An armadillo had died in her family's front yard, and its odor was attracting vultures. (If it had died in the midst of a field of bluebonnets, this would have achieved the trifecta of Texas wildlife!) The odor and the vultures (not the cleanest of birds) created a **negative externality,** and the Homeowners' Association was getting after her parents. Her father was squeamish about cleaning it up, but he hit upon a solution: He offered my student double her usual weekly allowance if she would remove the beast. This **compensating wage differential** was sufficient to induce her to supply her labor for the task, and the offending armadillo was removed.

Q: *Groups like this homeowners' association are formed to take care of issues such as this armadillo externality—the group's needs can be placed ahead of the individual's through various enforcement mechanisms. Do you think this is an efficient way to handle externalities? Which enforcement mechanisms do you think are most likely to be effective?*

18.16

It's the Tuesday before Thanksgiving. Thanksgiving is a holiday at my university, as is the day after Thanksgiving. But today is not, nor is tomorrow. Judging by the foot traffic around campus, a lot of students, most of whom live within a five-hour car ride, have already gone home. A lot of professors have canceled Wednesday classes, even though they aren't supposed to; and others have even canceled today's classes since students have asked me if I'm holding class today. (I answered with a resounding yes.) Those professors who have canceled are imposing a **negative externality** on me since I have to disappoint students who hope to blow off the whole week. So, too, the **equilibrium**—Thursday and Friday with no classes—is being pushed back to Wednesday, Thursday, and Friday with no classes. I envision a situation in which the university is pushed toward an equilibrium with no classes through the entire Thanksgiving week. Fortunately, such a situation comes at the cost of starting classes even earlier in August, and as long as university administrators are aware of this **trade-off,** perhaps they will hold the line and insist that faculty members hold classes on Tuesday and Wednesday of Thanksgiving week, as they should.

Q: *What incentive do you have for insisting that your professor holds class the day before Thanksgiving?*

18.17

A story on Yahoo.com news today mentions that the Philadelphia newspapers are running advertisements for a fake airline called Derrie-Air (get it?). The airline advertises that it is carbon-neutral, and that it charges by the passenger's weight: $1.40 per passenger pound from Philadelphia to Chicago, $2.25 per passenger pound from Philadelphia to Los Angeles. While quite mythical, this pricing structure is not unreasonable: The heavier people cost more to ship; and at a time when fuel prices are so high, this seems especially important and a good way of letting price reflect **marginal cost.** Also, heavier people spill over onto their neighbors' seats, generating **negative externalities** for the other passenger. So I hope a few real-world airlines take notes and think about charging extra for heavier passengers.

Q: *What would happen to this airline if all other airlines charged per seat regardless of the passengers' weights?*

18.18

It has been really cold in central Texas, which causes a problem for my wife and me each morning. We use sinks that face each other with a common wall between them. The same hot water pipe supplies the faucets in both sinks. Whoever washes first each morning must put up with 2 minutes of cold water before the hot water kicks in. This gives me an incentive to wash up second; that way, she bears the cost of the cold water and confers a **positive externality** on me. If it were anyone else other than my wife, I'd probably be very careful to go second and be the beneficiary of the **externality.** But because I love my wife and behave **altruistically** toward her, I try to go first as often as I can. Love conquers even economics.

Q: *What similar externalities exist in your household? Are you as **altruistic** toward the people there as I claim to be toward my wife?*

18.19

One of my colleagues just returned from vacation in the Florida Keys. He was excited that, at age 48, he had gone scuba diving for the first time. He remarked that, unfortunately, the water was quite rough and made him somewhat seasick. He felt worse and worse, had to return to the boat, and eventually was so ill that he "fed his lunch to the fishes." He noted, however, that he had at least created a **positive externality:** His activity attracted a large number of exotic fish, allowing other divers standing on the boat much better viewing that they otherwise would have had. Although his seasickness was not a **Pareto improvement** compared with the situation if he hadn't been sick (he was made worse off), at least some other people were better off as a result.

> **Q:** *If you were a tour-boat operator and read this, what might you do to make the fish-viewing trip better for ALL of the people taking the trip?*

18.20

A very common ailment in Korean summers and autumns is pinkeye (conjunctivitis), and the problem has been getting much worse in the past two years. My Korean co-author tells me, however, that the H1N1 virus has created a **positive externality** in Korea. These days, people who are worried about this new virus are encouraged to wash their hands more frequently, and they appear to be doing it. That has also sharply reduced cases of pinkeye. On net, I imagine that the economic costs of the swine-flu epidemic exceed the costs of the pinkeye outbreak. Nonetheless, it's always nice to note the silver lining in an otherwise dark cloud.

> **Q:** *Give other examples of positive externalities arising out of negative shocks.*

18.21

Peer pressure can generate **externalities,** both **positive** and **negative** ones. A pair of Israeli economists has examined this idea using data on major league baseball. They argue that whether the externalities within an organization are positive or negative will depend on the **incentives** that are created by one's peers' activities. If those activities create incentives that give you a reason to be more productive, you will work harder and be more productive; if they create incentives that make life cushy for you, you will slack off. They show that players' batting averages are higher when their team-mates are batting better. This makes sense, since improvements in my batting coupled with my teammates' better batting will increase the chances of winning the ballgame. When a team's pitchers are performing better, however, its batters do not do so well—their batting averages are lower. After all, if the pitcher has a no-hitter going, there is no need for batters to try to score huge numbers of runs to win the game.

Q: *Are there any analogies to this kind of behavior in basketball? Football? Soccer?*

18.22

My University lights the famous UT tower with burnt-orange lights after sports victories (and even victories in debate tournaments!), and includes a numeral 1 in white superimposed on the burnt or-ange if there is a national championship (and even to honor the occasional professor!). This sight warms the hearts of alumni and students, and I get a kick out of it too. I thus head to campus tonight to take a picture of the tower and enjoy what is surely a nearly pure **public good.** I am not alone—there are at least fifty other people around the campus taking pictures of the tower. Strangers are talk-ing to each other and seem to be enjoying having others around. This public good has generated the additional **positive externality** of camaraderie among all those who came to take pictures.

Q: *Is your enjoyment of public goods generally increased by others' enjoyment of those goods?*

18.23

In Germany, the land of serious recycling, we separate much of our waste into bio, packing, paper, and everything else ("all the rest, and only that," as the instructions in our apartment state). Of course, this doesn't include the three types of glass—white, green, and brown—that are to be carried to a set of common re-ceptacles two blocks from our apartment. Once I had to deposit an empty olive oil bottle in the green-glass container (on a Saturday, not on Sunday, since Sundays are forbidden—perhaps due to **ex-ternalities** created by the noise of crashing glass, perhaps for re-ligious reasons), but I wasn't at all sure the bottle was green and not brown. These stringent rules raise the price of using contain-ers and other things that are to be recycled. As such, they **decrease**

demand for such products and indirectly help the environment. Maybe this is the most important route by which recycling rules aid the environment!

Q: *There are rumors that the government in fact throws all three types of glass into the same place when it is collected. If you believe this, how will your behavior change?*

18.24

A colleague informs me that, in Finland, traffic violations are fined in proportion to a person's income—the fine is higher for people with higher incomes. This struck me as a good thing in terms of **equity**—why shouldn't the rich pay more than the poor if they misbehave? In terms of **efficiency,** it might make sense if the incentives that people respond to are in percentage terms instead of dollar terms—if the effect on behavior is smaller for a $10 fine on a rich person than on a poor person. Presumably, though, these fines are designed to reduce **negative externalities**—so that my bad driving doesn't increase somebody else's chance of injury or death. I drive a Honda Civic—so if my bad driving leads to an accident involving somebody else, the damage is small; if I drove a Hummer, the damage inflicted on them would be large. So, maybe on efficiency grounds the fines should be linked to the weight of the vehicle, not the driver's income. This might also be equitable, since the **income elasticity** of demand for Cadillacs, SUVs, Hummers, and other big automobiles is surely positive.

Q: *Would either of these changes result in a* **Pareto improvement** *over the current method of fines that we have in the U.S.?*

Transaction Costs

18.25

A newspaper story mentioned a bordello in Germany (where prostitution is legal) that charges customers a fixed fee, a bit over €100 ($140) for an evening of drinks, food and entertainment. This kind of pricing is common to amusement parks (Disneyland, for example), ski lifts, all-you-can-eat restaurants, and elsewhere. It is a way the firm can minimize the **transactions costs** of pricing each service and also, if the fixed price is set properly, to extract the entire

consumer surplus. With such a pricing scheme, however, the customers who choose to pay the fixed fee will differ from those who would buy the product if each item were priced separately. Visitors to Disneyland will disproportionately be those who will consume a lot of rides, skiers will be those who want to make a lot of runs, and bigger eaters will visit all-you-can-eat restaurants (for example, I never go to them because they're a bad deal for me).

Q: *How will this pricing scheme affect the kinds of customers that the bordello attracts?*

18.26

The *New York Times* ran a story stating that increasing numbers of married men are no longer wearing wedding rings. In interviews, a number of single women complained that they spend time in bars and at social occasions talking to men who turn out to be married. The women viewed the men's behavior as both predatory and dishonest and object to having been deceived. While wedding rings clearly have a ceremonial and even religious significance, from an economic point of view they are also important: They reduce **transaction costs.** Women seeking men will not waste their valuable time socializing with guys with wedding rings. In the story, some married men who wear wedding rings also noted that transaction costs are reduced in another way: Because the women they meet realize that the men are married, the men feel somewhat more relaxed talking to women who know they are not going to be "hitting on" them.

Q: *What other transactions costs are there in signaling one's dating status or preferences? Could we adopt other cultural symbols to minimize these?*

18.27

A *Sex and the City* episode has a scene in which Big takes Carrie out to a fancy restaurant. Big lights up a cigar. The maitre d' comes over and tells him there is no smoking in the restaurant. The **property rights** to the air in the restaurant belong to nonsmokers. Big shrugs, continues smoking, then stands up and asks each of the other five diners if it's okay with them if he smokes. He also says that he is buying drinks for all five of them. They all say that his smoking is fine. Big has thus incurred the transaction cost of buying the property rights to the air in the restaurant. Since he's happier, and since the other diners are happy to be getting free drinks, his actions represent a **Pareto improvement** for the community of diners in this restaurant, at this point in time.

>   **Q:** *What happens to Big's solution if every 5 minutes a new table of diners comes into the restaurant?*

18.28

In the movie *Blindness*, Julianne Moore's character is the only sighted person in a prison ward of blind people. Men in another ward have captured all the boxes of food and demand payment in valuables. Moore tells the others that each can give what he wants, but that he shouldn't expect to get fed if he doesn't give. If everybody were blind, any food brought into the ward would be a **common property resource**—nobody could see who was grabbing what. With Moore being sighted, however, she has control of the resource, can allocate it as she sees fit, and can prevent those who don't contribute from grazing the commons.

>   **Q:** *Are there are similar situations where, because of one unusual person, **property rights** exist for what had been or otherwise would be a common property resource?*

18.29

The U.S. Department of Labor is proposing to end the overtime exemption of "companions" —home assistants typically employed to assist and/or watch the infirm elderly—employed directly by an agency. (The exemption would remain for companions employed directly by a private individual.) This rule would lead to classic results: 1) Higher labor costs through agencies, no doubt passed on to older people in the form of higher prices, leading to less employment through agencies; 2) A shift to more companions employed directly by individuals. I'm not sure what the **demand elasticity** for companions is, but it is unlikely to be small. Moreover, the negative effect on jobs through agencies will be larger than the positive effect through increased direct employment. Also, agencies reduce **transaction costs** (including background checks, arranging tax payments, etc.), so this change will also raise those costs and reduce well-being. The only winners appear to be the bureaucrats who would have more rules to enforce and those agency companions who keep their jobs.

>   **Q:** *How would these changes affect the quality of people who wind up being employed as companions?*

CHAPTER 19

Taxes and Public Expenditures

Taxation

19.1

In the Beatles song "Taxman," the tax man says, "There's one for you, nineteen for me." The Beatles are complaining about the high **marginal tax rate** that they faced in the United Kingdom in the 1960s. Implicitly, each extra pound they earned left them only one shilling (one-twentieth of a pound in the old British money), with the remaining nineteen shillings going to the tax collector. This is clearly about the marginal tax rate, the tax on each extra bit of earnings, not the **average tax rate**, the ratio of taxes to total income. No tax system has an average tax rate of 95 percent on the entire tax base. The 95-percent marginal rate is also probably an exaggeration: Most systems have loopholes that allow some income to escape taxation when the rate is this steep. That Sir Paul McCartney is now a billionaire is pretty good evidence that the Beatles never really paid 95 percent of their earnings as taxes.

> **Q:** *What is the marginal tax rate on your earnings if you are working? What is your parent(s)' marginal tax rate? Are these the same as the average tax rates?*

19.2

A well-known economist published a scholarly article showing that there were fewer deaths late in December, and more deaths in early in January, in those years when the amount of tax on estates (assets left upon death) was lowered on January 1. An anecdote is not as good as statistical proof; but the death of my Dad's ninety-three-year-old uncle on January 2, 2004, made me a believer in the findings of this study. My great-uncle left an estate valued at $1.4

million. On January 1, the amount of an estate that escaped taxation rose from $1 million to $1.5 million. By living into 2004, he saved his heirs more than $160,000 in taxes (40 percent times $1.4 million minus $1 million) as compared with the tax liability if he had died on December 31. With an initial **marginal tax rate** of more than 40 percent, the extra two days meant a lot more for his heirs, and a lot less for the tax man. Did my uncle consciously choose to live two days more to save us taxes? Probably not; but incentives do not have to be consciously perceived to affect behavior, in this case much to the benefit of his heirs.

> **Q:** *The estate tax was phased out through 2009. What do you expect this did to the patterns of deaths that occurred late in December 2009 and early in January 2010?*

19.3

I played *Life* with some grandkids today, a much revised game from what we played with our kids. The paychecks you receive as you move along the board are taxed at a constant **marginal tax rate** of 50 percent, with an **exemption** of $10,000 of income. As such it mirrors fairly closely some **flat-tax** proposals, except the tax rate is far above what flat-tax advocates would like. The tax system in the game is **neutral** after the lowest income level, but the property system favors the rich: Except for one outlier in the middle range of house values, the expected percentage return on buying houses rises with their purchase price. Perhaps the game is realistic—it seems to favor the already rich!

> **Q:** *What kind of property tax system would you introduce to the game if you wanted to create more equality among players' wealth levels?*

19.4

The most annoying volunteer job I've ever done is that of treasurer at my synagogue—three years at one synagogue, and I was dumb enough to volunteer for three years at another. Trying to eke dues out of the small number of delinquent members had bad effects on my blood pressure. Synagogues and other religious organizations are **public goods**—it's easy to enjoy the services offered (pun intended) without paying one's fair share of the costs. Many European countries do it differently. In Germany, for example, when you move to a town you are asked to state your religious affiliation at the city office. Unless you say none, you are then assessed a surtax of 8 percent on your income tax liability. With a **progressive income tax,** this means that the rich pay a greater share of their income to support religious institutions than the poor. No need to go harassing delinquent members—it's pay to play. As a synagogue treasurer, I would have loved that; as a U.S. citizen, I realize that this is inconsistent with the separation of church and state in the U.S., and that it might be difficult to determine what constitutes a religious organization, a problem that has arisen in Germany.

Q: *Ignoring the problem of separation of church and state, what difficulties might arise if this system were instituted in the U.S.?*

19.5

Exodus 30:12-15 states that each man aged twenty or older is required to donate one-half shekel as an offering to the sanctuary. "The rich shall not give more, and the poor shall not give less." This would seem like a highly **regressive tax**—the same amount is required of citizens independent of their incomes—and it is. Even in biblical times, however, a half-shekel was not a lot of money so that the amount collected by this tax probably was not sufficient to provide for the upkeep of the sanctuary. Presumably, additional offerings were required and obtained, and they were based more on ability to pay. As such, total support for maintaining the sanctuary may have meant that the overall cost implied **progressive taxation.**

Q: *Ask your parents about how their religious organization is financed. Is the overall support progressive, neutral, or regressive across members' income levels?*

19.6

I just paid a fee of £5 (about $8) to enter a museum in London and was told by the ticket-taker to grab an envelope and send my receipt for the ticket into a government tax office. The envelope states that the museum will receive a **subsidy** of 28 percent of the ticket price if I do that. This use of the tax system differs from the U.S. in interesting ways. First, my giving to a museum at home doesn't generate direct tax benefits for the museum; instead, it lowers my federal taxes since I can take the donation as a **deduction,** thus lowering the amount on which I am taxed. This gives me an **incentive** to donate more than otherwise. Second, in Britain, a donation produces the same 28 percent benefit whether given by a rich or poor person. In the U.S., however, a donation by a very wealthy person saves her or him nearly 40 percent in taxes since that is the **marginal tax rate** for the richest people in the U.S.; for lower-income people, the tax saving is only 10 percent, which is their marginal tax rate.

> **Q:** *Which system, the U.S. or the British, do you think will get more total contributions for museums? In other words, think about the supply elasticity of charitable contributions under these two alternative methods.*

19.7

Costa Rica, like many smaller countries, charges a departure tax at its international airport. I pay a $17 tax, but Costa Rican citizens pay $41 and resident noncitizens pay $61. Why charge foreigners less? The issue is tax competition. As a small country competing for business and tourists, Costa Rica can't charge a huge amount. If it did, travelers, knowing this, would go elsewhere. Its own citizens have little choice: This is the only way they can exit the country conveniently. Moreover, given the amount of tax evasion, a departure tax is a good way to collect taxes, and it is fairly **progressive:** Richer Costa Ricans fly out of the country more often than do their poorer fellow citizens. The $61 tax on residents must be demand-based **price discrimination** against people who have an even lower **price elasticity of demand** for departures than citizens do—probably wealthy foreigners who make their homes in Costa Rica but maintain other citizenship.

> **Q:** *Why not charge resident foreigners a $1,000 tax each time they depart the country?*

19.8

The state of Washington imposed a licensing fee on cars that rose as a car's value increased. Fees on cars valued at more than $25,000 amounted to $600 per year. A referendum reduced this to a flat fee of $30 per car. Now, why would the average voter approve replacing a clearly **progressive tax** with a fixed-amount, obviously **regressive tax?** Either the average voter doesn't realize that this hurts him or her and helps the rich, or he or she believes that by cutting one tax there will be no offsetting increases in other taxes. Appealing to the average person to help reduce a tax that hits mainly the rich is a common ploy. A good example is the pressure brought (successfully) on Congress several years ago to repeal a special excise tax on boats costing more than $30,000. The argument was that the tax hurt the workers in the boat-building industry. Possibly so, but it requires a strange theory of **tax incidence** for that to be true.

> **Q:** *If you had been in the state of Washington at that time, would you have voted to repeal the tax? How would the repeal have helped or hurt you, and how does that affect your opinion on the fee referendum?*

19.9

Several years ago, the state of Texas surprised the public by creating a tax holiday the weekend before school started. School supplies, kids' clothing, and related items were temporarily exempted from the 8-percent state sales tax. Who really benefited from the tax holiday? What was the **tax incidence** of this temporary tax cut? That depended on how the supply and demand for these items responded to the tax cut and the resulting drop in the net price. It's hard to believe that demand responded much because by that weekend many people had already bought the back-to-school items. If not, they had to buy them then—an **inelastic demand.** That would have led to a big drop in the net price: Consumers reaped most of the benefit from the tax holiday. Since then, the state has been offering this holiday annually, and most people expect it. They are adjusting their spending patterns accordingly so that now there is a more **elastic demand** on that weekend. Retail stores can also plan around this date all year long and be sure that they reap part of the gains from the temporary—but now fully anticipated—tax holiday. Buyers and sellers now share the incidence of the tax cut.

> **Q:** *If you want to make sure that consumers get the benefits of the tax cut—that the incidence is entirely on them—how can you design tax holidays to do this?*

19.10

A California state assemblyman has proposed dealing with the state's huge budget shortfall by taxing pornography, including the production and sales of pornographic videos—by 25 percent. To an economist, this initially sounds like a good idea: An ideal tax is one that doesn't cause any change in behavior—that doesn't generate any **excess burden** on the economy. I believe the demand for pornography is quite **inelastic,** so I don't expect sales to be reduced much if porn prices rise as producers try and succeed in passing this tax along to consumers. But demand is only one side of the market: A tax only in California gives producers an incentive to move their operations elsewhere. I don't know how attached porn-video producers are to the Los Angeles area, which is a leader in this and all other aspects of the movie industry; but I wouldn't think that the fixed costs of production are very high, and I bet that workers in this industry are fairly mobile, too. That being the case, this tax might generate a substantial **deadweight loss,** as a lot of production shifts to other states that don't impose the tax. The tax might raise revenue—that depends on how many producers go elsewhere; but it will certainly reduce output in this major California industry and cost the California economy some jobs.

    Q: *How might the discussion of this change if the tax were imposed nationwide, by the federal government?*

19.11

I'm lecturing at the University of Essex and going from office to office chatting with people about their research. This is hard physical labor—I repeatedly go down one or two flights of stairs in this rabbit warren, walk down a hall, up the stairs in the adjoining building, then back down another hall. What a waste—why? The answer is that the British government imposes a value-add tax on building extensions so that, if the buildings were joined on each floor, the newer ones would count as extensions and would be heavily taxed. To avoid this, the University struck a deal with the tax man to allow one internal door between adjoining buildings, allowing what is merely an extension to be treated as a new edifice and thus escape taxation. The only problem is that, as usual, taxes create a **deadweight loss,** as my well-exercised, tired knees now illustrate. I doubt the building's planners considered the cost of this loss when they agreed to this subterfuge.

    Q: *What type of incentives does this tax create? How would it change the planning process for new buildings?*

19.12

In his posthumous novel *The Pale King,* David Foster Wallace describes a fictional **progressive** sales tax in Illinois that imposes higher rates the larger the amount that's purchased. Sounds good and fair, but it contributes to substantial **deadweight loss:** People buy a few things, take them to their cars, then come back and buy more. Auto dealers sell parts separately to reduce the **average tax rate** on consumers. If this were real, the deadweight loss would be borne especially by low-income people. Those who feel pinched for cash but whose time is less valuable would be more likely to engage in tax-avoiding activities like repeated small purchases.

> **Q:** *Is there any way to impose a progressive sales tax, one that rises with income, without incurring costs like these?*

Government Programs

19.13

Newspapers are full of stories about companies that offer to locate in a state or city in exchange for tax breaks: no state corporate income taxes or local property taxes for an extended period. Others add direct **subsidies** in their requests to state and local governments. Perhaps the most visible claimants are professional sports franchises. Do these subsidies pay off for taxpayers? A reasonable criterion is that the discounted value of the extra taxes generated by the extra business and jobs created should at least equal the tax breaks and subsidies offered to the companies. I doubt that governments do much better than this breakeven level. The reason is that the companies and sports franchises behave like **monopolists** in bargaining with the various governments that are competing to get a company to locate. As monopolists bargaining with competing governments, they can extract, in the form of tax breaks, every bit of **economic rent** that the locality might have gotten from the deal. Sports franchises do even better: Citizens seem willing to pay higher taxes or give up public services for the prestige of having a major-league sports franchise in the city.

> **Q:** *How would the amount of tax breaks that are offered change if the company was one that needed to use particular mineral resources that are located in only two places in the U.S.? Why does this outcome differ from the one described in the vignette?*

19.14

I am officially old (by definition of the U.S. Census Bureau). As an economist I am "hung up" on this age. Why? Because the life-cycle theories of **utility maximization** that describe patterns of consumption are based on a retirement age; and 65 was enshrined as that age by the **Social Security** Act of 1935 (even though its predecessor, Bismarck's German legislation of 1889, set the pension age at 70). The problem that underlies Social Security and other countries' public pension programs is that the average time from 65 to death has been rising very rapidly—five years for men, seven for women since 1938 in the U.S. The U.S. has gone a bit of the way—66 is now the regular age for Social Security, and 67 will be in 2021. But that is nowhere near enough, given rises in longevity. The solution is simple—raise the age of regular benefits by a year four times, once every five years from 2015 until 2030. That removes most of the Social Security deficit—and the average retiree could still expect to live at least as long, and draw benefits for at least as long, as Americans who retired at 65 when the program began.

Q: *Do you think you will be receiving Social Security benefits when you retire?*

19.15

Some economists at Louisiana State University are working on a proposal to exempt textbooks from sales taxes in Baton Rouge, currently a whopping 9%. I'm all in favor of cutting sales taxes, which are generally not **progressive;** but textbooks are a **luxury** good—college education is disproportionately undertaken by the offspring of higher-income families. Why subsidize higher-income college students still further? The **elasticity of demand for** textbooks is probably quite small—professors assign the same number of textbooks; and students used to buy them locally. With more students purchasing textbooks from the Internet today, the elasticity is probably much higher locally. There was little **excess burden** before; and with the expansion of the Internet the burden is still small since people can escape the tax with minimal effort.

Q: *If students order textbooks from out-of-state, it is likely that they will not have to pay any sales tax. Given that fact, how would removing the sales tax on textbooks affect local booksellers?*

19.16

Texas raises most of its tax revenue from the sales tax. We are one of only seven states that lack a personal income tax. Even with the exclusion of groceries from the sales tax, it is likely that the tax is **regressive.** Our legislators are now proposing that state-supported universities be limited to tuition increases not exceeding 5 percent per year. The bill's author believes that this will force the legislature to increase appropriations for higher education, raising the state up from its near-bottom position in public support offered for colleges and universities. Even if this belief were correct, would the substitution of tax revenue for tuition revenue be desirable? I don't think so! Tuition is paid by students and their parents—and the average college student at public universities in this and other states comes from a family whose income is well above the median. The proposal would thus substitute regressive taxes for somewhat **progressive** tuition payments. The days of taxing the poor to support the rich are surviving well here in Texas!

Q: *Think about other goods and services provided by the government, such as funding for the arts. Which do you think are primarily enjoyed by the rich, and which are primarily enjoyed by the poor?*

19.17

The Texas sales tax is 6.25 percent, and Austin adds on 2 percentage points. I've always thought we were high in this category. Before a current vacation in Colorado, I noticed that the Colorado state sales tax rate is only 2.9 percent. On my first purchase in Steamboat Springs, though, the tax rate was 8.4 percent—the town adds on 5.5 percentage points to its state sales tax rate. Annoying to me—but sensible, and probably **efficient** and **equitable.** After all, much of the purchasing is by tourists like me—and our demand for goods here is probably quite **inelastic**—so the **excess burden** of the tax is small. Also, this is a pretty fancy tourist destination, so the tax is probably somewhat **progressive** overall. Finally, as my wife notes, without such a tax we wouldn't be doing our share of paying for the public services that the town provides and that we enjoy.

Q: *Suppose a nearby town adds a sales tax of only 1 percent. How would this affect the incidence of the tax, and how would you expect locals and tourists to react?*

19.18

A student of mine tells me that she lives in the District of Columbia. I remark that out-of-state tuition at Texas must be a burden. She replies that it isn't: As a D.C. resident, she can pay in-state tuition at any U.S. public university. Essentially, the average U.S. taxpayer

subsidizes the higher education of the offspring of D.C. residents. I would bet that students taking advantage of this subsidy come from much higher-than-average income D.C. families—higher, too, than the average American taxpayer. As with setting tuition for in-state students below **average cost,** here, too, the subsidy is disequalizing. The difference is that in the D.C. case it's the well-off in one city being subsidized by the average taxpayer elsewhere, while for non-D.C. students the average taxpayer in a state subsidizes the higher education of the upper-middle class of that state.

Q: *How could we reduce the subsidies that the average taxpayer in your state provides for the education of the upper-middle class in your state?*

CHAPTER 20

International Economics

Comparative Advantage and Globalization

20.1

A student mentioned that, as a high-school swimmer, he was the best in the conference in the breast stroke. Yet when the coach was putting together the medley relay team, he was assigned to swim the butterfly stroke. Why would the coach put the best breast stroker on a different stroke? The reason is very simple: Other team members were almost as fast at the breast stroke as my student, but all were far inferior at the butterfly. My student had an **absolute advantage** at both the breast stroke and the butterfly, but a **comparative advantage** at swimming the butterfly stroke. The coach realized the medley team's overall time would be lower with the student doing the butterfly.

> **Q:** *Have you come across any examples like this in team sports in which you have participated?*

20.2

We did two hours of volunteer work on Maui trying to remove sea grape, an invasive species. Twelve people had to divide the tasks of using large shears, raking brush, and hauling away all the cuttings. The group started off with most people switching among the several tasks. Pretty soon, it became clear that some people had **comparative advantages** at certain tasks (my wife at raking), while others had comparative and **absolute advantages** at other tasks (a burly, retired ophthalmic surgeon at cutting with shears). Productive groups generally learn quickly how to maximize output in situations like this, pushing the **production possibility frontier** outward, even with no guidance from a manager. Some people in the group (like me) were uniformly relatively good (or bad) at all tasks (had no obvious comparative advantage) so that their skills (or lack thereof) led them to spend the time alternating among all the tasks. I would think that primitive farming groups and, even further back in time, groups of hunters quickly learned who was relatively and absolutely good at which tasks.

Q: *Under what kinds of circumstances will people learn more or less quickly what the appropriate allocation of tasks is? Think about examples from things that you have done with a group.*

20.3

I do most of the dinner cooking during the week. My wife is a better cook than I am, and she likes to cook more than I do. Also, my average earnings per hour worked exceed hers. So why am I cooking, if she has a **comparative advantage** in cooking, likes it better, and earns less on average per hour? The reason is that our decisions, like those of most people, are made based on **marginal,** not average considerations. Even though I earn more than she does, my time is quite flexible; and I don't earn more by rigidly sticking to an 8 AM to 6 PM schedule. As an attorney she needs to be in her office from 8 AM to 6 PM on most days so that the value of her time right before dinnertime is higher than mine. Our decision to have me cook dinner is a rational response to differences in the prices of our time at the margin. I cook because my time is less valuable than hers when the cooking must be done.

Q: *Are there similar arrangements in your household so that a person who might be less productive at a task does it because his or her value of time varies with the day or week?*

20.4

In the movie *Michael Clayton*, starring George Clooney, the title character had been a courtroom attorney in the prosecutor's office, but now is a "fixer"—a deal-maker—in a large private firm. He hates his job and suggests to his boss that he might like to go back to trial work. His boss tells him that he was a good trial lawyer, but that there are lots of good trial lawyers. He says too that Clooney is a great fixer, and those are very scarce. Implicitly, his boss is saying that Clooney has both an **absolute advantage** and a **comparative advantage** as a fixer.

Q: *Would you expect him to make a higher salary as a fixer or as a trial lawyer? In general, what can you surmise about the relationship between wages and having a comparative advantage in a rare skill set?*

20.5

We file into a tent for a wedding reception. On one side is the guest book, on the other side is the bar offering the initial refreshments. We want to sign the guest book, but more important is getting glasses of wine soon without getting caught in a large line. Almost instinctively and after forty-two years of marriage, my wife and I know our **comparative and absolute advantages.** Her handwriting is good, mine is dreadful. My arms are longer than hers. She makes an immediate beeline to sign the guest book, and I head straight for the bar, having ascertained what she wants to drink. Very soon she has signed the book and I have two glasses of merlot. The efficiency gains from marriage are well known, and for most couples they grow over time.

> **Q:** *Give examples of situations when you, with a friend or relative, have faced similar situations. How and why did you split up the tasks?*

20.6

A discussion in the movie *Harold and Kumar Go to White Castle* illustrates the fact that, when talking about people's activities, **comparative advantage** is not the only thing that matters. Harold asks why, with his perfect MCAT scores and great grades, Kumar doesn't want to go to medical school. Kumar responds by noting that, "Just because [. . . *deleted for reasons of propriety*] doesn't mean that he has to be a porn star." Our comparative advantage generates our earnings opportunities—Kumar might be much better off financially, given his skills, choosing medicine. But **preferences** matter too, and Kumar would like to be a slacker—he wants to maximize **utility,** not income. His response to Harold suggests that he would rather earn less doing something that he finds enjoyable than earn a lot in medicine, which he doesn't enjoy.

> **Q:** *You are now choosing a career, or you will be soon. Are you picking the highest-paying one possible, or do considerations other than pay enter your decision?*

20.7

My colleagues laughed at me today when I mentioned I was doing my income taxes myself rather than using an accountant. They argued that, given the price of my time—my **wage rate**—I should hire a professional. They ignore the fact that **comparative advantage** works in production, but it must be modified in consumption activities, as those can alter **utility** beyond any monetary gains (or losses). In an occupation with few opportunities to exhibit one's macho characteristics, doing my own tax return is my chance to go *mano a mano* with the federal government. I get a real kick from finding a legitimate **deduction** that had not previously occurred to me. That I also learn more about the tax structure, its incentives and burdens, and can use this information in my principles lectures, are additional reasons not to hire a pro.

Q: *Think of what your parents do with their time. Are there things they do for which it would be cheaper to hire someone than do it themselves?*

20.8

A fellow economist mentioned the unusual behavior of his eighteen-year-old and fifteen-year-old daughters. The older one, a freshman in college, brings her laundry home and expects the younger daughter to launder it. The younger daughter complies— but each time she keeps the piece of clothing that she likes most. Their father told this to the older sister, who laughed and said that's okay; when she comes home and her little sister is away she takes some of the little sister's clothing. Both sisters know all this, and both seem to view it as a way of trading. Like most trading that is voluntary, both sisters are better off. There are **gains from trade** in "stealing" each other's clothes!

Q: *What will happen to the gains from this kind of trade as the sisters' preferences for the clothing they purchase become more similar?*

20.9

The mayor of an isolated town in Queensland, Australia, was excoriated for making the following statement: "May I suggest that if there are five blokes to every girl, we should find out where there are beauty-disadvantaged women and ask them to proceed to Mt. Isa." He is simply recognizing that, in the dating/marriage markets, looks are one of the commodities traded; and there is substantial evidence suggesting that better-looking women marry men with more **human capital**—men who can earn more. That the mayor is asking ugly women to come to Mt. Isa is just an attempt to get them where their scarcity might allow them to mitigate their "disadvantage" and benefit from the **surplus** of single men. **Gains from trade** make sense to this economist, although the mayor's statement is somewhat crude. Interestingly, the head of the Chamber of Commerce noted that, "There's a lot of anger circulating among the community. . . there's a lot of women voicing their opinions." I wonder if the women's anger is at the mayor's crudeness, or whether it is a standard response by domestic **monopolists** who are threatened with foreign competition??

> **Q:** *If the town were full of women and a female mayor were to make a similar statement, what type of men would she suggest come to Mt. Isa?*

20.10

There have been several news stories about Americans' increasing willingness to **outsource** medical care. This is not just a matter of importing goods since the care must be administered to Americans who temporarily locate in foreign countries. The trend is caused by the high price of medical care to the uninsured in America compared with the much lower prices elsewhere. One man went to Belgium for a knee operation, which cost one third what it would cost here, even including the price of an air ticket. In fact, it's no longer just the uninsured doing this, as several states' Blue Cross insurers are now encouraging people to shop internationally by offering the same coverage for procedures at approved foreign hospitals as in American hospitals. If this continues, I expect that the **competition** will force American hospitals and doctors to begin cutting prices—so this trend will help slow the growth of medical costs here.

> **Q:** *Does this type of outsourcing cause a loss of jobs in the U.S. in this example? Who is hurt by it?*

20.11

We took our visiting twelve-year-old granddaughter out to dinner last night. She insisted on ordering *edamame*, which I, too, love. I discovered it at age 60 and would never have seen it in the U.S. at age twelve in 1955. Earlier in the day, I had bought a *cherimoya* at the local grocery store. These examples illustrate an additional benefit of **globalization**—the import of goods and, more important perhaps, information on and even local growing of different foods.

Since there's evidence that variety increases **utility,** this expansion is an additional, typically unacknowledged benefit of globalization.

Q: *Go to your locally grocery store, talk to your parents and grandparents and determine what other foods simply did not exist in the U.S. fifty years ago?*

20.12

Typically, production is **outsourced** to low-wage countries as a way of producing labor-intensive goods at prices that consumers in industrialized economies will pay. This type of **globalization** illustrates how companies respond to changing labor costs and changing **comparative advantage.** All of this occurs as part of the production process. A recent story on Yahoo! illustrates how people in industrialized economies have begun to outsource their leisure—how they are now **substituting** the inexpensive labor time of workers in developing countries for their own time that has a high **opportunity cost.** Several companies in China have started employing young people to play computer games on behalf of game players in wealthy countries. The Chinese workers are paid to spend time to take the player's character through the more routine phases of the computer game, at which point the game player takes over his or her character. This enables the player in the rich country to avoid spending time in boring activities, and use the time saved to get more pleasure out of the more complex and interesting parts of the games.

Q: *This is a pretty unusual type of outsourcing. Can you find other examples that are equally strange?*

Trade and Related Policies

20.13

In the late 1990s, China "went green"—after severe flooding on the Yangtze River due to deforestation, the country started enforcing laws against illegal logging and made a serious effort to achieve sustainable forests. At the same time it reduced **tariffs** on imported logs. The result was just what economic theory would predict: With tighter restrictions on Chinese logging, the **supply curve** of domestically produced logs shifted to the left, raising prices in China. At the same time, the lower tariff, coupled with the rise in domestic prices, induced a huge influx of foreign logs (a sixteen-fold increase in just five years). While Chinese forests are being better protected, the greater **incentives** for illegal logging in countries such as Indonesia and Brazil, that the growth in Chinese demand for imports has produced, have resulted in more rapid deforestation elsewhere. This story shows that it is difficult to maintain a more open economy and be pro-environment in a global economy in which other countries are less concerned about environmental issues.

Q: *If you were a Chinese citizen, how would you feel about the changes that have occurred as a result of the changes in policy?*

20.14

U.S. candy producers are complaining that the high domestic price of sugar is forcing them to move production abroad, where they can buy sugar at the much lower world price. U.S. sugar growers are heavily protected, and the U.S. price is much higher than the world price. But that has been true for at least forty years. Equilibrium doesn't change unless some underlying factor has changed, so high sugar prices can't be the cause. What has changed is that **tariffs** on manufactured goods have been lowered fairly steadily, particularly within North America under the North American Free Trade Agreement (NAFTA). Since much of the imported candy comes from Canadian plants, lower tariffs (in the case of NAFTA: zero tariffs) seem like the cause of the relocation of candy plants. But the candy manufacturers are correct about one thing: Lowering domestic sugar prices to the world price would reduce the cost disadvantages of producing here and at least partly stem losses in domestic output.

Q: *What would lowering U.S. sugar prices do to the market value of Canadian candy companies that are potential takeover targets by American firms?*

20.15

With the continuing drought in South Texas, the issue of how to allocate scarce water resources has flared up again. Rice farmers south of Austin want water from the Colorado River for their crops; yet the two storage lakes on the river, which provide most of the Austin area's drinking water, are less than half full. A rice farmer says, "Water availability should be based on sound hydrology and not on political pressure." WRONG! It should be based on neither—it should be based on economics: What is the **opportunity cost** of the water? In particular, one might ask why the U.S. is growing rice at all. It is hard to believe we have a **comparative advantage** in rice-growing and that it shouldn't all be imported. That's especially true about rice grown in dry South Texas. We grow rice because of entrenched interests that obtained water rights many years ago. The rice farmers get heavily **subsidized** water precisely because of the political pressure this rice farmer deplores—and they now want to compound the effects of bad policy.

Q: *What would happen to rice prices in the U.S. if the U.S. stopped subsidizing the use of water to grow rice?*

20.16

A story in *The Economist* illustrates the folly of imposing **tariffs** in an industry where **average cost** varies across producers. The U.S. imposed tariffs averaging 27 percent on imports of lumber from Canada. You would think this would hurt Canadian lumber producers, and it did. But it also forced them to concentrate production in their most efficient mills, while the U.S. continued to try to produce at relatively inefficient mills. The result is that more U.S. mills have closed than Canadian ones. Not surprisingly, to limit competition still further, the U.S. lumber industry would like to replace tariffs with **quotas.** By limiting the amount imported from Canada, this would guarantee that the Canadians' continuing greater efficiency cannot give them an advantage over the increasingly relatively inefficient U.S. firms.

Q: *Would the U.S. consumer be better off with these tariffs or with the quotas that U.S. lumber companies would like?*

20.17

One of the most famous writings in economics is Frederic Bastiat's *A Petition from the Candlemakers*, a spoof written in the 1800s in which the candlemakers petition the government to impose a **tariff** on their biggest competitor—the sun! Life apparently almost imitates art. American candlemakers have managed to persuade the federal government that Chinese candles are being **dumped** on the U.S. market. The U.S. manufacturers have a tremendous incentive to claim this: Under a recent change in federal regulations, penalties on foreign companies for dumping are paid to the American companies that sue successfully. Not only do the U.S. companies reduce competition, they also receive a **subsidy** from their foreign competitors. If I ran a company, I would prefer such an antidumping regulation to a tariff. Both help to insulate my product from foreign competition; but unlike tariff payments, which go into the federal Treasury, the fines for dumping would go into my company's treasury!

> **Q:** *Other than the political power of domestic companies, is there any economic reason that might make sense to let the U.S. companies receive the penalties assessed on their foreign competitors?*

20.18

Today, imports account for ninety percent of U.S. shrimp production. The U.S. Department of Commerce has approved protective **tariffs** against some shrimp imports in an **antidumping** case brought by U.S. shrimp producers. Domestic producers sell fresh shrimp, while many of the imports are farm raised, using cheap labor and inexpensive feeds. Not surprisingly, the **total cost** of imported shrimp is lower; but are the foreigners selling at a price below **average variable cost,** which is supposed to be the definition of dumping? I doubt it; they are selling a lower-quality product. The domestic producers are making complaints that are standard when a U.S. producer faces foreign competition. The domestic producers benefit from the tariff; and the federal bureaucracy has every incentive to enlarge itself by approving more such tariffs. It is thus not surprising that these lawsuits succeed. What is sad is that the American consumer, who seems to be willing to consume lower-quality but cheaper farm-raised imports, must now face higher prices of those imports. The consumer will not be able to benefit from greater efficiency in domestic production that stiffer competition from imports might have generated.

> **Q:** *What if the U.S. just imposed tariffs on imports of farm-raised shrimp, leaving any imports of ocean-raised shrimp untaxed? Would that solve the U.S. producers' problems?*

Tips on Hunting for Economics Everywhere in Part III

1. When someone postpones an activity, what does that imply about the rate of return on that activity compared with the cost of borrowing? Think about how your own willingness to postpone gratification has changed over your life.
2. Ask yourself why people's wages differ, and search for the underlying determinants. Look for differences by demographic group, education and training, skills, kinds of activities undertaken, and other potential sources. How do you think your earnings will change over your life?
3. Examine your own job hunting and consider why you accepted or failed to accept jobs you were offered. What does your behavior imply about your attitudes toward work?
4. Look for cases where the activity of a person, firm, or company affects the well being of others in surprising ways. Look for public goods and free rides, and both positive and negative externalities. Look for these in your family, in your dealings with roommates and classmates.
5. Consider how outcomes differ depending on who has property rights. How do groups try to overcome initial grants of property rights? How are transaction costs structured to alter outcomes?
6. Watch for responses to changes in marginal tax rates, especially when the tax rate rises or falls sharply. Look at how behavior differs in response to changes in average and marginal rates. Think about the burden and incidence of the taxes you see. Look for ways in which your own behavior changes because of a tax that you face.
7. Look for instances of the use of comparative advantage in your own activities, for example, in dividing tasks with friends, family and roommates, and in changing patterns of international trade. Is comparative advantage being accounted for properly?

G*lossary*

Absolute advantage Higher actual productivity than other producers.

Addiction Increasing satisfaction from a good resulting from prior consumption of that good.

Adverse selection People sorting into a program so that the average quality of those choosing it is reduced.

Altruism Deriving satisfaction from increases in the satisfaction of someone else.

Arbitrage Buying in a location where price is low, selling where it is high.

Auction A sale at which the seller elicits price offers from a group of potential buyers.

Average fixed cost Total fixed cost divided by the number of units produced.

Average product The ratio of output to the quantity of an input.

Average tax rate Total taxes divided by the total amount that is taxed.

Average total cost Total cost (fixed plus variable) divided by the number of units produced.

Average variable cost Total variable cost divided by the number of units produced.

Ban A government prohibition on the sale of some good or service.

Bilateral monopoly A market relationship in which the seller has monopoly power and the buyer has monopsony power.

Change in demand A shift in the amount people wish to buy at any given price; usually due to changes in income, prices of related goods, tastes, or market size.

Common property resource A good whose consumption cannot be limited, that cannot be owned by one or a few consumers.

Comparative advantage Relatively greater productivity in an activity.

Compensating wage differential Extra pay for an unpleasant aspect of an occupation.

Competitive equilibrium A situation in a competitive market in which no firms have an incentive to enter or exit because there is no economic profit.

Complements A pair of goods related so that, when the price of one falls, the amount of the other sold rises.

Consumer surplus The excess of the amount consumers are willing to pay for a good over its market price.

Deadweight loss The output lost to an economy because a price shifted away from a competitive optimum.

Demand curve A downward-sloping relationship between quantity demanded and price along which income, prices of related goods, tastes, and market size are held constant.

Derived demand Demand in one market that is the result of demand from another market.

Diminishing marginal productivity Decreasing extra output as more units of a variable input are combined with fixed inputs.

Diminishing marginal utility Decreasing extra satisfaction from each additional unit of a good or service consumed.

Discount rate The extra fraction, D, required to make someone indifferent between having \$1 now and having \$$[1 + D]$ a year from now.

Discounting period The amount of time in the future over which returns are received and discounted back to the present.

Discrimination Treating objectively identical people differently.

Diseconomies of scale Long-run average costs that increase as a firm increases output.

Disequilibrium An imbalance between market forces, especially supply and demand.

Dominant strategy A strategy that is best no matter what the other party does.

Dumping Selling a product in a foreign country at a price below average variable cost.

Duopoly A market with only two sellers.

Economic profit Revenue minus input costs (including opportunity cost).

Economic rent The excess of the returns to an input above its opportunity cost.

Economies of scale Long-run average cost that decreases as a firm increases output.

Efficiency Using all resources and producing all goods in a way that minimizes cost and maximizes consumer surplus.

Elastic demand Quantity demanded decreasing by more than one percent with each one percent rise in price.

Endgame problem An incentive for people or firms to alter behavior near the end of a relationship.

Entry barrier An impediment that prevents firms from entering a market.

Equilibrium price The price that equates the demand and the supply for a good or service.

Equity Fairness.

Excess burden The activities undertaken or avoided as a result of the imposition of a tax.

Extensive margin The decision between doing something at all and not doing it at all.

Externality A cost or benefit conferred on others by the maximizing behavior of a person, firm, or government.

Fixed cost Input cost that does not vary in the short run because it has already been incurred.

Free rider Someone who benefits from a public good without paying for it.

General equilibrium The equating of demand and supply in all markets at the same time.

Globalization The expansion of trade and production across international borders.

Human capital Skills and knowledge embodied in workers as a result of previous investments of time and goods.

Hyperbolic discounting Attaching a higher discount rate to dollars postponed over the near future than to dollars postponed for the same length of time but further in the future.

Import quotas Numerical limits on the amounts of particular goods allowed to be imported.

Income elasticity of demand The percentage change in quantity purchased in response to a one-percent increase in income.

Independence of irrelevant alternatives The choice between a pair of alternatives is not altered by an offer of a third alternative that is inferior to one or both of the pair.

Inefficient Not using all existing resources to maximize the value of output.

Inelastic demand Quantity demanded decreasing by less than one percent with each one-percent rise in price.

Inferior good A good with a negative income elasticity of demand.

Intensive margin The decision about how much of something to do, given that you will be doing at least some of it.

Jumping the gun Moving before the previous equilibrium in order to gain a competitive advantage.

Labor force participation Being employed or looking for work.

Labor-intensive technology One that uses relatively a lot of labor and relatively little of other inputs.

Labor theory of value The notion that the value of goods stems from workers' current or past efforts.

Long-run average cost The minimum average cost of producing at a particular level of output if the firm plans to produce that amount forever.

Long-term employment contract Relationship between an employer and employee that explicitly of implicitly binds them together for several periods of time

Luxury A good with an income elasticity of demand greater than one.

Marginal cost The change in total cost that occurs when output increases by one unit.

Marginal product The change in total product that occurs when an input is increased by one unit.

Marginal revenue product The change in revenue that occurs when an input is increased by one unit.

Marginal subsidy A subsidy applied only to changes in the amount of an activity undertaken or good purchased.

Marginal tax rate The change in taxes when the amount taxed increases by one unit.

Marginal utility The change in utility from a good when the amount consumed of that good increases by one unit.

Market demand curve The sum at each price of the demand curves of all the individuals in the market.

Matching Bringing together buyers and sellers so that they enter into a trade.

Minimum wage A price floor on a wage rate.

Monopolist The single seller of a good.

Monopolistic competition A market characterized by many sellers of similar but not identical goods.

Monopoly A market with only one seller.

Monopsony A market with only one buyer.

Moral hazard An incentive created by some program that causes people to alter their behavior in a way that raises program costs.

Nash equilibrium A strategic situation in which no side in a game has any incentive to alter its strategy.

Necessity A good with an income elasticity of demand less than one but greater than zero.

Negative externality A cost imposed on others by the maximizing behavior of a person, firm, or government.

Neutral tax A tax that is neither progressive nor regressive.

Normal profits The profit rate that would arise in equilibrium in a perfectly competitive market.

Oligopolist One of a small number of sellers in a market.

Oligopoly A market characterized by few sellers.

On-the-job training Investment in human capital through acquiring skills at work.

Outsourcing Buying goods or services from firms outside one's own economy.

Opportunity cost The value of an input, good, or service in its best alternative use.

Pareto-improving A change that improves the well-being of at least one person without reducing anyone else's well-being.

Pareto optimal Not being able to improve the well-being of one person without reducing at least one other's well-being.

Patent A government grant of a monopoly over some product or process.

Payoff bimatrix A matrix that shows the payoffs to each player under each combination of possible strategies in a game.

Perfect competition A market form characterized by many firms, easy entry/exit, and a homogeneous product.

Positive externality A benefit conferred on others by the maximizing behavior of a person, firm, or government.

Poverty line The income deemed necessary by the government to avoid being defined as poor.

Predatory pricing Setting price below average variable cost.

Present discounted value The discounted value of a stream of future income or returns.

Price ceiling An upper limit imposed on a market price.

Price discrimination Charging different prices to buyers of a good or service.

Price elasticity of demand The percentage change in quantity demanded when price rises by one percent.

Price floor A lower limit imposed on a market price.

Prisoners' dilemma A game in which both sides have incentives that lead them to an equilibrium inferior to a collusive equilibrium.

Producer surplus The excess of the price received over the price for which a producer is willing to sell the good or service.

Product differentiation Creating characteristics of products to distinguish them from other products and make their demand less elastic.

Production possibility frontier A curve indicating a trade-off between two goods and showing the maximum combinations of them that can be produced with the available resources.

Profit The difference between revenue and cost.

Profit-maximizing Seeking the highest available difference between revenue and cost.

Progressive tax A tax with an average tax rate that rises with the amount taxed.

Property rights Control over a good, service, or set of rules.

Public good A good whose consumption by one person does not reduce the amount available to be consumed by other people.

Rationing Setting an upper limit on the quantity of a good or service that a consumer is allowed to purchase.

Regressive tax A tax with an average tax rate that falls with the amount taxed.

Regulated An industry that has its quantity and/or price determined in part through a government agency.

Repeated game A strategic interaction that occurs several times.

Revenue Quantity times price.

Risk-averse Preferring a choice with a higher chance of an average return to one with higher chances of large gains or large losses.

Shortage An excess of demand over supply at the current price.

Social norm The rules that a group uses for appropriate and inappropriate values, beliefs, attitudes, and behaviors.

Social Security A federal program, enacted in 1935, initially only providing retirement benefits for most Americans who had worked for pay.

Separate markets In the case of price discrimination, a seller's effort to ensure that those who are only eligible to buy a product at a high price are unable to buy it at a low price.

Speculation Buying a product at one point in time, hopefully cheaply, and selling it at a later date, hopefully at a higher price.

Subgame perfect A strategy in a dynamic game that yields the player the best outcome in all future periods.

Subsidy An amount paid, typically by the government, to reduce the price consumers or firms must pay for a good, service, or productive input.

Substitutes A pair of goods related so that when the price of one falls, the amount of the other that is sold falls.

Superior good A good with a positive income elasticity of demand.

Superstars People whose talents generate immense earnings.

Supply curve An upward-sloping relationship between quantity supplied and price along which technology and input costs are held constant.

Surplus An excess of supply over demand at the current price.

Tariff A tax on an imported good or service.

Tax credit A dollar-for-dollar reduction in tax liability, computed after the total tax liability is determined.

Tax deduction A reduction in the amount of income subject to tax that results from one's spending on activities the government wishes to encourage.

Tax exemption A reduction in the amount of income subject to tax that results from having more people in the household.

Tax incidence The share of a tax borne by each side in the market for the taxed good or service.

Technological change An improvement in methods of production or organization that allows greater output with no additional inputs and thus lowers cost.

Tied sale A product supplied competitively must be purchased together with a monopolized product.

Total cost The sum of fixed cost and variable cost.

Tournament In sports and firms, a competition with payoffs designed to elicit the optimal effort from the participants.

Trade-off A choice between two goods or services that, because of scarcity, requires forgoing some of one to obtain more of the other.

Transaction costs Costs of changing the ownership of property rights.

Two-part tariff A fixed price to do something, plus an additional price for each extra amount purchased.

Utility Satisfaction.

Variable cost Input cost that changes as output changes.

G*uide to Vignettes*

List of Vignettes by Chapter

N = new to this edition; **Indicates author's favorite vignette in book.
F = "author's favorite." (N&F indicates both new and favorite.)

Chapter 3 — Demand and Supply—Quantity and Price in Unrestricted Markets

Chapter 4 — Demand and Supply—Quantity and Price in Restricted Markets

N = new to this edition; **Indicates author's favorite vignette in book.
F = "author's favorite." (N&F indicates both new and favorite.)

N = new to this edition; **Indicates author's favorite vignette in book.
F = "author's favorite." (N&F indicates both new and favorite.)

N = new to this edition; **Indicates author's favorite vignette in book.
F = "author's favorite." (N&F indicates both new and favorite.)

Chapter 9   Firms and Competitive Markets in the Long Run

Equilibrium

The Role of Market Size

Chapter 10   Competitive Markets—Responses to Shocks

Changes in Technology and Costs

Shifts in Industry Demand

Chapter 11   Efficiency and Well-Being

N = new to this edition; **Indicates author's favorite vignette in book.
F = "author's favorite." (N&F indicates both new and favorite.)

Chapter 12   Monopoly and Monopolistic Competition

Monopoly

Monopolistic Competition

Chapter 13   Price Discrimination

Chapter 14   Oligopoly (Including Game Theory)

Games

N = new to this edition; **Indicates author's favorite vignette in book.
F = "author's favorite." (N&F indicates both new and favorite.)

N = new to this edition; **Indicates author's favorite vignette in book.
F = "author's favorite." (N&F indicates both new and favorite.)

Chapter 17   Human Capital, Discrimination, and Labor-Market Policy

Education and Training

Discrimination

Policy and Poverty

Chapter 18   Public Goods, Externalities, and Property Rights

Public Goods

Externalities

N = new to this edition; **Indicates author's favorite vignette in book.
F = "author's favorite." (N&F indicates both new and favorite.)

Chapter 19   Taxes and Public Expenditures

Taxation

Government Programs

Chapter 20   International Economics

Comparative Advantage and Globalization

N = new to this edition; **Indicates author's favorite vignette in book.
F = "author's favorite." (N&F indicates both new and favorite.)

List of Vignettes in Alphabetical Order

N = new to this edition; **Indicates author's favorite vignette in book.
F = "author's favorite." (N&F indicates both new and favorite.)